IMPERIALISM

IMPERIALISM:

From the Colonial Age to the Present

Essays by Harry Magdoff

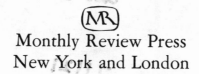

Monthly Review Press
New York and London

Copyright © 1978 by Harry Magdoff
All rights reserved

Library of Congress Cataloging in Publication Data
Magdoff, Harry.
    Imperialism: from the colonial age to the present.

    1. Imperialism—History. 2. Economic history—
1750-1918. 3. Economic history—1918- I. Title.
JC359.M26   325'.3   77-76167
ISBN 0-85345-426-4

Monthly Review Press
62 West 14th Street, New York, N.Y. 10011
47 Red Lion Street, London WC1R 4PF

Manufactured in the United States of America

10 9 8 7 6 5 4 3 2 1

Contents

Introduction

Although the essays collected in this volume were written at different times and for special occasions, they are essentially further explorations of themes I raised in *The Age of Imperialism* (New York: Monthly Review Press, 1969). Apart from two rejoinders to several critics of that book, the bulk of the material was prepared in response to various invitations to participate in seminars and conferences on imperialism (in New Delhi, at Oxford and Yale, and at an annual convention of the American Economic Association), to contribute a lengthy article on European expansion since 1763 for the new fifteenth edition of the *Encyclopaedia Britannica*, and to write introductions to two books dealing with imperialism.

The articles are grouped here under three headings: History, Theory and the Third World, and Reply to Critics. These divisions are by the very nature of the case arbitrary, since the topics interweave and necessarily overlap. The subject of imperialism is quintessentially a historical one, and the theoretical quest therefore needs to be aimed at differentiating and explaining major historical trends. Both themes, the historical and the theoretical, also crop up in the rejoinders to critics.

The frequently met attempt to construct a theory of imperialism that is essentially isolated from major problems of historical differentiations creates false issues for Marxists and non-Marxists alike, since it leads to a search for an analytical framework that is, in the words of one commentator, "watertight and self-contained." The trouble with "watertight" theories in this area is that they tend to become calcified into oversimplified and mechanical stimulus-response explanations. They accordingly are unsuitable, because they are unable to cope with the contemporaneous diversity of socioeconomic structures among nations, the many complex factors that contribute to historical change, and the intricate relations between economics, politics, ideology, and culture. On the other hand, those scholars who, without an adequate theoretical framework, concentrate on the historical aspects, either get lost in a welter of detail or end up with meaningless generalizations. An example of the latter is the reliance on such supposedly explanatory devices as the universal prevalence of a drive for power among rulers of nations, with a consequent neglect of the close interrelations between power, wealth, and the sources of wealth in different social systems.

An important source of the difficulty is that empire-building, territorial expansion, and domination of weaker by stronger powers—features commonly associated with the term *imperialism*—have a long history. Despite this appearance of universality, however, two questions insistently thrust themselves upon students of modern imperialism. First, are there analytically significant differences between such drives in precapitalist and capitalist times? And second, what is the explanation for the almost simultaneous outburst of a renewed wave of expansion by a number of leading nations in the late nineteenth century, accompanied by a marked intensification of the power struggle among these states?

These are not idle academic questions, nor are they merely matters of intellectual curiosity. As a matter of fact, the contrast between the genesis and role of expansionism in capitalist and other social systems is central to an understanding of the nature and structure of capitalism, as well as to an appreciation of the unique features of the imperialism of capitalist states. In former social systems, the economic root of expansionism was the exaction of tribute: in effect, the appropriation of the surplus available or obtainable from militarily weaker societies. In the main, the earlier "imperialisms" left the economic basis of conquered or dominated territories intact. Plunder, piracy, capture of slaves, and the establishment of colonies—these were the familiar hallmarks of the early empire-builders.

To be sure, direct robbery was not spurned by the emerging capitalist nations. But the enhancement of their wealth and power eventually required much more than the mere transfer of an already existing foreign surplus. What was new in this mode of production was its inner necessity to produce and sell goods on an ever enlarged scale. And because of this, the geographic spread of capitalist nations resulted in the alteration of the economic base of the rest of the world in ways that would aid and abet the *generation of an ever growing surplus within the home countries.* In short, the economies and societies of the conquered or dominated areas were transformed, adapted, and manipulated to serve as best they could the imperatives of capital accumulation at the center.

This contrast in the modes of expansionism is highlighted in changes which occurred during the evolution of capitalism itself. The initial geographical spread of the European countries bordering on the Atlantic Ocean was closely tied in with the rise of mercantile capitalism. During that period, when manufacturing activity was relatively underdeveloped and in the main subservient to merchant capital, the wealth and power of the expanding European nations (and of the settlers from these lands) was augmented from four sources: (1) the takeover of a major share of the traditional intra-Asian trade, after the traditional merchants had been eliminated and the Europeans had become the masters of the world's sea routes; (2) the seizure of the gold and silver of the Americas as well as the treasures found in other conquered territories; (3) the procurement of products native to Asia and the Americas for which demand existed or could be stimulated at home; and (4) the development of the African slave trade. The core of this activity was the direct appropriation of the surplus of dominated territories; and the wars among European powers were largely, though not exclusively, concerned with the division of the spoils of commerce and of colonial possessions. Ultimately, however, there were limits to this type of "imperialism." As long as productivity was fairly stagnant and most of the people of the world produced barely enough for their own use, there could not be much growth in the surplus that could be stolen.

Expansionism took a new lease on life with the blossoming of an economic system that depended on continuous revolution in the methods of production. For this the accelerated advance in world commerce had paved the way. The accompanying increases in production for exchange and in the use of money contributed to the disintegration in parts of Western Europe of the feudal mode of production and set the stage for the transition to full-blown capitalism. But the latter did not develop at the same time and in equal measure in all the nations that had led the commercial revolution of the sixteenth and seventeenth centuries. The new mode of production matured only in those countries where the necessary groundwork had been evolving since medieval times and where the state and class relations provided a sufficiently favorable environment.

Capitalism was most successful where industrial capital replaced merchant capital as the dominant force in the economic and political affairs of the nation. Factory production spread, technologies were continually changed to raise labor productivity and expand the scale of production, and the securing of markets became a major concern. Although the process of industrialization contributed to the growth of internal markets, domestic demand was not always sufficient to enable the risk-taking industrialists to recoup their costs and make a profit. As a result, the international economic, political, and military activity of the more advanced capitalist nations became increasingly involved in transforming foreign economies to create a new supply of customers. The driving force was no longer merely one of procuring foreign products; in addition, and often more important, was the pressure to grab every opportunity to carve out new markets or capture existing ones.

This does not mean that each and every act of expansion was in response to a specific economic need or pressure. Many diverse factors were at work. Fortune-seeking adventurers; business promoters and land speculators; millions of migrants fleeing from economic, political, and religious oppression; ambitious military chiefs and colonial administrators; political leaders aiming to cope with internal problems, notably to counteract growing working-class consciousness and struggle—these were among the actors who played important roles in, and helped fashion the concrete aspects of, the vast spread of Europe (and Europeans) over the globe during the past centuries.

At the root of all this movement, however, was a vigorously growing capitalism as it evolved from its birth during the creation of world commerce to a system that flourished in proportion to its expansion on a worldwide scale. In the words of Joan Robinson, "few would deny that the extension of capitalism into new territories was the mainspring of . . . the 'vast secular boom' of the last two hundred years."[1] This secular boom was nourished by the essential dynamic of the socioeconomic organism on which it rested: the persistent search for new profitable investments, spurred by competition among investors for markets.

The difficulty with many analyses of expansionism and imperialism is that they separate out and isolate some of the contributing elements and in so doing fail to see the whole picture. For example, the international nature of competition is customarily treated solely in terms of relative productive efficiencies, thereby ignoring decisive historical factors that created and continue to modify the international division of labor. Foreign markets did not spring up automatically. They often required disruptions of existing economic bases of dominated areas, disintegration of local production, and artificial stimulation of production for exchange and the use of money. Military power has been used to encourage advantageous trade and other economic relations. Above all, control and influence in international money markets, international banking, insurance, and shipping have been, and continue to be, major instruments in firming up and maintaining a hold on trade channels. Even if a country's conquest of territory and enlargement of its sphere of influence may have occurred without any relation to a specific trade goal, nevertheless by adding weight to one or more of the elements that directly or indirectly strengthen the dominating country's overall competitive position, the trade factor may be extremely important in initiating and sustaining the overall process of expansion.

Failure to examine the capitalist organism as a whole also results in a tendency to overlook the uneven development of capitalism with its varying effects on the needs of capital accumulation in different countries at different times. Thus, there are those who insist that unless a simple economic "law" can be found which applies equally to the geographical spread of Portugal, tsarist Russia, and Great Britain, any logical connection between capitalism and expansionism must be denied. Precisely these examples, however, are in fact useful illustrations of the nature and role of capitalist expansionism at contrasting stages of development and in different historical contexts. Although contemporaneous, Great Britain's territorial expansion in the mid-nineteenth century took place under the impact of a mature industrial capitalism, while that of Russia in the same period occurred during a slow transition from merchant to industrial capitalism. (The trends in both countries are examined in the first essay, European Expansion Since 1763.) The case of Portugal illuminates another important aspect of the issues discussed in this book: how the hierarchical relations of the world capitalist system unfolded. The role of England's military protection of Portugal, the consequent special trade favors received by England, and the resulting contribution made by the gold flowing from Portugal's Brazilian colony to the establishment

of London as the gold bullion market of the world are discussed in the fifth essay, Economic Myths and Imperialism.

The pressing need for historical differentiation arises
especially with respect to the changes during the late nineteenth century, when new colonial powers entered the scene
(including for the first time an Asian nation, Japan), when
the search for and acquisition of new colonies was revitalized
(notably, the scramble for Africa), and when a struggle for
hegemony among the leading powers emerged in full force. It
was in this period, also, that the term *imperialism* came into
widespread use. Subsequently, Lenin led the way in limiting
the term to this stage of capitalism in order to distinguish its
unique features from earlier processes of expansionism. The
significance of this distinction is explored in the second
essay, Imperialism: A Historical Survey, as well as in the first,
and there is no need to dwell on the matter in this introduction. But I think it would be useful to refer briefly to three
prevalent misconceptions about this period that must be
guarded against.

First, it should be pointed out that even though Marxists
stress the expansionist imperatives of capitalism, it does not
follow that they hold to the theme that every instance of
territorial aggrandizement is impelled by immediate economic interests in the acquired area. In this connection, Paul
Sweezy's observations of thirty-six years ago concerning this
question are worth recalling. Working within the Marxist
framework, he carefully explained and emphasized the role
of *protective* and *anticipatory* annexations:

> Much of this renewed activity in empire building [in the late
> nineteenth century] was of a protective or anticipatory character.
> When one country lays claim to an area, it follows as a matter of
> course that the nationals of other countries will at the very least
> be at a serious disadvantage in doing business there. Con-
> sequently, though English capitalists may have little to gain
> through annexation by their own country, they may have much
> to lose through annexation by France or Germany. As soon as
> rivals appear on the scene, each country must make every effort
> to protect its position against the incursion of the others. The

result may appear to be a net loss, but this is only because the measurement is made from an irrelevant base. What is important is not the loss or gain compared to the pre-existing situation, but rather the loss or gain compared to the situation which would have prevailed had a rival succeeded in stepping in ahead. This is a principle of wide application in the economics of monopoly; when applied to the building of colonial empires it may appropriately be referred to as the principle of protective annexation. Closely related in some ways is the urge to annex territories which, though of little or no present value, nevertheless may become valuable in the future. This may be called the principle of anticipatory annexation. Protective and anticipatory annexations played a very important part in the late-nineteenth-century scramble for still unclaimed parts of the earth's surface. Finally, we must not forget considerations of a strategic nature. An empire must be defensible from a military standpoint, and this obviously implies the need for well-placed land and sea bases, lines of communication, and so forth.[2]

A second misconception is involved in confining the economic significance of domination to access to raw materials, investment opportunities, and/or markets. In this way the great and sometimes overriding importance of financial and balance-of-payments considerations is overlooked and implicitly denied. A notable case is India's role in strengthening one of Great Britain's major sources of wealth and power: its hegemonic position as an international financial center before World War I. This relationship has been analyzed in an interresting recent book by Marcello de Cecco in which India's role is summarized as follows:

India had assumed in the twenty-five years under discussion [1890-1914] the role of a protagonist of the international settlements system: her trade surplus with the rest of the world and her trade deficit with England allowed the latter to square her international settlements on current account. This enabled her to use the income from her overseas investment for further investment abroad, and to give back to the international monetary system the liquidity she had absorbed as investment income.

This, however, was not the only reason why India had an important place in the international monetary system. The reserves on which the Indian monetary system was based provided a large *masse de manoeuvre* which British monetary authorities could use to supplement their own reserves and to keep London the center of the international monetary system.[3]

The third area of confusion arises from restricting the definition of imperialism solely to the relation between rich and poor nations. This relation has of course been a crucial feature of expansionism throughout the ages. What is essentially new, however, about the imperialism of the capitalist period, and especially that of the past hundred years, is the prevalence of tension and conflict among a number of leading powers. Rich and powerful as these advanced capitalist nations may appear to be, none of them has ever been omnipotent, and they are all repeatedly subject to many threats and setbacks arising from internal as well as external contradictions. Because each of them suffers from disadvantages and weaknesses, they are all, whatever their position in the hierarchy of the imperialist network, constantly under challenge. At the same time, they are all striving to improve their relative positions vis-à-vis their rivals, to reach a higher rung on the ladder of international trade, investment, and finance. In such a competitive environment, the stronger nations seek to influence and control weaker ones, not only for direct exploitation, but to use them as resources in the inter-imperialist power struggle.

These aspects of imperialism—especially the power conflict at the various levels of the hierarchy of nations, the struggle for hegemony in the international monetary system, and the role of the periphery in the inter-power struggles at the core—have been among the most neglected areas of investigation and should, in my opinion, be high on the agenda for future research in this field.

Notes

1. Introduction to Rosa Luxemburg, *The Accumulation of Capital* (New York: Monthly Review Press, 1964), p. 28.
2. Paul M. Sweezy, *The Theory of Capitalist Development—Principles of Marxian Political Economy*, reprinted. (1942; New York: Monthly Review Press, 1964), pp. 302-3.
3. Marcello de Cecco, *Money and Empire, The International Gold Standard,1890-1914* (Oxford: Basil Blackwell, 1974), p. 62. The rest of the fourth chapter, in which this passage occurs, supplies evidence and analyzes still another aspect of India's financial role in the world economy: "India had played a similar role in the period immediately preceding, when she had stemmed world inflation by absorbing huge quantities of silver which would have otherwise glutted the Western markets. It is a common belief that India was always the silver standard country *par excellence.* This belief, like many others, has proved to be false. Silver was imposed on India by the British." (p. 62)

A Technical Note

I would like to take this opportunity to raise what parliamentarians might call a point of personal privilege. In *The Age of Imperialism* I had occasion to make a statistical comparison showing an increase in earnings of U.S. foreign investments as a percent of all after-tax profits on operations of domestic nonfinancial corporations from approximately 10 percent in 1950 to about 22 percent in 1964 (pp. 182-83).* These estimates have been attacked as invalid on grounds which, if correct, would indicate either bad faith or woeful ignorance on my part. I am afraid, however, that it is my critics who need to do their homework.

To the best of my knowledge, the criticism was first made by Professor Robert Tucker of Johns Hopkins, then expanded upon by Professor Benjamin Cohen of Tufts, and later repeated or referred to, assuming the critique to be valid, by Professor Barrington Moore of Harvard and others.[1] Two errors were alleged: (1) the data on profits from foreign investment included profits of financial corporations, while those relating to domestic corporations excluded financial corporations; and (2) the data on foreign profits (which con-

---

* The earnings of domestic nonfinancial earnings include that portion of foreign earnings transferred to the parent corporation.

sisted primarily of income from direct investment of U.S. corporations) were *before* taxes, and those on profits of domestic corporations were *after* taxes. Such noncomparability, it was argued, stacked the deck.*

Let us take up these points in order. Obviously, a meaningful ratio, or percentage, can only be obtained if the numerator and denominator measure comparables. The proper approach, in my opinion, would have been to exclude financial corporations in both the numerator and denominator. The reason for this was that financial corporations in the United States include a wide variety of activities that are essentially domestic, such as, for example, extending installment credit and other consumer loans, casualty and life insurance, and real estate transactions. The data, however, were not available at that time to permit exclusion of financial corporations from the numerator. I therefore undertook a study of the question based on examination of indirect data and interviews with statisticians experienced in the field, and concluded that the net income of financial corporations from foreign operations was relatively negligible. (Remember that the comparison covered the period from 1950 to 1965, a period prior to the major explosion of foreign-branch banking.) Based on the results of this study, it became clear to me that including the profits of financial corporations in the numerator while excluding them from the denominator would produce a much more reasonable approximation of comparability than any other method.

Now, since that time the Commerce Department has published a special survey of U.S. direct investment abroad in which data on net income from foreign operations of finan-

---

* Professor Cohen added other wrinkles, charging, for example, that my data exaggerated the case since they included profits of all foreign investment, which are larger than profits of investment in Third World countries. This is almost too silly and obvious to argue about, since I clearly indicated that my purpose was to measure the significance of *all* U.S. foreign investment. He could, if he wished, dispute the significance of the question the data were intended to answer. But that is quite another matter from implying that the intention was to inflate the magnitudes involved.

cial corporations can be found. It is therefore possible to check my judgment against official figures. While it would have been better to have such data for 1964, the year Professor Tucker uses to challenge my percentages, the special survey unfortunately deals only with 1966. But the years are so close, and, as we will soon see, the magnitudes so small, that the utilization of the 1966 survey should give us a fairly good idea of what all the shouting is about. The net income of foreign finance and insurance operations, including earnings abroad from royalties, fees, and services, came to $288 million in 1966.[2] Had an equivalent figure been deducted from the numerator, the "perfect" comparable percent of earnings from nonfinancial operations abroad (relative to the earnings from domestic corporate operations) for 1964 would show up as 21.7 percent instead of the 22.7 percent estimate in *The Age of Imperialism.* Anyone acquainted with the frequent and sizeable revisions made by the Department of Commerce of their corporate profits statistics will surely recognize that this difference is less than the margin of error in the basic data. Also, it should be noted, the percentage stated in the text of *The Age of Imperialism* was conservatively rounded off to 22, and if one were to round off the newly corrected one it would still be 22.

Insignificant as the first point turns out to be, the second criticism advanced by the critics is indeed potentially of major proportions. A comparison of profits before taxes in the numerator with profits after taxes in the denominator would be tantamount to an egregious falsification. The trouble here is that the professors did not take the trouble to read the text published in the government's statistical publications. Had they bothered to do this, they would have discovered that the Commerce Department data on net earnings of foreign affiliates of U.S. corporations are net *after* taxes, and not, as they assumed, *before* taxes. Here, for example, is the standard definition stated time and again alongside the published statistics: "Net earnings measures the U.S. owners' share, based on percentage of ownership, in the after-tax net earnings of foreign affiliates."[3]

The shoe, then, is on the other foot. It is Professors Tucker and Cohen who, in their eagerness to expose alleged falsification of data by radicals, fall into the noncomparability trap. The "corrected" alternate percentages they present are constructed by putting before-tax profits in the denominator, thereby comparing after-tax foreign profits with before-tax domestic profits. As for *The Age of Imperialism*, the data on corporate profits in the numerator and the denominator are both *after* taxes.

There might still have been a potential for error in my calculations, since the taxes deducted from earnings of foreign affiliates are those collected by the host countries. If the tax rates in the latter were substantially lower than those in the United States, then I would indeed have been overstating the importance of foreign earnings. But based on a study of tax rates and consultations with tax attorneys I had concluded the opposite to be the case. This judgment was substantiated in a recent government study. A sample survey made by the Department of Commerce for 1970 reveals that the foreign affiliates covered by the sample had an effective tax rate of 45.1 percent, while the U.S. parent corporations had an effective tax rate of only 39.2 percent.[4]

Notes

1. Robert W. Tucker, *The Radical Left and American Foreign Policy* (Baltimore: The Johns Hopkins Press, 1971), p. 128; Benjamin J. Cohen, *The Question of Imperialism* (New York: Basic Books, 1973), pp. 136-37; and Barrington Moore, Jr., *Reflections on the Causes of Human Misery* (Boston: Beacon Press, 1972), p. 124.
2. U.S. Department of Commerce, *U.S. Direct Investments Abroad 1966, Part I: Balance of Payments Data* (Washington, D.C.: Superintendent of Documents, 1970), pp. 70 and 147.
3. Ibid., p. 18.
4. Robert B. Leftwich, "U.S. Multinational Companies: Profitability, Financial Leverage, and Effective Income Tax Rates," *Survey of Current Business*, May 1974, p. 34.

HISTORY

1

European Expansion Since 1763

The global expansion of Western Europe between the 1760s and the 1870s differed in several important ways from the expansionism and colonialism of previous centuries. Along with the rise of the Industrial Revolution, which economic historians generally trace to the 1760s, and the continuing spread of industrialization in the empire-building countries came a shift in the strategy of trade with the colonial world. Instead of being primarily buyers of colonial products (and frequently under strain to offer sufficient salable goods to balance the exchange), as in the past, the industrializing nations increasingly became sellers in search of markets for the growing volume of their machine-produced goods. Furthermore, over the years there occurred a decided shift in the composition of demand for goods produced in the colonial areas. Spices, sugar, and slaves became relatively less important with the advance of industrialization, concomitant with a rising demand for raw materials for industry (e.g., cotton, wool, vegetable oils, jute, dyestuffs) and food for the swelling industrial areas (wheat, tea, coffee, cocoa, meat, butter).

This article originally appeared in volume 4 of the fifteenth edition of the Encyclopaedia Britannica, copyright © 1974 by Encyclopaedia Britannica, Inc.

This shift in trading patterns entailed, in the long run, changes in colonial policy and practice as well as in the nature of colonial acquisitions. The urgency to create markets and the incessant pressure for new materials and food were eventually reflected in colonial practices, which sought to adapt the colonial areas to the new priorities of the industrializing nations. Such adaptation involved major disruptions of existing social systems over wide areas of the globe. Before the impact of the Industrial Revolution, the changes forced upon the non-European world were largely confined to: (1) occupying areas that supplied precious metals, slaves, and tropical products then in large demand; (2) establishing white-settler colonies along the coast of North America; and (3) setting up trading posts and forts and applying superior military strength to achieve the transfer to European merchants of as much existing world trade as was feasible. However disruptive these changes may have been to the societies of Africa, South America, and the isolated plantation and white-settler colonies, the social systems over most of the earth outside Europe nevertheless remained much the same as they had been for centuries (in some places for millennia). These societies, with their largely self-sufficient small communities based on subsistence agriculture and home industry, provided poor markets for the mass-produced goods flowing from the factories of the technologically advancing countries; nor were the existing social systems flexible enough to introduce and rapidly expand the commercial agriculture (and, later, mineral extraction) required to supply the food and raw material needs of the empire-builders.

The adaptation of the nonindustrialized parts of the world to become more profitable adjuncts of the industrializing nations embraced, among other things: (1) overhaul of existing land and property arrangements, including the introduction of private property in land where it did not previously exist, as well as the expropriation of land for use by white settlers or for plantation agriculture; (2) creation of a labor supply for commercial agriculture and mining by means of direct forced labor and indirect measures aimed at generating a body of wage-seeking laborers; (3) spread of the use of money and exchange of commodities by imposing money payments for taxes and land rent and by inducing a decline of home industry; and (4) where the precolonial society already had a developed industry, curtailment of production and exports by native producers.

The classic illustration of this last policy is found in India. For centuries India had been an exporter of cotton goods, to such an extent that Great Britain for a long period imposed stiff tariff duties to protect its domestic manufacturers from Indian competition. Yet, by the middle of the nineteenth century, India was receiving one-fourth of all British exports of cotton piece goods and had lost its own export markets.

Clearly, such significant transformations could not get very far in the absence of appropriate political changes, such as the development of a sufficiently cooperative local elite, effective administrative techniques, and peace-keeping instruments that would assure social stability and environments conducive to the radical social changes imposed by a foreign power. Consistent with these purposes was the installation of new, or amendments of old, legal systems that would facilitate the operation of a money, business, and private land economy. And tying it all together was the imposition of the culture and language of the dominant power.

The changing nature of the relations between centers of empire and their colonies, under the impact of the unfolding Industrial Revolution, was also reflected in new trends in colonial acquisitions. While in preceding centuries colonies, trading posts, and settlements were in the main, except for South America, located along the coastline or on smaller islands, the expansions of the late eighteenth century and especially of the nineteenth century were distinguished by the spread of the colonizing powers, or of their emigrants, into the interior of continents. Such continental extensions, in general, took one of two forms, or some combination of the two: (1) the removal of the indigenous peoples by killing them off or forcing them into specially reserved areas, thus providing room for settlers from Western Europe who then developed the agriculture and industry of these lands under the social system imported from the mother countries; or (2) the conquest of the indigenous peoples and the transformation of their existing societies to suit the changing needs of the more powerful militarily and technically advanced nations.

At the heart of Western expansionism was the growing disparity in technologies between those of the leading European nations and those of the rest of the world. Differences between the level of technology in Europe and some of the regions on other continents were not especially great in the early part of the eighteenth century. In fact, some of the crucial technical knowledge used in Europe at that time came originally from Asia. During the eighteenth century, however, and at an accelerating pace in the nineteenth and twentieth centuries, the gap between the technologically advanced countries and technologically backward regions kept on increasing despite the diffusion of modern technology by the colonial powers. The most important aspect of this disparity was the technical superiority of Western armaments, for this superiority enabled the West to impose its will on the much larger colonial populations. Advances in communication and transportation, notably railroads, also became important tools for consolidating foreign rule over extensive territories. And along with the enormous technical superiority and the colonizing experience itself came important psychological instruments of minority rule by foreigners: racism and arrogance on the part of the colonizers and a resulting spirit of inferiority among the colonized.

Naturally, the above description and summary telescope events that transpired over many decades and the incidence of the changes varied from territory to territory and from time to time, influenced by the special conditions in each area, by what took place in the process of conquest, by the circumstances at the time when economic exploitation of the possessions became desirable and feasible, and by the varying political considerations of the several occupying powers. Moreover, it should be emphasized that expansion policies and practices, while far from haphazard, were rarely the result of long-range and integrated planning. The drive for expansion was persistent, as were the pressures to get the greatest advantage possible out of the resulting opportunities. But the expansions arose in the midst of intense rivalry among major powers that were concerned with the distribution of power on the continent of Europe itself as well as with ownership of overseas territories. Thus, the issues of national power, national wealth, and military strength shifted more and more to the world stage as commerce and territorial acquisitions spread over larger segments of the globe. In fact, colonies were themselves often levers of military power —sources of military supplies and of military manpower and bases for navies and merchant marines. What appears, then, in tracing the concrete course of empire is an intertwining of the struggle for hegemony between competing national powers, the maneuvering for preponderance of military strength, and the search for greatest advantage practically obtainable from the world's resources.

European Colonial Activity (1763-c. 1875)

Stages of history rarely, if ever, come in neat packages: the roots of new historical periods begin to form in earlier eras, while many aspects of an older phase linger on and help shape the new. Nonetheless, there was a convergence of developments in the early 1760s, which, despite many qualifications, delineates a new stage in European expansionism and especially in that of the most successful empire-builder, Great Britain. It is not only the Industrial Revolution in Great Britain that can be traced to this period but also the consequences of England's decisive victory over France in the Seven Years' War and the beginnings of what turned out to be the second British Empire. As a result of the Treaty of Paris, France lost nearly the whole of its colonial empire, while Britain became, except for Spain, the largest colonial power in the world.

The second British Empire. The removal of threat from the strongest competing foreign power set the stage for Britain's conquest of India and for operations against the North American Indians to extend British settlement in Canada and westerly areas of the North American continent. In addition, the new commanding position on the seas provided an opportunity for Great Britain to probe for additional markets in Asia and Africa and to try to break the Spanish trade monopoly in South America. During this period, the scope of British world interests broadened dramatically to cover the South Pacific, the Far East, the South Atlantic, and the coast of Africa.

The initial aim of this outburst of maritime activity was not so much the acquisition of extensive fresh territory as the attainment of a far-flung network of trading posts and maritime bases. The latter, it was hoped, would serve the interdependent aims of widening foreign commerce and controlling ocean shipping routes. But in the long run many of these initial bases turned out to be stepping-stones to future territorial conquests. Because the indigenous populations did not always take kindly to foreign incursions into their homelands, even when the foreigners limited themselves to small enclaves, penetration of interiors was often necessary to secure base areas against attack.

Loss of the American colonies. The path of conquest and territorial growth was far from orderly. It was frequently diverted by the renewal or intensification of rivalry between, notably, England, France, Spain, and the Low Countries in colonial areas and on the European continent. The most severe blow to Great Britain's eighteenth century dreams of empire, however, came from the revolt of the thirteen American colonies. These contiguous colonies were at the heart of the old, or what is often referred to as the first, British Empire, which consisted primarily of Ireland, the North American colonies, and the plantation colonies of the West Indies. Ironically, the elimination of this core of the first British Empire was to a large extent influenced by the upsurge of empire building after the Seven Years' War. Great Britain harvested from its victory in that war a new expanse of territory about equal to its prewar possessions on the North

American continent: French Canada, the Floridas, and the territory between the Alleghenies and the Mississippi River. The assimilation of the French Canadians, control of the Indians and settlement of the trans-Allegheny region, and the opening of new trade channels created a host of problems for the British government. Not the least of these were the burdensome costs to carry out this program on top of a huge national debt accumulated during the war. To cope with these problems, new imperial policies were adopted by the mother country: raising (for the first time) revenue from the colonies; tightening mercantile restrictions, imposing firm measures against smuggling (an important source of income for colonial merchants), and putting obstacles in the way of New England's substantial trade with the West Indies. The strains generated by these policies created or intensified the hardships of large sections of the colonial population and, in addition, disrupted the relative harmony of interests that had been built up between the mother country and important elite groups in the colonies. Two additional factors, not unrelated to the enlargement of the British Empire, fed the onset and success of the American War of Independence (1775-1783): first, a lessening need for military support from the mother country once the menacing French were removed from the continent, and, second, support for the forces of the American Revolution from the French and Spanish, who had much to fear from the enhanced sea power and expansionism of the British.

The shock of defeat in North America was not the only problem confronting the British society. Ireland—in effect, a colonial dependency—also experienced a revolutionary upsurge, giving added significance to attacks by leading British free traders against existing colonial policies and even at times against colonialism itself. But such criticism had little effect except as it may have hastened colonial administrative reforms to counteract real and potential independence movements in dependencies such as Canada and Ireland.

Conquest of India. Apart from reforms of this nature, the aftermath of American independence was a diversion of

British imperial interests to other areas—the beginning of the settlement of Australia being a case in point. In terms of amount of effort and significance of results, however, the pursuit of conquest in India took first place. Starting with the assumption of control over the province of Bengal (after the Battle of Plassey in 1757) and especially after the virtual removal of French influence from the Indian Ocean, the British waged more or less continuous warfare against the Indian people and took over more and more of the interior. The Marathas, the main source of resistance to foreign intrusion, were decisively defeated in 1803, but military resistance of one sort or another continued until the middle of the nineteenth century. The financing and even the military manpower for this prolonged undertaking came mainly from India itself. As British sovereignty spread, new land-revenue devices were soon instituted, which resulted in raising the revenue to finance the consolidation of power in India and the conquest of other regions, breaking up the old system of self-sufficient and self-perpetuating villages, and supporting an elite whose self-interests would harmonize with British rule.

Global expansion. Except for the acquisition of additional territory in India and colonies in Sierra Leone and New South Wales, the important additions to British overseas possessions between the Seven Years' War and the end of the Napoleonic era came as prizes of victory in wars with rival European colonial powers. In 1763 the first British Empire was primarily focused on North America. By 1815, despite the loss of the thirteen colonies, Britain had a second empire, one that straddled the globe from Canada and the Caribbean in the Western Hemisphere around the Cape of Good Hope to India and Australia. This empire was sustained by and in turn was supported by maritime power that far exceeded that of any of Britain's European rivals.

Policy changes. The half century of global expansion is only one aspect of the transition to the second British Empire. The operations of the new empire in the longer run also reflected decisive changes in British society. The replacement of mercantile by industrial enterprise as the main source of national wealth entailed changes to make national and colonial policy more consistent with the new hierarchy of interests. The restrictive trade practices and monopolistic privileges that sustained the commercial explosion of the sixteenth and most of the seventeenth centuries—built around the slave trade, colonial plantations, and monopolistic trading companies—did not provide the most effective environment for a nation on its way to becoming the workshop of the world.

The desired restructuring of policies occurred over decades of intense political conflict: the issues were not always clearly delineated, interest groups frequently overlapped, and the balance of power between competing vested interests shifted from time to time. The issues were clearly drawn in some cases, as for example over the continuation of the British East India Company's trade monopoly. The company's export of Indian silk, muslins, and other cotton goods was seen to be an obstacle to the development of markets for competing British manufactures. Political opposition to this monopoly was strong at the end of the eighteenth century, but the giant step on the road to free trade was not taken until the early decades of the nineteenth century: termination of the Indian trade monopoly in 1813 and the Chinese trade monopoly in 1833.

In contrast, the issues surrounding the strategic slave trade were much more complicated. The West Indies plantations relied on a steady flow of slaves from Africa. British merchants and ships profited not only from supplying these slaves but also from the slave trade with other colonies in the Western Hemisphere. In fact, the British were the leading slave traders, controlling at least half of the transatlantic slave trade by the end of the eighteenth century. But the influential planter and slave-trade interests had come under vigorous and unrelenting attack by religious and humanitarian leaders and organizations, who propelled the issue of abolition to the forefront of British politics around the turn of the nineteenth century. Historians are still unraveling the threads of conflicting arguments about the priority of causes in the final abolition of the slave trade and, later, of slavery itself, because economic as well as political issues were at play: glutted sugar markets (to which low-cost producers in competing colonies contributed) stimulated thoughts about controlling future output by limiting the supply of fresh slaves; the compensation paid to plantation owners by the British government at the time of the abolition of slavery rescued many planters from bankruptcy during a sugar crisis, with a substantial part of the compensation money being used to pay off planters' debts to London bankers. Moreover, the battle between proslavery and antislavery forces was fought in an environment in which free-trade interests were challenging established mercantilist practices and the West Indies sugar economy was in a secular decline.

The British were not the first to abolish the slave trade. Denmark had ended it earlier, and the United States Constitution, written in 1787, had already provided for its termination in 1808. But the British Act of 1807 formally forbidding the slave trade was followed up by diplomatic and naval pressure to suppress the trade. By the 1820s Holland, Sweden, and France had also passed antislave-trade laws. Such laws and attempts to enforce them by no means stopped the trade, so long as there was buoyant demand for this commodity and good profit from dealing in it. Some decline in the demand for slaves did follow the final emancipation in 1833 of slaves in British possessions. On the other hand, the demand for slaves elsewhere in the Americas took on new life—e.g., to work the virgin soils of Cuba and Brazil and to pick the rapidly expanding U.S. cotton crops to feed the voracious appetite of the British textile industry. Accordingly, the number of slaves shipped across the Atlantic accelerated at the same time Britain and other maritime powers outlawed this form of commerce.

Involvement in Africa. Although Britain's energetic activity to suppress the slave trade was far from effective, its diplomatic and military operations for this end led it to much greater involvement in African affairs. Additional colonies were acquired—Sierra Leone in 1808, Gambia in 1816, and the Gold Coast in 1821—to serve as bases for suppressing the slave trade and for stimulating substitute commerce. British naval squadrons touring the coast of Africa, stopping and inspecting suspected slavers of other nations, and forcing African tribal chiefs to sign antislavery treaties did not halt the expansion of the slave trade, but they did help Britain attain a commanding position along the western coast of Africa, which in turn contributed to the expansion of both its commercial and colonial empire.

The growth of informal empire. The transformation of the old colonial and mercantilist commercial system was completed when, in addition to the abolition of slavery and the slave trade, the Corn Laws and the Navigation Acts were repealed in the late 1840s. The repeal of the Navigation Acts acknowledged the new reality: the primacy of Britain's navy and merchant shipping. The repeal of the Corn Laws (which had protected agricultural interests) signaled the maturation of the Industrial Revolution. In the light of Britain's manufacturing supremacy, exclusivity and monopolistic trade restraints were less important than, and often detrimental to, the need for ever-expanding world markets and sources of inexpensive raw materials and food.

With the new trade strategy, under the impetus of freer trade and technical progress, came a broadening of the concept of empire. It was found that the commercial and financial advantages of formal empire could often be derived by informal means. The development of a worldwide trade network, the growth of overseas banking, the export of capital to less advanced regions, the leading position of London's money markets—all under the shield of a powerful and mobile navy—led to Great Britain's economic preeminence and influence in many parts of the world, even in the absence of political control.

Anticolonial sentiment. The growing importance of informal empire went hand in hand with increased expressions of dissatisfaction with the formal colonial empire. The critical approach to empire came from leading statesmen, government officials in charge of colonial policy, the free traders, and the philosophic Radicals (the latter, a broad spectrum of opinion-makers often labeled the Little Englanders, whose voices of dissent were most prominent in the years between 1840 and 1870). Taking the long view, however, some historians question just how much of this current of political thought was really concerned with the transformation of the British Empire into a Little England. Those who seriously considered colonial separation were for the most part thinking of the more recent white-settler colonies, such as Canada, Australia, and New Zealand, and definitely not of independence for India nor, for that matter, for Ireland. Differences of opinion among the various political factions naturally existed over the best use of limited government finance, colonial administrative tactics, how much foreign territory could in practice be controlled, and such issues as the costs of friction with the United States over Canada. Yet, while there were important differences of opinion on the choice between formal and informal empire, no important conflict arose over the desirability of continued expansion of Britain's world influence and foreign commercial activity. Indeed, during the most active period of what has been presumed to be anticolonialism, both the formal and informal empires grew substantially: new colonies were added, the territory of existing colonies was enlarged, and military campaigns were conducted to widen Britain's trading and investment area, as in the Opium Wars of the mid-nineteenth century (see *Penetration of the West in Asia,* p. 44 below).

Decline of colonial rivalry. An outstanding development in colonial and empire affairs during the period between the Napoleonic Wars and the 1870s was an evident lessening in conflict between European powers. Not that conflict disappeared entirely, but the period as a whole was one of relative calm compared with either the almost continuous wars for colonial possessions in the eighteenth century or the revival of intense rivalries during the latter part of the nineteenth and early twentieth centuries. Instead of wars among colonial powers, the period witnessed wars against colonized peoples and their societies, incident either to initial conquest or to the extension of territorial possessions farther into the interior. Examples are Great Britain in India, Burma, South Africa (the Kaffir Wars), New Zealand (the Maori Wars); France in Algeria and Indochina; the Low Countries in Indonesia; Russia in Central Asia; and the United States against the North American Indians.

Contributing to the abatement of intercolonial rivalries was the undisputable supremacy of the British Navy during these years. The increased use of steamships in the nineteenth century helped reinforce this supremacy: Great Britain's ample domestic coal supply and its numerous bases around the globe (already owned or newly obtained for this purpose) combined to make available needed coaling stations. Over several decades of the nineteenth century and until new developments toward the end of the century opened up a new age of naval rivalry, no country was in a position to challenge Britain's dominance of the seas. This may have temporarily weakened Britain's acquisitive drive: the motive of preclusive occupation of foreign territory still occurred, but it was not as pressing as at other times.

On the whole, despite the relative tranquility and the rise of anticolonial sentiment in Britain, the era was marked by a notable wave of European expansionism. Thus, in 1800 Europe and its possessions, including former colonies, claimed title to about 55 percent of the earth's land surface: Europe, North and South America, most of India, and small sections along the coast of Africa. But much of this was merely claimed; effective control existed over a little less than 35 percent, most of which consisted of Europe itself. By 1878—that is, before the next major wave of European acquisitions began—an additional 6,500,000 square miles (16,800,000 square kilometers) were claimed; during this period, control was consolidated over the new claims and over all the territory claimed in 1800. Hence, from 1800 until 1878, actual European rule (including former colonies in North and South America) increased from 35 to 67 percent of the earth's land surface.

Decline of the Spanish and Portuguese empires. The early nineteenth century, however, did witness a conspicuous exception to the trend of colonial growth, and that was the decline of the Portuguese and Spanish empires in the Western Hemisphere. The occasion for the decolonization was provided by the Napoleonic Wars. The French occupation of the Iberian Peninsula in 1807, combined with the ensuing years of intense warfare until 1814 on that peninsula (between the British and French and their respective allies), effectively isolated the colonies from their mother countries. During this isolation the long-smouldering discontents in the colonies erupted in influential nationalist movements, revolutions of independence, and civil wars. The stricken mother countries could hardly interfere with events on the South American continent, nor did they have the resources, even after the Peninsular War was over, to bring enough soldiers and armaments across the Atlantic to suppress the independence forces.

Great Britain could have intervened on behalf of Spain and Portugal, but it declined. British commerce with South America had blossomed during the Napoleonic Wars. New vistas of potentially profitable opportunities opened up in those years, in contrast with preceding decades when British penetration of Spanish colonial markets consisted largely of smuggling to get past Spain's mercantile restrictions. The British therefore now favored independence for these colonies and had little interest in helping to reimpose colonial rule, with its accompanying limitations on British trade and investment. Support for colonial independence by the British came in several ways: merchants and financiers provided loans and supplies needed by insurrectionary governments; the British navy protected the shipment of those supplies and the returning specie; and the British government made it clear to other nations that it considered South American countries independent. The British forthright position on independence, as well as the availability of the British navy to support this policy, gave substance to the U.S. Monroe Doctrine of 1823, which the United States had insufficient strength at that time to really enforce.

After some fifteen years of uprisings and wars, Spain by 1825 no longer had any colonies in South America itself, retaining only the islands of Cuba and Puerto Rico. During the same period Brazil achieved its independence from Portugal. The advantages to the British economy made possible by the consequent opening up of the Latin American ports were eagerly pursued, facilitated by commercial treaties signed with these young nations. The reluctance of France to recognize their new status delayed French penetration of their markets and gave an advantage to the British. In one liberated area after another, brokers and commercial agents arrived from England to ferret out business opportunities. Soon the continent was flooded with British goods, often competing with much weaker native industries. Actually, Latin America provided the largest single export market for British cotton textiles in the first half of the nineteenth century.

Despite the absence of formal empire, the British were able to attain economic preeminence in South America. Spanish and Portuguese colonialism had left a heritage of disunity and conflict within regions of new nations and between nations, along with conditions that led to unstable alliances of ruling elite groups. While this combination of weaknesses militated against successful self-development, it was fertile ground for energetic foreign entrepreneurs, especially those who had technically advanced manufacturing capacities, capital resources, international money markets, insurance and shipping facilities, plus supportive foreign policies. The early orgy of speculative loans and investments soon ended. But before long, British economic penetration entered into more lasting and self-perpetuating activities, such as promoting Latin American exports, providing railroad equipment, constructing public works, and supplying banking networks. Thus, while the collapse of the Spanish and Portuguese empires led to the decline of colonialism in the Western Hemisphere, it also paved the way for a significant expansion of

Britain's informal empire of trade, investment, and finance during the nineteenth century.

The emigration of European peoples. European influence around the globe increased with each new wave of emigration from Europe. Tides of settlers brought with them the Old World culture and, often, useful agricultural and industrial skills. An estimated 55,000,000 Europeans left their native lands in the 100 years after 1820, the product chiefly of two forces: (1) the push to emigrate as a result of difficulties arising from economic dislocations at home, and (2) the pull of land, jobs, and recruitment activities of passenger shipping lines and agents of labor-hungry entrepreneurs in the New World. Other factors were clearly also at work, such as the search for religious freedom, escape from tyrannical governments, avoidance of military conscription, and the desire for greater upward social and economic mobility. Such motives had existed throughout the centuries, however, and they are insufficient to explain the massive population movements that characterized the nineteenth century. Unemployment induced by rapid technological changes in agriculture and industry was an important incentive for English emigration in the mid-1800s. The surge of German emigration at roughly the same time is largely attributable to an agricultural revolution in Germany, which nearly ruined many farmers on small holdings in southwest Germany. Under English rule, the Irish were prevented from industrial development and were directed to an economy based on export of cereals grown on small holdings. A potato blight, followed by famine and eviction of farm tenants by landlords, gave large numbers of Irish no alternative other than emigration or starvation. These three nationalities—English, German, and Irish—composed the largest group of migrants in the 1850s. In later years Italians and Slavs contributed substantially to the population spillover. The emigrants spread throughout the world, but the bulk of the population transfer went to the Americas, Siberia, and Australasia. The population outflow, greatly facilitated by European supremacy outside Europe, helped ease the social pressures and probably abated the dangers of social upheaval in Europe itself.

Advance of the U.S. frontier. The outward movement of European peoples in any substantial numbers naturally was tied in with conquest and, to a greater or lesser degree, with the displacement of indigenous populations. In the United States, where by far the largest number of European emigrants went, acquisition of space for development by white immigrants entailed activity on two fronts: competition with rival European nations and disposition of the Indians. During a large part of the nineteenth century, the United States remained alert to the danger of encirclement by Europeans, but in addition the search for more fertile land, pursuit of the fur trade, and desire for ports to serve commerce in the Atlantic and Pacific oceans nourished the drive to penetrate the American continent. The most pressing points of tension with European nations were eliminated during the first half of the century: purchase of the Louisiana Territory from France in 1803 gave the United States control over the heartland of the continent; settlement of the War of 1812 ended British claims south of the 49th parallel up to the Rocky Mountains; Spain's cession of the Floridas in 1819 rounded out the Atlantic coastal frontier; and Russia's (in 1824) and Great Britain's (in 1846) relinquishment of claims to the Oregon territory gave the United States its window on the Pacific. The expansion of the United States, however, was not confined to liquidating rival claims of overseas empires; it also involved taking territory from neighboring Mexico. United States settlers wrested Texas from Mexico in 1836, and war against Mexico (1846–1848) led to the U.S. annexation of the Southwest region between New Mexico and Utah to the Pacific Ocean.

Diplomatic and military victories over the European nations and Mexico were but one precondition for the transcontinental expansion of the United States. In addition, the Indian tribes sooner or later had to be rooted out to clear the new territory. At times, treaties were arranged with Indian tribes, by which vast areas were opened up for white settlement. But even where peaceful agreements had been reached, the persistent pressure of the search for land and commerce created recurrent wars with Indian tribes that were seeking to retain their homes and their land. On the whole, room for the new settlers was obtained by forced removal of natives to as yet nonwhite-settled land—a process that was repeated as white settlers occupied ever more territory. Massacres during wars, susceptibility to infectious European diseases, and hardships endured during forced migrations all contributed to the decline in the Indian population and the weakening of its resistance. Nevertheless, Indian wars occupied the United States army's attention during most of the nineteenth century, ending with the eventual isolation of the surviving Indians on reservations set aside by the U.S. government.

The New Imperialism (c. 1875-1914)

Reemergence of colonial rivalries. Although there are sharp differences of opinion over the reasons for, and the significance of, the "new imperialism," there is little dispute that at least two developments in the late nineteenth and in the beginning of the twentieth century signify a new departure: (1) notable speedup in colonial acquisitions, and (2) an increase in the number of colonial powers.

New acquisitions. The annexations during this new phase of imperial growth differed significantly from the expansionism earlier in the nineteenth century. While the latter was substantial in magnitude, it was primarily devoted to the consolidation of claimed territory (by penetration of continental interiors and more effective rule over indigenous populations) and only secondarily to new acquisitions. On the other hand, the new imperialism witnessed a burst of activity in carving up as yet independent areas: taking over almost all Africa, a good part of Asia, and many Pacific islands. This new vigor in the pursuit of colonies is reflected in the fact that the rate of new territorial acquisitions of the new imperialism was almost three times that of the earlier period. Thus, the increase in new territories claimed in the first seventy-five years of the nineteenth century averaged about 83,000 square miles (210,000 square kilometers) a year. As against this, the colonial powers added an average of about 240,000 square miles (620,000 square kilometers) a year between the late 1870s and World War I (1914-1918). By the beginning of that war, the new territory claimed was for the most part fully conquered, and the main military resistance of the indigenous populations had been suppressed. Hence, in 1914, as a consequence of this new expansion and conquest on top of that of preceding centuries, the colonial powers, their colonies, and their former colonies extended over approximately 85 percent of the earth's surface. Economic and political control by leading powers reached almost the entire globe, for, in addition to colonial rule, other means of domination were exercised in the form of spheres of influence, special commercial treaties, and the subordination that lenders often impose on debtor nations.

New colonial powers. This intensification of the drive for colonies reflected much more than a new wave of overseas activities by traditional colonial powers, including Russia. The new imperialism was distinguished particularly by the emergence of additional nations seeking slices of the colonial pie: Germany, the United States, Belgium, Italy, and, for the first time, a non-European power, Japan. Indeed, this very multiplication of colonial powers, occurring in a relatively short period, accelerated the tempo of colonial growth. Unoccupied space that could potentially be colonized was limited. Therefore, the more nations there were seeking additional colonies at about the same time, the greater was the premium on speed. Thus, the rivalry among the colonizing nations reached new heights, which in turn strengthened the motivation for preclusive occupation of territory and for attempts to control territory useful for the military defense of existing empires against rivals.

The impact of the new upsurge of rivalry is well illustrated in the case of Great Britain. Relying on its economic preeminence in manufacturing, trade, and international finance as well as on its undisputed mastery of the seas during most of the nineteenth century, Great Britain could afford to relax in the search for new colonies, while concentrating on consolidation of the empire in hand and on building up an informal empire. But the challenge of new empire-builders, backed up by increasing naval power, put a new priority on Britain's desire to extend its colonial empire. On the other hand, the more that potential colonial space shrank, the greater became the urge of lesser powers to remedy disparities in size of empires by redivision of the colonial world. The struggle over contested space and for redivision of empire generated an increase in wars among the colonial powers and an intensification of diplomatic maneuvering.

Rise of new industrialized nations. Parallel with the emergence of new powers seeking a place in the colonial sun and the increasing rivalry among existing colonial powers was the rise of industrialized nations able and willing to challenge Great Britain's lead in industry, finance, and world trade. In the mid-nineteenth century Britain's economy outdistanced by far its potential rivals. But, by the last quarter of that century, Britain was confronted by restless competitors seeking a greater share of world trade and finance; the Industrial Revolution had gained a strong foothold in these nations, which were spurred on to increasing industrialization with the spread of railroad lines and the maturation of integrated national markets.

Moreover, the major technological innovations of the late nineteenth and early twentieth centuries improved the competitive potential of the newer industrial nations. Great Britain's advantage as the progenitor of the first Industrial Revolution diminished substantially as the newer products and sources of energy of what has been called a second Industrial Revolution began to dominate industrial activity. The late starters, having digested the first Industrial Revolution, now had a more equal footing with Great Britain: they were all starting out more or less from the same base to exploit the second Industrial Revolution. This new industrialism, notably featuring mass-produced steel, electric power and oil as sources of energy, industrial chemistry, and the internal-combustion engine, spread over Western Europe, the United States, and eventually Japan.

A world economy. To operate efficiently, the new industries required heavy capital investment in large-scale units. Accordingly, they encouraged the development of capital markets and banking institutions that were large and flexible enough to finance the new enterprises. The larger capital markets and industrial enterprises, in turn, helped push forward the geographic scale of operations of the industrialized nations: more capital could now be mobilized for foreign loans and investment, and the bigger businesses had the resources for the worldwide search for, and development of, the raw materials essential to the success and security of their investments. Not only did the new industrialism generate a voracious appetite for raw materials, but food for the swelling urban populations was now also sought in the far corners of the world. Advances in ship construction (steamships using steel hulls, twin screws, and compound engines) made feasible the inexpensive movement of bulk raw materials and food over long ocean distances. Under the pressures and opportunities of the later decades of the nineteenth century, more and more of the world was drawn upon as primary producers for the industrialized nations. Self-contained economic regions dissolved into a world economy, involving an international division of labor whereby the leading industrial nations made and sold manufactured products and the rest of the world supplied them with raw materials and food.

New militarism. The complex of social, political, and economic changes that accompanied the new industrialism and the vastly expanded and integrated world commerce also provided a setting for intensified commercial rivalry, the rebuilding of high tariff walls, and a revival of militarism. Of special importance militarily was the race in naval construction, which was propelled by the successful introduction and steady improvement of radically new warships that were steam driven, armor-plated, and equipped with weapons able to penetrate the new armor. Before the development of these new technologies, Britain's naval superiority was overwhelming and unchallengeable. But because Britain was now obliged in effect to build a completely new navy, other nations with adequate industrial capacities and the will to devote their resources to this purpose could challenge Britain's supremacy at sea.

The new militarism and the intensification of colonial rivalry signaled the end of the relatively peaceful conditions of the mid-nineteenth century. The conflict over the partition of Africa, the South African War (the Boer War), the Sino-Japanese War, the Spanish-American War, and the Russo-Japanese War were among the indications that the new imperialism had opened a new era that was anything but peaceful.

The new imperialism also represented an intensification of tendencies that had originated in earlier periods. Thus, for example, the decision by the United States to go to war with Spain cannot be isolated from the long-standing interest of the United States in the Caribbean and the Pacific. The defeat of Spain and the suppression of the independence revolutions in Cuba and the Philippines finally gave substance to the Monroe Doctrine: the United States now became the dominant power in the Caribbean, and the door was opened for acquisition of greater influence in all of Latin America. Possession of the Philippines was consistent with the historic interest of the United States in the commerce of the Pacific, as it had already manifested by its long interest in Hawaii (annexed in 1898) and by an expedition by Commodore Matthew Perry to Japan in 1853.

Historiographic debate. The new imperialism marked the end of vacillation over the choice of imperialist military and political policies; similar decisions to push imperialist programs to the forefront were arrived at by the leading industrial nations over a relatively short period. This historical conjuncture requires explanation and still remains the subject of debate among historians and social scientists. The pivot of the controversy is the degree to which the new imperialism was the product of primarily economic forces and in particular whether it was a necessary attribute of the capitalist system.

Serious analysts on both sides of the argument recognize that there is a multitude of factors involved: the main protagonists of economic imperialism recognize that political, military, and ideological influences were also at work; similarly, many who dispute the economic imperialism thesis acknowledge that economic interests played a significant role. The problem, however, is one of assigning priority to causes.

Economic imperialism. The father of the economic interpretation of the new imperialism was the British liberal economist John Atkinson Hobson. In his seminal study, *Imperialism: A Study* (first published in 1902), he pointed to the role of such drives as patriotism, philanthropy, and the spirit of adventure in advancing the imperialist cause. As he saw it, however, the critical question was why the energy of these active agents takes the particular form of imperialist expansion. Hobson located the answer in the financial interests of the capitalist class as "the governor of the imperial engine." Imperialist policy had to be considered irrational if viewed from the vantage point of the nation as a whole: the economic benefits derived were far less than the costs of wars and armaments; and needed social reforms were shunted aside in the excitement of imperial adventure. But it was rational, indeed, in the eyes of the minority of financial interest groups. And the reason for this, in Hobson's view, was the persistent congestion of capital in manufacturing. The pressure of capital needing investment outlets arose in part from a maldistribution of income: low mass-consuming power blocks the absorption of goods and capital inside the country. Moreover, the practices of the larger firms, especially those operating in trusts and combines, foster restrictions on output, thus avoiding the risks and waste of overproduction. Because of this, the large firms are faced with limited opportunities to invest in expanding domestic production. The result of both the maldistribution of income and monopolistic behavior is a need to open up new markets and new investment opportunities in foreign countries.

Hobson's study covered a broader spectrum than the analysis of what he called its economic taproot. It also examined the associated features of the new imperialism, such as political changes, racial attitudes, and nationalism. The book as a whole made a strong impression on, and greatly influenced, Marxist thinkers who were becoming more involved with the struggle against imperialism. The most influential of the Marxist studies was a small book written by Lenin in 1916, *Imperialism: The Highest Stage of Capitalism.* Despite many similarities, at bottom there is a wide gulf between Hobson's and Lenin's frameworks of analysis and also between their respective conclusions. While Hobson saw the new imperialism serving the interests of certain capitalist groups, he believed that imperialism could be eliminated by social reforms while maintaining the capitalist system. This would require restricting the profits of those classes whose interests were closely tied to imperialism and attaining a more equitable distribution of income so that consumers would be able to buy up a nation's production. Lenin, on the other hand, saw imperialism as being so closely integrated with the structure and normal functioning of an advanced capitalism that he believed that only the revolutionary overthrow of capitalism, with the substitution of socialism, would rid the world of imperialism.

Lenin placed the issues of imperialism in a context broader than the interests of a special sector of the capitalist class. According to Lenin, capitalism itself changed in the late nineteenth century; moreover, because this happened at pretty much the same time in several leading capitalist nations, it explains why the new phase of capitalist development came when it did. This new phase, Lenin believed, involves political and social as well as economic changes; but its economic essence is the replacement of competitive capitalism by monopoly capitalism, a more advanced stage in which finance capital, an alliance between large industrial and banking firms, dominates the economic and political life of society. Competition continues, but among a relatively small number of giants who are able to control large sectors of the national and international economy. It is this monopoly capitalism and the resulting rivalry generated among monopoly capitalist nations that foster imperialism; in turn, the processes of imperialism stimulate the further development of monopoly capital and its influence over the whole society.

The difference between Lenin's more complex paradigm and Hobson's shows up clearly in the treatment of capital export. Like Hobson, Lenin maintained that the increasing importance of capital exports is a key figure of imperialism, but he attributed this phenomenon to much more than pressure from an overabundance of capital. He also saw the acceleration of capital migration arising from the desire to obtain exclusive control over raw material sources and to get a tighter grip on foreign markets. He thus shifted the emphasis from the general problem of surplus capital, inherent in capitalism in all its stages, to the imperatives of control over raw materials and markets in the monopoly stage. With this perspective, Lenin also broadened the concept of imperialism. Because the thrust is to divide the world among monopoly interest groups, the ensuing rivalry extends to a struggle over markets in the leading capitalist nations as well as in the less advanced capitalist and colonial countries. This rivalry is intensified because of the uneven development of different capitalist nations: the latecomers aggressively seek a share of the markets and colonies controlled by those who got there first, who naturally resist such a redivision. Other forces—political, military, and ideological—are at play in shaping the contours of imperialist policy, but Lenin insisted that these influences germinate in the seedbed of monopoly capitalism.

Noneconomic imperialism. Perhaps the most systematic alternative theory of imperialism was proposed by Joseph Alois Schumpeter, one of the best known economists of the first half of the twentieth century. His essay "Zur Soziologie des Imperialismus" ("The Sociology of Imperialism") was first published in Germany in the form of two articles in 1919. Although Schumpeter was probably not familiar with Lenin's *Imperialism* at the time he wrote his essay, his arguments were directed against the Marxist currents of thought of the early twentieth century and in particular against the idea that imperialism grows naturally out of capitalism. Unlike other critics, however, Schumpeter accepted some of the components of the Marxist thesis, and to a certain extent he followed the Marxist tradition of looking for the influence of class forces and class interests as major levers of social change. In doing so, he in effect used the weapons of Marxist thought to rebut the essence of Marxist theory.

A survey of empires, beginning with the earliest days of written history, led Schumpeter to conclude that there are three generic characteristics of imperialism: (1) At root is a persistent tendency to war and conquest, often producing nonrational expansions that have no sound utilitarian aim. (2) These urges are not innate in man. They evolved from critical experience when peoples and classes were molded into warriors to avoid extinction; the warrior mentality and the interests of warrior classes live on, however, and influence events even after the vital need for wars and conquests disappears. (3) The drift to war and conquest is sustained and conditioned by the domestic interests of ruling classes, often under the leadership of those individuals who have the most to gain economically and socially from war. But for these factors, Schumpeter believed, imperialism would have been swept away into the dustbin of history as capitalist society ripened; for capitalism in its purest form is antithetical to imperialism: it thrives best with peace and free trade. Yet despite the innate peaceful nature of capitalism, interest groups do emerge that benefit from aggressive foreign conquests. Under monopoly capitalism the fusion of big banks and cartels creates a powerful and influential social group that pressures for exclusive control in colonies and protectorates, for the sake of higher profits.

Notwithstanding the resemblance between Schumpeter's discussion of monopoly and that of Lenin and other Marxists, a crucial difference does remain. Monopoly capitalism in Lenin's frame of reference is a natural outgrowth of the previous stage of competitive capitalism. But according to

Schumpeter, it is an artificial graft on the more natural competitive capitalism, made possible by the catalytic effect of the residue from the preceding feudal society. Schumpeter argued that monopoly capitalism can only grow and prosper under the protection of high tariff walls; without that shield there would be large-scale industry but no cartels or other monopolistic arrangements. Because tariff walls are erected by political decisions, it is the state and not a natural economic process that promotes monopoly. Therefore, it is in the nature of the state—and especially those features that blend the heritage of the previous autocratic state, the old war machine, and feudal interests and ideas along with capitalist interests—that the cause of imperialism will be discovered. The particular form of imperialism in modern times is affected by capitalism, and capitalism itself is modified by the imperialist experience. In Schumpeter's analysis, however, imperialism is neither a necessary nor inevitable product of capitalism.

Quest for a general theory of imperialism. The main trend of academic thought in the Western world is to follow Schumpeter's conclusion—that modern imperialism is not a product of capitalism—without paying close attention to Schumpeter's sophisticated sociological analysis. Specialized studies have produced a variety of interpretations of the origin or reawakening of the new imperialism: for France, bolstering of national prestige after its defeat in the Franco-Prussian War of 1870–1871; for Germany, Bismarck's design to stay in power when threatened by political rivals; for England, the desire for greater military security in the Mediterranean and India. These reasons—along with other frequently mentioned contributing causes, such as the spirit of national and racial superiority and the drive for power—are still matters of controversy with respect to specific cases and to the problem of fitting them into a general theory of imperialism. For example, if it is found that a new colony was acquired for better military defense of existing colonies, the questions still remain as to why the existing colonies were acquired in the first place and why it was considered necessary to defend them rather than to give them up. Similarly, explanations in terms of the search for power still have to account for the close relationship between power and wealth, because in the real world adequate economic resources are needed for a nation to hold on to its power, let alone to increase it. Conversely, increasing a nation's wealth often requires power. As is characteristic of historical phenomena, imperialist expansion is conditioned by a nation's previous history and the particular situation preceding each expansionist move. Moreover, it is carried forth in the midst of a complex of political, military, economic, and psychological impulses. It would seem, therefore, that the attempt to arrive at a theory that explains each and every imperialist action— ranging from a semifeudal Russia to a relatively undeveloped Italy to an industrially powerful Germany—is a vain pursuit. But this does not eliminate the more important challenge of constructing a theory that will provide a meaningful interpretation of the almost simultaneous eruption of the new imperialism in a whole group of leading powers.

Penetration of the West in Asia

Russia's eastward expansion. European nations and Japan at the end of the nineteenth century spread their influence and control throughout the continent of Asia. Russia, because of its geographic position, was the only occupying power whose Asian conquests were overland. In that respect there is some similarity between Russia and the United States in the forcible outward push of their continental frontiers. But there is a significant difference: the United States advance displaced the indigenous population, with the remaining Indians becoming wards of the state. On the other hand, the Russian march across Asia resulted in the incorporation of alien cultures and societies as virtual colonies of the Russian Empire, while providing room for the absorption of Russian settlers.

Although the conquest of Siberia and the drive to the Pacific had been periodically absorbing Russia's military

energies since the sixteenth century, the acquisition of additional Asian territory and the economic integration of previously acquired territory took a new turn in the nineteenth
century. Previously, Russian influence in its occupied territory was quite limited, without marked alteration of the
social and economic structure of the conquered peoples.
Aside from looting and exacting tribute from subject tribes,
the major objects of interest were the fur trade, increased
commerce with China and in the Pacific, and land. But
changes in nineteenth-century Russian society, especially
those coming after the Crimean War (1853–1856), signaled a
new departure. First, Russia's resounding defeat in that war
temporarily frustrated its aspirations in the Balkans and the
Near East; but, because its dynastic and military ambitions
were in no way diminished, its expansionist energies turned
with increased vigor to its Asian frontiers. Second, the emancipation of the serfs in 1861, which eased the feudal restrictions on the landless peasants, led to large waves of migration
by Russians and Ukrainians—first to Siberia and later to
Central Asia. Third, the surge of industrialization, foreign
trade, and railway building in the post-Crimean War decades
paved the way for the integration of Russian Asia, which
formerly, for all practical purposes, had been composed of
separate dependencies, and for a new type of subjugation for
many of these areas, especially in Central Asia, in which the
conquered societies were "colonized" to suit the political and
economic needs of the conqueror.

This process of acquisition and consolidation in Asia
spread out in four directions: Siberia, the Far East, the
Caucasus, and Central Asia. This pursuit of tsarist ambitions
for empire and for warm-water ports involved numerous
clashes and conflicts along the way. Russian expansion was
ultimately limited not by the fierce opposition of the native
population, which was at times a stumbling block, but by the
counterpressure of competitive empire builders, such as Great
Britain and Japan. Great Britain and Russia were mutually
alarmed as the distances between the expanding frontiers of
Russia and India shortened. One point of conflict was finally

resolved when both powers agreed on the delimitation of the northern border of Afghanistan. A second major area of conflict in Central Asia was settled by an Anglo-Russian treaty in 1907 to divide Persia into two separate spheres of influence, leaving a nominally independent Persian nation.

As in the case of Afghanistan and Persia, penetration of Chinese territory produced clashes with both the native government and other imperialist powers. At times China's preoccupation with its struggle against other invading powers eased the way for Russia's penetration. Thus, in 1860, when Anglo-French soldiers had entered Peking, Russia was able to wrest from China the Amur Province and special privileges in Manchuria (Northeast Provinces) south of the Amur River. With this as a stepping-stone, Russia took over the seacoast north of Korea and founded the town of Vladivostok. But, because the Vladivostok harbor is icebound for some four months of the year, the Russians began to pay more attention to getting control of the Korean coastline, where many good year-round harbors could be found. Attempts to acquire a share of Korea, as well as all of Manchuria, met with the resistance of Britain and Japan. Further thrusts into China beyond the Amur and maritime provinces were finally thwarted by defeat in 1905 in the Russo-Japanese War.

The partitioning of China. The evolution of the penetration of Asia was naturally influenced by a multiplicity of factors—economic and political conditions in the expanding nations, the strategy of the military officials of the latter nations, the problems facing colonial rulers in each locality, pressures arising from white settlers and businessmen in the colonies, as well as the constraints imposed by the always limited economic and military resources of the imperialist powers. All these elements were present to a greater or lesser extent at each stage of the forward push of the colonial frontiers by the Dutch in Indonesia, the French in Indochina (Vietnam, Laos, Cambodia), and the British in Malaya, Burma, and Borneo.

Yet, despite the variety of influences at work, three general types of penetration stand out. One of these is expansion designed to overcome resistance to foreign rule. Resistance, which assumed many forms ranging from outright rebellion to sabotage of colonial political and economic domination, was often strongest in the border areas farthest removed from the centers of colonial power. The consequent extension of military control to the border regions tended to arouse the fears and opposition of neighboring states or tribal societies and thus led to the further extension of control. Hence, attempts to achieve military security prompted the addition of border areas and neighboring nations to the original colony.

A second type of expansion was a response to the economic opportunities offered by exploitation of the colonial interiors. Traditional trade and the free play of market forces in Asia did not produce huge supplies of raw materials and food or the enlarged export markets sought by the industrializing colonial powers. For this, entrepreneurs and capital from abroad were needed, mines and plantations had to be organized, labor supplies mobilized, and money economies created. All these alien intrusions functioned best under the firm security of an accommodating alien law and order.

The third type of expansion was the result of rivalry among colonial powers. When possible, new territory was acquired or old possessions extended in order either to preclude occupation by rivals or to serve as buffers for military security against the expansions of nearby colonial powers. Where the crosscurrents of these rivalries prevented any one power from obtaining exclusive control, various substitute arrangements were arrived at: parts of a country were chipped off and occupied by one or more of the powers; spheres of influence were partitioned; unequal commercial treaties were imposed—while the countries subjected to such treatment remained nominally independent.

The penetration of China is the outstanding example of this type of expansion. In the early nineteenth century the middle part of eastern Asia (Japan, Korea, and China), containing about half the Asian population, was still little affected by Western penetration. By the end of the century,

Korea was on the way to becoming annexed by Japan, which had itself become a leading imperialist power. China remained independent politically, though it was already extensively dominated by outside powers. Undoubtedly, the intense rivalry of the foreign powers helped save China from being taken over outright (as India had been). China was pressed on all sides by competing powers anxious for its trade and territory: Russia from the north, Great Britain (via India and Burma) from the south and west, France (via Indochina) from the south, and Japan and the United States (in part, via the Philippines) from the east.

The Opium Wars. The first phase of the forceful penetration of China by Western Europe came in the two Opium Wars. Great Britain had been buying increasing quantities of tea from China, but it had few products that China was interested in buying by way of exchange. A resulting steady drain of British silver to pay for the tea was eventually stopped by Great Britain's ascendancy in India. With British merchants in control of India's foreign trade and with the financing of this trade centered in London, a three-way exchange developed: the tea Britain bought in China was paid for by India's exports of opium and cotton to China. And because of a rapidly increasing demand for tea in England, British merchants actively fostered the profitable exports of opium and cotton from India.

An increasing Chinese addiction to opium fed a boom in imports of the drug and led to an unfavorable trade balance paid for by a steady loss of China's silver reserves. In light of the economic effect of the opium trade plus the physical and mental deterioration of opium users, Chinese authorities banned the opium trade. At first this posed few obstacles to British merchants, who resorted to smuggling. But enforcement of the ban became stringent toward the end of the 1830s; stores of opium were confiscated, and warehouses were closed down. British merchants had an additional and long-standing grievance because the Chinese limited all trade by foreigners to the port of Canton.

In June 1840 the British fleet arrived at the mouth of the

Canton River to begin the first Opium War. The Chinese capitulated in 1842 after the fleet reached the Yangtze, Shanghai fell, and Nanking was under British guns. The resulting Treaty of Nanking—the first in a series of commercial treaties China was forced to sign over the years—provided for: (1) cession of Hong Kong to the British crown; (2) the opening of five treaty ports, where the British would have residence and trade rights; (3) the right of British nationals in China who were accused of criminal acts to be tried in British courts; and (4) the limitation of duties on imports and exports to a modest rate. Other countries soon took advantage of this forcible opening of China; in a few years similar treaties were signed by China with the United States, France, and Russia.

The Chinese, however, tried to retain some independence by preventing foreigners from entering the interior of China. With the country's economic and social institutions still intact, markets for Western goods, such as cotton textiles and machinery, remained disappointing: the self-sufficient communities of China were not disrupted as those in India had been under direct British rule, and opium smuggling by British merchants continued as a major component of China's foreign trade. Western merchants sought further concessions to improve markets. But meanwhile China's weakness, along with the stresses induced by foreign intervention, was further intensified by an upsurge of peasant rebellions, especially the massive fourteen-year Taiping Rebellion of 1850–1864.

The Western powers took advantage of the increasing difficulties by pressing for even more favorable trade treaties, culminating in a second war against China (1856–1860), this time by France and England. Characteristically, the Western powers invading China played a double role: in addition to forcing a new trade treaty, they also helped to sustain the Chinese ruling establishment by participating in the suppression of the Taiping Rebellion; they believed that a Taiping victory would result in a reformed and centralized China, more resistant to Western penetration. China's defeat in the second war with the West produced a series of treaties, signed at Tientsin with Britain, France, Russia, and the United States, which brought the Western world deeper into China's affairs. The Tientsin treaties provided, among other things, for the right of foreign nationals to travel in the interior, the right of foreign ships to trade and patrol on the Yangtze River, the opening up of more treaty ports, and additional exclusive legal jurisdiction by foreign powers over their nationals residing in China.

Foreign privileges in China. Treaties of this general nature were extended over the years to grant further privileges to foreigners. Furthermore, more and more Western nations—including Germany, Italy, Denmark, the Low Countries, Spain, Belgium, and Austria-Hungary—took advantage of the new opportunities by signing such treaties. By the beginning of the twentieth century, some ninety Chinese ports had been opened to foreign control. While the Chinese government retained nominal sovereignty in these ports, de facto rule was exercised by one or more of the powers: in Shanghai, for example, Great Britain and the United States coalesced their interests to form the Shanghai International Settlement. In most of the treaty ports, China leased substantial areas of land at low rates to foreign governments. The consulates in these concessions exercised legal jurisdiction over their nationals, who thereby escaped China's laws and tax collections. The foreign settlements had their own police forces and tax systems and ran their own affairs independently of nominally sovereign China.

These settlements were not the only intrusion on China's sovereignty. In addition, the opium trade was finally legalized, customs duties were forced downward to facilitate competition of imported Western goods, foreign gunboats patrolled China's rivers, and aliens were placed on customs-collection staffs to ensure that China would pay the indemnities imposed by various treaties. In response to these indignities and amid growing antiforeign sentiment, the Chinese government attempted reforms to modernize and develop sufficient strength to resist foreign intrusions. Steps were taken to master Western science and technology, erect shipyards and arsenals, and build a more effective army and navy. The reforms, however, did not get very far; they did not tackle the roots of China's vulnerability, its social and political structure; and they were undertaken quite late, after foreign nations had already established a strong foothold. Also, it is likely that the reforms were not wholehearted because two opposing tendencies were at play: on the one hand, a wish to seek independence and, on the other hand, a basic reliance on foreign support by a weak Manchu government beset with rebellion and internal opposition.

The Open Door Policy. In any event, preliminary attempts to Westernize Chinese society from within did not deter further foreign penetration; nor did the subsequent revolution in 1911 succeed in freeing China from Western domination. Toward the end of the nineteenth century, under the impact of the new imperialism, the spread of foreign penetration accelerated. Germany entered a vigorous bid for its sphere of influence; Japan and Russia pushed forward their territorial claims; and United States commercial and financial penetration of the Pacific, with naval vessels patrolling Chinese rivers, was growing rapidly. But at the same time this mounting foreign interest also inhibited the outright partition of China. Any step by one of the powers toward outright partition or sizable enlargement of its sphere of influence met with strong opposition from other powers. This led eventually to the Open Door Policy, advocated by the United States, which limited or restricted exclusive privileges of any one power vis-à-vis the others. It became generally accepted after the antiforeign Boxer Rebellion of 1900 in China. With the foreign armies that had been brought in to suppress the rebellion now stationed in North China, the danger to the continued existence of the Chinese government and the danger of war among the imperialist powers for their share of the country seemed greater than ever. Agreement on the Open Door Policy helped to retain both a compliant native government and equal opportunity for commerce, finance, and investment by the more advanced nations.

Japan's rise as a colonial power. Japan was the only Asian country to escape colonization from the West. European nations and the United States tried to "open the door," and to some extent they succeeded; but Japan was able to shake off the kind of subjugation, informal or formal, to which the rest of Asia succumbed. Even more important, it moved onto the same road of industrialization as did Europe and the United States. And instead of being colonized it became one of the colonial powers.

Japan had traditionally sought to avoid foreign intrusion. For many years, only the Dutch were permitted to have a trading depot, confined to an island (Deshima) near the port of Nagasaki. No other foreigners were permitted to land in Japan, though Russia, France, and England tried, but with little success. The first significant crack in Japan's trade and travel barriers was forced by the United States in an effort to guarantee and strengthen its shipping interests in the Far East. Japan's guns and ships were no match for those of Commodore Perry in his two U.S. naval expeditions to Japan in 1853 and 1854. The Japanese, well aware of the implications of foreign penetration through observing what was happening to China, tried to limit Western trade to two ports. In 1858, however, Japan agreed to a full commercial treaty with the United States, followed by similar treaties with the Low Countries, Russia, France, and Britain. The treaty pattern was familiar: more ports were opened; resident foreigners were granted extraterritorial rights, as in China; import and export duties were predetermined, thus removing control that Japan might otherwise exercise over its foreign trade.

Many attempts have been made to explain why a weak Japan was not taken over as a colony or, at least, did not follow in China's footsteps. Despite the absence of a commonly accepted theory, two factors were undoubtedly crucial. On the one hand, the Western nations did not pursue their attempts to control Japan as aggressively as they did elsewhere. In Asia the interests of the more aggressively expanding powers had centered on India, China, and the immediately surrounding areas. When greater interest developed in a possible breakthrough in Japan in the 1850s and 1860s, the leading powers were occupied with other pressing affairs, such as the 1857 Indian mutiny, the Taiping Rebellion, the Crimean War, French intervention in Mexico, and the United States Civil War. International jealousy may also have played a role in deterring any one power from trying to gain exclusive control over the country. On the other hand, in Japan itself, the danger of foreign military intervention, a crisis in its traditional feudal society, the rise of commerce, and a disaffected peasantry led to an intense internal power struggle and finally to a revolutionary change in the country's society and a thoroughgoing modernization program, one that brought Japan the economic and military strength to resist foreign nations.

The opposing forces in Japan's civil war were lined up between the supporters of the ruling Tokugawa family, which headed a rigid hierarchical feudal society, and the supporters of the emperor Meiji, whose court had been isolated from any significant government role. The civil war culminated in 1868 in the overthrow of the Tokugawa government and the restoration of the rule of the emperor. The Meiji Restoration also brought new interest groups to the center of political power and instigated a radical redirection of Japan's economic development. The nub of the changeover was the destruction of the traditional feudal social system and the building of a political, social, and economic framework conducive to capitalist industrialization. The new state actively participated in the turnabout by various forms of grants and guarantees to enterprising industrialists and by direct investment in basic industries such as railways, shipbuilding, communications, and machinery. The concentration of resources in the industrial sector was matched by social reforms that eliminated feudal restrictions, accelerated mass education, and encouraged acquisition of skills in the use of Western technology. The ensuing industrialized economy provided the means for Japan to hold its own in modern warfare and to withstand foreign economic competition.

Soon Japan not only followed the Western path of internal

industrialization, but it also began an outward aggression resembling that of the European nations. First came the acquisition and colonization of neighboring islands: Ryukyu Islands (including Okinawa), the Kuril Islands, Bonin Islands, and Hokkaido. Next in Japan's expansion program was Korea, but the opposition of other powers postponed the transformation of Korea into a Japanese colony. The pursuit of influence in Korea involved Japan in war with China during 1894–1895, at the end of which China recognized Japan's interest in Korea and ceded to Japan Taiwan, the Pescadores, and southern Manchuria. At this point rival powers interceded to force Japan to forgo taking over the southern Manchuria peninsula. While France, Britain, and Germany were involved in seeking to frustrate Japan's imperial ambitions, the most direct clash was with Russia over Korea and Manchuria. Japan's defeat of Russia in the war of 1904–1905 procured for Japan the lease of the Liaotung Peninsula, the southern part of the island of Sakhalin, and recognition of its "paramount interest" in Korea. Still, pressure by Britain and the United States kept Japan from fulfillment of its plan to possess Manchuria outright. By the early twentieth century, however, Japan had, by means of economic and political penetration, attained a privileged position in that part of China, as well as colonies in Korea and Taiwan and neighboring islands.

The Partition of Africa

By the turn of the twentieth century, the map of Africa looked like a huge jigsaw puzzle, with most of the boundary lines having been drawn in a sort of game of give-and-take played in the foreign offices of the leading European powers. The division of Africa, the last continent to be so carved up, was essentially a product of the new imperialism, vividly highlighting its essential features. In this respect, the timing and the pace of the scramble for Africa are especially noteworthy. Before 1880 colonial possessions in Africa were relatively few and limited to coastal areas, with large sections of the coastline and almost all the interior still independent. By 1900 Africa was almost entirely divided into separate territories controlled by European nations. The only exceptions were Liberia, generally regarded as being under the special protection of the United States; Morocco, conquered by France a few years later; Libya, later taken over by Italy; and Ethiopia.

The second feature of the new imperialism was also strongly evident. It was in Africa that Germany made its first major bid for membership in the club of colonial powers: between May 1884 and February 1885, Germany announced its claims to territory in Southwest Africa, Togoland, Cameroon, and part of the East African coast opposite Zanzibar. Two smaller nations, Belgium and Italy, also entered the ranks, and even Portugal and Spain once again became active in bidding for African territory. The increasing number of participants in itself sped up the race for conquest. And with the heightened rivalry came more intense concern for preclusive occupation, increased attention to military arguments for additional buffer zones, and, in a period when free trade was giving way to protective tariffs and discriminatory practices in colonies as well as at home, a growing urgency for protected overseas markets. Not only the wish but also the means were at hand for this carving up of the African pie. Repeating rifles, machine guns, and other advances in weaponry gave the small armies of the conquering nations the effective power to defeat the much larger armies of both the advanced and the technically backward peoples of Africa. Rapid railroad construction provided the means for military, political, and economic consolidation of continental interiors. With the new steamships, men and materials could be moved to Africa with greater dispatch, and bulk shipments of raw materials and food from Africa, prohibitively costly for some products in the days of the sailing ship, became economically feasible and profitable.

Penetration of Islamic North Africa was complicated, on the one hand, by the struggle among European powers for control of the Mediterranean Sea and, on the other hand, by the suzerainty that the Ottoman Empire exercised to a greater or lesser extent over large sections of the region. Developments in both respects contributed to the wave of partition toward the end of the nineteenth century. First, Ottoman power was perceptibly waning: the military balance had tipped decisively in favor of the European nations, and Turkey was becoming increasingly dependent on loans from European centers of capital (in the late 1870s Turkey needed half of its government income just to service its foreign debt). Second, the importance of domination of the Mediterranean increased significantly after the Suez Canal was opened in 1869.

France was the one European nation that had established a major beachhead in Islamic North Africa before the 1880s. At a time when Great Britain was too preoccupied to inter-fere, the French captured the fortress of Algiers in 1830. Frequent revolts kept the French army busy in the Algerian interior for another fifty years before all Algeria was under full French rule. While Tunisia and Egypt had been areas of great interest to European powers during the long period of France's Algerian takeover, the penetration of these countries had been informal, confined to diplomatic and financial maneuvers. Italy, as well as France and England, had loaned large sums to the ruling *beys* of Tunisia to help loosen that country's ties with Turkey. The inability of the *beys* to service the foreign debt in the 1870s led to the installation of debt commissioners by the lenders. Tunisia's revenues were pledged to pay the interest due on outstanding bonds; in fact, the debt charges had first call on the government's income. With this came increased pressure on the people for larger tax payments and a growing popular dissatisfaction with a government that had "sold out" to foreigners. The weakness of the ruling group, intensified by the danger of popular revolt or a military coup, opened the door further for formal occupation by one of the interested foreign powers. When Italy's actions showed that it might be preparing for outright possession, France jumped the gun by invading Tunisia in

1881 and then completed its conquest by defeating the rebellions precipitated by this occupation.

The Europeans in North Africa. The course of Egypt's loss of sovereignty resembled somewhat the same process in Tunisia: easy credit extended by Europeans, bankruptcy, increasing control by foreign-debt commissioners, mulcting of the peasants to raise revenue for servicing the debt, growing independence movements, and finally military conquest by a foreign power. In Egypt, interimperialist rivalry, mainly between Great Britain and France, reached back to the early nineteenth century but was intensified under the circumstances of the new imperialism and the construction of the Suez Canal. By building the Suez Canal and financing Egypt's ruling group, France had gained a prominent position in Egypt. But Britain's interests were perhaps even more pressing because the Suez Canal was a strategic link to its empire and its other Eastern trade and colonial interests. The successful nationalist revolt in the 1880s, headed by the Egyptian army, imminently threatened the interests of both powers. France, occupied with war in Tunisia and with internal political problems, did not participate in the military intervention to suppress the revolt. Great Britain bombarded Alexandria in 1882, landed troops, and thus obtained control of Egypt. Unable to find a stable collaborationist government that would also pay Egypt's debts and concerned with suppressing not only the rebellion but also a powerful anti-Egyptian Mahdist revolt in the Sudan, Britain completely took over the reins of government in Egypt.

The rest of North Africa was carved up in the early twentieth century. France, maneuvering for possession of Morocco, which bordered on her Algerian colony, tried to obtain the acquiescence of the other powers by both secret and open treaties granting Italy a free hand in Libya, allotting to Spain a sphere of influence, and acknowledging Britain's paramountcy in Egypt. France had, however, overlooked Germany's ambitions, now backed by an increasingly effective army and navy. The tension created by Germany led to an international conference at Algeciras in 1906, which produced a short-lived compromise, including recognition of France's paramount interest, Spanish participation in policing Morocco, and an open door for the country's economic penetration by other nations. But France's vigorous pursuit of her claims, reinforced by the occupation of Casablanca and surrounding territory, precipitated critical confrontations, which reached their peak in 1911 when French troops were suppressing a Moroccan revolt and a German cruiser appeared before Agadir in a show of force. The resulting settlements completed the European partition of North Africa: France obtained a lion's share of Morocco; in return, Germany received a large part of the French Congo; Italy was given the green light for her war with Turkey over control of Tripoli, the first step in her eventual acquisition of Libya; and Spain was enabled to extend her Río de Oro protectorate to the southern frontier of Morocco. The more or less peaceful trade-offs by the occupying powers differed sharply from the long, bitter, and expensive wars they waged against the indigenous peoples and rulers of Islamic North Africa to solidify European rule.

The race for colonies in sub-Saharan Africa. The partition of Africa below the Sahara took place at two levels: (1) on paper—in deals made among colonial powers who were seeking colonies partly for the sake of the colonies themselves and partly as pawns in the power play of European nations struggling for world dominance—and (2) in the field—in battles of conquest against African states and tribes and in military confrontations among the rival powers themselves. This process produced, over and above the ravages of colonialism, a wasp's nest of problems that was to plague African nations long after they achieved independence. Boundary lines between colonies were often drawn arbitrarily, with little or no attention to ethnic unity, regional economic ties, tribal migratory patterns, or even natural boundaries.

Before the race for partition, only three European powers —France, Portugal, and Britain—had territory in tropical Africa, located mainly in West Africa. Only France had moved into the interior along the Senegal River. The other French colonies or spheres of influence were located along the Ivory Coast and in Dahomey and Gabon. Portugal held on to some coastal points in Angola, Mozambique (Moçambique), and Portuguese Guinea. While Great Britain had a virtual protectorate over Zanzibar in East Africa, its actual possessions were on the west coast in Gambia, the Gold Coast, the Sierra Leone, all of them surrounded by African states that had enough organization and military strength to make the British hesitate about further expansion. Meanwhile, the ground for eventual occupation of the interior of tropical Africa was being prepared by explorers, missionaries, and traders. But such penetration remained tenuous until the construction of railroads and the arrival of steamships on navigable waterways made it feasible for European merchants to dominate the trade of the interior and for European governments to consolidate conquests.

Once conditions were ripe for the introduction of railroads and steamships in West Africa, tensions between the English and French increased as each country tried to extend its sphere of influence. As customs duties, the prime source of colonial revenue, could be evaded in uncontrolled ports, both powers began to stretch their coastal frontiers, and over-lapping claims and disputes soon arose. The commercial penetration of the interior created additional rivalry and set off a chain reaction. The drive for exclusive control over interior areas intensified in response to both economic competition and the need for protection from African states resisting foreign intrusion. This drive for African possessions was intensified by the new entrants to the colonial race who felt menaced by the possibility of being completely locked out.

Perhaps the most important stimulants to the scramble for colonies south of the Sahara were the opening up of the Congo Basin by Belgium's king, Leopold II, and Germany's energetic annexationist activities on both the east and west coasts. As the dash for territory began to accelerate, fifteen nations convened in Berlin in 1884 for the West African Conference, which, however, merely set ground rules for the ensuing intensified scramble for colonies. It also recognized the Congo Free State ruled by King Leopold, while insisting that the rivers in the Congo Basin be open to free trade. From his base in the Congo, the king subsequently took over mineral-rich Katanga, transferring both territories to Belgium in 1908.

In West Africa, Germany concentrated on consolidating its possessions of Togoland and Cameroon (Kamerun), while England and France pushed northward and eastward from their bases: England concentrated on the Niger region, the center of its commercial activity, while France aimed at joining its possessions at Lake Chad within a grand design for an empire of contiguous territories from Algeria to the Congo. Final boundaries were arrived at after the British had defeated, among others, the Ashantis, the Fanti Confederation, the Opobo kingdom, and the Fulani; and the French won wars against the Fon kingdom, the Tuaregs, the Mandingos, and other resisting tribes. The boundaries determined by conquest and agreement between the conquerors gave France the lion's share: in addition to the extension of its former coastal possessions, France acquired French West Africa and French Equatorial Africa, while Britain carved out its Nigerian colony.

In Central Africa, the intercolonial rivalries chiefly involved the British, the Portuguese, the South African Republic of the Transvaal, the British-backed Cape Colony, and the Germans. The acquisitive drive was enormously stimulated by dreams of wealth generated by the discovery of diamonds in Griqualand West and gold in Matabeleland. Encouraged by these discoveries, Cecil Rhodes (heading the British South Africa Company) and other entrepreneurs expected to find gold, copper, and diamonds in the regions surrounding the Transvaal, among them Bechuanaland, Matabeleland, Mashonaland, and Trans-Zambezia. In the ensuing struggle, which involved the conquest of the Nbele and Shona peoples, Britain obtained control over Bechuanaland and, through the British South Africa Company, over the areas later designated as the Rhodesias and Nyasaland. At the same time, Portugal moved inland to seize control over the colony of Mozambique. It was clearly the rivalries of stronger powers, especially the concern of Germany and France over the extension of British rule in Central Africa, that enabled a weak Portugal to have its way in Angola and Mozambique.

The boundary lines in East Africa were arrived at largely in settlements between Britain and Germany, the two chief rivals in that region. For the first area of friction—Zanzibar, where Britain had de facto control over the sultanate, and the future Tanganyika, where German colonization was spreading—separate spheres of influence were established in the 1886 Anglo-German agreement. But, as German control approached Lake Victoria, the headwaters of the Upper Nile, Britain visualized a potential menace to its rule at the other end of the Nile in Egypt. Captain Frederick (later Lord) Lugard and his African troops were sent by the Imperial British East Africa Company to take over Buganda at the northern shore of Lake Victoria. A final division of the area coveted by both powers was reached in an overall Anglo-German treaty of 1890: Britain obtained the future Uganda and recognition of its paramount interest in Zanzibar and Pemba in exchange for ceding the strategic North Sea island of Heligoland (Helgoland) and noninterference in Germany's acquisition of the Karagwe and Haya countries of Tanganyika, Ruanda, and Urundi. As part of its consolidation of control over Uganda and its resources, Britain began to build an East African railroad to the coast, establishing the East African Protectorate (later Kenya) over the area through which the railroad was to be built.

Rivalry in Northeast Africa between the French and British focused on domination of the upper end of the Nile, for, as mentioned earlier, it was generally believed that control of the Nile waters would eventually determine who controlled Egypt. The third European power in this region, Italy, had established itself at two ends of Ethiopia, in an area on the Red Sea that the Italians called Eritrea and in Italian Somaliland along the Indian Ocean. Italy's inland thrust led to war with Ethiopia and defeat at the hands of the

Ethiopian army at Aduwa in 1896. Ethiopia, surrounded by Italian and British armies, had turned to French advisers. The unique victory by an African state over a European army strengthened French influence in Ethiopia and enabled France to stage military expeditions from Ethiopia as well as from the Congo in order to establish footholds on the Upper Nile. The resulting race between British and French armies ended in a confrontation at Fashoda in 1898, with the British army in the stronger position. War was narrowly avoided in a settlement that completed the partition of the region: eastern Sudan was to be ruled jointly by Britain and Egypt, while France was to have the remaining Sudan from the Congo and Lake Chad to Darfur.

Germany's entrance into South Africa through occupation and conquest of South West Africa touched off an upsurge of British colonial activity in that area, notably the separation of Basutoland (Lesotho) as a crown colony from the Cape Colony and the annexation of Zululand. The thorn in the side of British interests, however, was the independence of the Transvaal, which was rich in gold, had its own ambitions to expand, and was a potential area of German infiltration. Confident because of its superiority at Fashoda and in the acquisitive spirit of the new imperialism, London provoked war with the Boers during 1899–1902, at the end of which Britain obtained sovereignty over the Transvaal as well as the Afrikaner Orange Free State.

World War I and the Interwar Period (1914–1939)

Postwar redivision of colonies. Following the well-trodden path of dividing foreign territory in the ministries of the great powers, the victors in World War I—with the exception of the United States, which sought to enhance its influence in the international community through an independent strategy— carved up among themselves the colonial possessions of the defeated nations. Germany was forced to renounce title to overseas possessions in the 1919 Treaty of Versailles. Turkey's colonies were being divided even before it formally relinquished its claims in the 1923 Treaty of Lausanne. The reassignment of colonies took the form of mandates under Article 22 of the League of Nations Covenant, under which the League entrusted its international responsibility to govern these territories to particular states.

Three classes of mandates were established: (1) Class A mandates were set up for areas formerly belonging to the Turkish Empire that were expected to become independent in the near future. Under this arrangement, Syria and Lebanon were assigned to France and Iraq, Palestine, and Transjordan to Great Britain. (2) Class B mandates were established as typical colonies but were kept administratively separate from existing colonies. In this category were the African territories other than South West Africa: Togoland and the Cameroons were divided between France and Great Britain; Tanganyika was given to Great Britain; and Ruanda-Urundi to Belgium. (3) Class C mandates were imposed on South West Africa (given to the Union of South Africa) and the Pacific Islands (divided between Great Britain, Australia, New Zealand, and Japan). In these mandates the new owners were free to integrate the acquired territories as they saw fit.

Rise of independence movements. While the great powers were pursuing their redivision activities, a wave of nationalist independence movements spread throughout the colonial world, influencing colonial affairs and eventually leading to decolonization after World War II. While the seeds of nationalism had long been planted and nourished by foreign repression. World War I and related developments heightened national consciousness and stimulated new forms of independence movements. In the Arab world this trend was notably stimulated by the contrast between the imposed mandates and the wartime promises of independence made by the Allies in return for support on the Turkish front. It soon became clear that, while these promises were being made, the Allies had been carving up the Turkish Empire among themselves. In addition, Britain's Balfour Declaration of 1917 and the League of Nations Palestine Mandate of 1922—both negotiated behind the backs of the Arabs—announced the intent of setting aside Palestine as a Jewish homeland, thus further inflaming Arab nationalism while raising the hopes of the Jews. One result of the growing nationalist movements in the Middle East was the independence obtained by Egypt in 1922 and by Iraq in 1932,* although the treaties establishing these independent nations provided for continuation of Britain's military presence and influence; nor did the grant of limited independence interfere with Britain's dominant position in the Middle East or its ability to obtain by far the lion's share of the region's oil reserves.

Another major war-related stimulus to the new surge of nationalism was the Russian Revolution of 1917, which fired the imagination of the colonial masses, especially in Asia, for it showed the common people that they could rebel and manage their own affairs despite the opposition of imperialist powers. Also of major significance was the fact that the Soviet Union declared itself to be anti-imperialist, renounced imperialist privileges, and opened up the tsarist archives to reveal the secret processes of imperialist negotiations. In the 1919 Karakhan Manifesto to the Chinese People, the Bolsheviks offered to return territory taken from China by the tsarist regime, to renounce outstanding claims to the indemnity for the Boxer Rebellion in 1900, and to give up extraterritorial rights. Less dramatic but still influential was the example supplied by the winning of independence in southern Ireland and the creation of the independent Irish Free State in 1923.

But such external factors did not so much create the nationalist upsurge as, at most, they gave added impetus to an already powerful urge of the colonial peoples to free themselves from the political, social, and economic exploitation. In several areas nationalism gave rise to active rebellion,

---

* Although the British protectorate over Egypt was abolished in 1922, Egypt cannot be considered to have become independent until 1954, when an agreement was signed with Great Britain that arranged for the total withdrawal of British armed forces from Egyptian territory. Likewise, the real beginning of Iraq's independence occurred in 1947 with the final evacuation of British troops.

in others to various forms of political and trade-union movements. In Morocco the rising led by Abd el-Krim continued
throughout World War I and lasted until 1926. An unsuccessful Communist-led uprising occurred in Java and Sumatra
against Dutch rule in the mid-1920s. In tropical Africa the
rejection of colonialism and the struggle for freedom were
frequently clothed in religious dress, with separatist sects
gathering large and militant followings. In both religious and
secular organizations, uprisings against rulers as well as
against specific grievances, such as conscription, taxation, and
forced labor, burst forth at various times in the Belgian
Congo, French Sudan, southern Nigeria, Liberia, Upper
Volta, and other territories. The Chinese Communist Revolution began in the late 1920s. And it was after World War I
that the Indian National Congress developed as a truly mass
organization based on civil disobedience to British authorities.

Realignments among the colonial powers. Over and above
the redivision of the colonies of the defeated nations, World
War I also brought about changes in the relative positions of
the victors in the colonial world. Outstanding in this regard
was the ascendancy of the United States vis-à-vis Great Britain. With the growth of both U.S. and Japanese naval power,
Britain rapidly lost her dominant position on the seas, especially in the Pacific. This change also increased United
States influence in Canada and Australia. The wartime weakening of the British economy along with the strengthening of
the United States financial position as a major supplier of the
Allies allowed the United States soon to become the leading
capital market, to expand its international banking and overseas investment, and to compete with Great Britain for the
world's oil reserves. Long before the war, the United States
had already begun to advance its influence in Latin America,
most markedly in Central America, where, by military intervention and occupation, Cuba, the Dominican Republic,
Panama, Nicaragua, and Haiti had in effect become U.S.
protectorates. Starting with the war-induced disruptions of
trading and investment patterns, Latin America increasingly

came within the United States, instead of the British, economic and political orbit during the years between World War I and World War II.

World War I also provided new opportunities for Japan to further its imperial ambitions. In 1915, while war was raging in Europe, Japan presented China with Twenty-one Demands, which, if accepted, would have placed China under virtual Japanese control. United States and British pressure led to moderation of the demands, but Japan did force on China treaties that gave it an upper hand over the other foreign nations in that country. This favored position was further exploited by Japan in its invasion of Manchuria in 1931 and the establishment of a puppet government there. The next major step in Japan's drive for hegemony in Asia, to create the Greater East Asia Co-Prosperity Sphere, came in the form of a war for the conquest of China, which acted as a powerful stimulus to both nationalist and revolutionary movements in China. This war began in 1937 and lasted until Japan's defeat at the end of World War II.

Additional impetus for expansionist aggression during the interwar years came from the two European fascist nations in the midst of the Great Depression of the 1930s. Demand for repossession of Germany's former colonies cropped up from time to time among leaders of the Weimar Republic, but it did not become a central feature of government policy until the Nazis came to power. Although the Nazi program featured this goal, the strategy of conquest concentrated primarily on building an empire in Central and Eastern Europe. Benito Mussolini's regime, on the other hand, took advantage of the uncertainties and shifting alliances among the European powers to enlarge Italy's empire in Northeast Africa. In 1935 an Italian army invaded Ethiopia, a fellow member of the League of Nations, and followed up military victory by annexation of Ethiopia in the following year.

The Aftermath of World War II

Decolonization. While colonialism was still on the rise in the interwar years, World War II led not merely to an intensified and better organized nationalism but to a complete reversal of the expansionist trends of the preceding centuries. Now, all the large colonial empires began to shrink, to be replaced by a host of new politically independent nations. Illustrative of the difference is the contrast between the Pan-African congresses, including Africans and African descendants on other continents, held at the end of each war. The Second Pan-African Congress, held in Paris in 1919, appealed to the Allies meeting at the same time at the Versailles Peace Conference for greater representation of Africans in colonial governments, for the abolition of slave and forced labor, and for other reforms in harsh colonial rule. In marked contrast, the Fifth Pan-African Congress, held in Manchester in 1945, adopted resolutions demanding an end to all forms of economic and political imperialism and advocated the use of force to attain independence for Africa, if all other methods failed. These were no idle threats, for within tropical Africa mass-movement political parties were emerging, better organized, more radical, and more militant than in the past. In addition, they could now call on black African soldiers with field experience and knowledge of complex weapons gained in World War II.

Japanese occupation of numerous European possessions in Asia and the Pacific, and the movements of resistance by indigenous peoples to this occupation, shook the colonial system in that part of the world. Aside from the major warfare against the Japanese by the Chinese Communists and Nationalists, popular armed resistance had gained momentum in Indochina, Indonesia, Burma, and the Philippines. And even where there was no Japanese occupation, the weakening of the hold over the colonies by the mother countries engaged in a life-and-death struggle with the Axis powers raised the will of colonial peoples to resist. Thus, for example, by war's end, India was clearly on the verge of revolt against an enfeebled Britain, which was no longer able to exercise as much control over its empire as it had in the past, its naval power having been severely depleted. With an equally depleted treasury Britain could not undertake the creation of the modern air force, aircraft carriers, and air bases needed to defend its globe-straddling empire. Nor, in the light of the ferment in the colonies, could Britain any longer use colonial troops to maintain law and order. Similar practical weaknesses and limitations soon applied to other colonial powers as well—to France, the Netherlands, and Belgium.

The one power with sufficient strength at the end of the war to attempt the maintenance of the old colonial system trod a tortuous path amid conflicting trends. The United States was interested at one and the same time in (1) rebuilding the Western European nations as allies in the struggle against the Soviet Union; (2) countering social revolutions that would close the door to United States trade and investment; (3) enlarging its own sphere of influence in the very areas where its allies had prior claim; and (4) minimizing the influence the Soviet Union might obtain through support of anticolonial liberation movements. Such a complex of motives and aims at times served to intensify imperial wars against postwar colonial liberation movements, while in other cases it facilitated the transition to political independence.

In the final analysis, the explanation of the tidal wave of decolonization that followed World War II is to be found in the interaction of three elements: (1) the realignment of world power, with the United States and the Soviet Union emerging as the leading giants; (2) the declining ability of the old colonial powers to hold on to all of their far-flung empires; and (3) the evolution of independence and resistance movements becoming strong enough in one country after another to force the issue. If a further generalization can be made, it is that the transition to independence came sooner and with less bloodshed wherever the mother country was more confident that it was turning over power to governments that would remain in its economic and political orbit. The most intense and longest lasting warfare occurred where the independence movements were not only nationalist but also revolutionary—where independence might be expected to bring confiscation of foreign investments, severance of economic ties with the former mother country, and probably a shift to the orbit of a socialist country. To this must be added one other important influence: the role that large white-settler populations played in intensifying the struggle against national liberation, as in Algeria, and in blocking a transfer of power to the indigenous population, as in Southern Rhodesia.

The first nations to gain independence either during or right after the war were the Philippines (1946), where independence had long been promised by the United States, and the mandate states of Lebanon (1941), Syria (1941), and Transjordan (1946).* The remaining Middle East mandate, Palestine, did not attain sovereignty until 1948, because the partition imposed on this land contained the seeds of an Arab-Jewish war, from which emerged the actual division of Palestine, primarily between Jordan (formerly Transjordan) and the new state of Israel.

When the United Nations charter was drafted, it was expected that all the League of Nations mandates, other than those in the Middle East, would be placed under a UN trusteeship arrangement. The Republic of South Africa, however, refused to give up its control of South West Africa. The United Nations in 1968 declared South West Africa (Namibia) under direct UN control, but, as of 1973, it was still a colony of the Republic of South Africa. All other mandated territories, including Japan's, and the Italian colonies were either granted independence or became UN trust territories. By 1973 the original eleven UN trust territories had dwindled to two: New Guinea, administered by Australia, and the Trust Territory of the Pacific Islands, under United States control.

---

* Termination of the mandates over Syria and Lebanon was announced by the three French military authorities in 1941. The independence of these countries, however, did not take place until all foreign troops were withdrawn in 1946.

The states next in line for independence, after the Philippines and the Middle East, were British possessions in Asia. In Burma the national army had rebelled against Japanese occupation, and the people clearly expected freedom after the defeat of Japan. British procrastination stimulated a widespread strike in 1946, and by 1948 Burma attained its independence. Ceylon became a separate member of the British Commonwealth in the same year. Steps toward the independence of India began in the midst of the war when Japanese troops threatened Burma and eastern India, and a desperate Britain was seeking active help from the Indians. The British offer of independent dominion status in 1942 was rejected by the Indian nationalists as inadequate and dangerous because it stimulated the idea of partition of India. When independence finally came in 1947, the subcontinent was indeed divided, under British guidance, between India and Pakistan, producing massive migrations of Muslims fleeing to Pakistan and Hindus to India. In India, as later in the British African and West Indian possessions, the colonial peoples were not given the option of calling their own congresses to design their own political systems. As much as possible was done in the transfer of power by all the colonial powers to keep the new nations within the framework of the established economic, political, and military interests of the former mother country. Malaya, for instance, did not get independence until 1957 because of British involvement in the defeat of a communist-led revolution that lasted eight years.

Revolution and warfare dominated the nationalist developments in the rest of Asia. With the establishment of the People's Republic of China in 1949, after many years of civil war and war against the Japanese invasion, all vestiges of imperialism were eliminated from that country except for the British colony of Hong Kong, the Portuguese colony of Macau, and the United States sphere of influence in Taiwan. The Netherlands, with the aid of British troops, tried to reoccupy Indonesia when the Japanese left but was unable to do so in four years of war against the Republic of Indonesia, which finally became fully independent in 1949. The French were also unsuccessful in trying to reconquer Indochina. The war against the Japanese had produced a strong national army and liberation movement in Indochina, which, in addition to independence, aimed for basic social and economic changes. After nine years of intense, large-scale war, the French army, massively aided economically and morally by the United States, suffered major defeat, notably at the Battle of Dien Bien Phu. At a 1954 international peace conference in Geneva, an agreement was reached to recognize the independence of Laos, Cambodia, and Vietnam. As for Vietnam, a military demarcation line was drawn at approximately the 17th parallel to facilitate the truce and pave the way for elections under the supervision of an international commission to unite the Northern and Southern zones. South Vietnam, where U.S. influence became paramount, decided not to go along with the unification elections scheduled for July 1956 by the Geneva Agreement. This was followed by rebellion in South Vietnam, U.S. major military support of the South Vietnamese government, and massive air attacks on North Vietnam, until a cease-fire was reached in 1973.

In North Africa, independence began to be realized in the 1950s: Libya in 1951 and Morocco and Tunisia in 1956. Liberation was promoted by strong nationalist movements in these countries and in the latter two was accompanied by considerable violence as the French tried to repress these movements. Efforts at repression did not, however, last long, for French military resources were heavily engaged in Indochina and Algeria; and by 1954 France had lost the flower of its officer corps in Vietnam. The major revolutionary effort in Algeria started at the end of 1954. It developed into a long and bitter eight-year war that involved a large part of the French army and brought France itself to a major internal political crisis, ending in a victory for the Algerian liberation struggle in 1962.

The countries of tropical Africa were the last to gain their independence. As late as 1956 there were only three independent nations in tropical Africa: Liberia, Ethiopia, which had regained its sovereignty in 1941 after the Allies had defeated the Italian army in East Africa; and the Sudan, which was separated from Egypt in 1956. But once France, Great Britain, and Belgium recognized that the tide of nationalism could not be stopped in Africa without an overwhelming commitment of resources and without raising embarrassing political problems in the United Nations, the floodgates were opened. Only Portugal and the Republic of South Africa held back. Widespread strikes and uprisings in Ghana, Kenya, Tanganyika, Northern Rhodesia, and French West and Equatorial Africa shook the foundations of colonial rule. Pressure from newly independent nations, from the Soviet Union and the People's Republic of China, and from such political initiatives as the anticolonial Asian-African Conference held in 1955 in Bandung (Indonesia) contributed to a deluge of African decolonization movements. The decisive crack in the imperialist front came when Ghana (formerly the Gold Coast) became a self-governing nation in 1957. In the next five years, from 1958 to 1962, twenty-three new independent nations were established in tropical Africa; and from 1963 to 1968 an additional ten independent nations came into being there. In a number of the new societies, special economic and military links with the former mother country were retained.

In Rhodesia (formerly Southern Rhodesia) the white settlers managed to seize control. Thus, while Rhodesia is technically still a British colony, in 1965 it became de facto a separate nation ruled by the white minority. Portugal still holds on to its African possessions.* In Portuguese Guinea, Angola, and Mozambique, nationalist guerrilla forces have long been actively fighting for liberation. To counter these revolutionary activities, Portugal, the military resources of which are bolstered by its membership in the North Atlantic Treaty Organization, has sent large armies to its colonies.

---

*Since this article was written, Guinea-Bissau, Angola, and Mozambique have won independence.

Neocolonialism. The rapid decline in colonialism stimulated the rise of alternative means of domination by the more
powerful nations. Control and influence by means other than
outright colonial possession is hardly a new phenomenon.
Indeed, informal empire has been an important ingredient
throughout the evolution of capitalism as a means to secure
markets and access to raw materials. Along with outright
colonialism, informal empire helped to shape and sustain the
international division of labor between the advanced manufacturing nations and those supplying raw materials and food.
But the spread of informal empire as a substitute for formal
colonial rule and the introduction of new mechanisms of
control have been so pervasive since World War II as to give
rise to the term neocolonialism. The term and the ideas
underlying it are of course highly controversial. While conventional thought in the United States and Western Europe
generally rejects the validity of the term, in the former
colonial world the existence of the phenomenon of neocolonialism is commonly recognized and discussed.

What is usually meant by neocolonialism is the existence
of considerable foreign direction over a nominally independent nation. In its narrowest sense, this means a high degree of
influence over a country's economic affairs and economic
policy by an outside nation or by foreign business interests,
usually entailing influence over political and military policy
as well. In addition, the term is used to suggest the predominance of the culture and values of the former colonial
powers.

Aside from the cultural and ideological traditions carried
over from colonial times, as in the educational and civil-
service systems, the very technique of decolonization provided the framework of neocolonialism in many countries.
The continued membership by former French and British
colonies in the currency zones of the mother countries, for
instance, facilitated the perpetuation of existing trade relations. Various other techniques were newly adopted or prolonged to maintain economic ties, such as preferential tariff
arrangements and quota systems for the marketing of exports

from former colonial areas. Most important, however, was the continuity of the basic economic structures that had evolved in the colonies and mandated territories over many years to meet the specific needs of the metropolitan centers. This had resulted in economic and financial dependency on those financial and industrial centers. The pattern of resource allocation had thus been shaped and administered largely by foreign investors, bankers, and merchants. In the absence of a fundamental redirection of economic resources in the new nations and with the continuance and even enlargement of foreign business activity, the fundamental relations of colonialism and the old international division of labor inevitably persisted even after political independence was gained.

Perhaps the most important factor in the development of neocolonialism was the vastly expanded world role played by the United States. Coming out of World War II as the most powerful economic and military nation on earth, the United States assumed the mantle of leadership of the non-communist world and set itself the task of organizing and managing, as far as practically possible, that part of the world. To the United States' leaders, as well as those of its allies, the main danger confronting the capitalist world was the spread of communism. A high priority was therefore given to keeping as much of the world as possible economically and politically hospitable to the continuation of traditional patterns of trade and investment. Hence, it was essential to prevent social revolutions that might involve confiscation of foreign-owned assets or otherwise lead to limitations of trade and investment opportunities and access to raw materials.

As part of its strategy of containing the socialist countries and preventing or suppressing social revolutions, the United States built up a vast network of military bases around the world, many of them located in the former colonial countries. This network was supplemented by vigorous diplomatic and military action in countries where, in the United States' view, dangerous developments were threatening. The major war waged in Vietnam was the most drastic of these actions. An outstanding illustration of a lesser but effective operation was the overthrow of the Mosaddeg government in Iran in 1953, which had nationalized the foreign-owned oil industry. Similarly, in the following year, the United States organized the military overthrow of a regime in Guatemala that had nationalized United States–owned banana plantations. Other cases included the landing of marines in Lebanon in 1958 and the Dominican Republic in 1965 to control the course of events in those countries in a sense favorable to the United States.

Among the newer techniques of control was the extensive use of grants and loans for military and economic assistance. Military assistance has clearly been a tool to strengthen friendly nations and maintain the status quo. There are, however, conflicting interpretations on the uses of economic aid. The accepted view in the Western donor countries is that such aid is part of a humanitarian program by which the rich share some of their wealth with the poor. The contrary opinion is that this aid is used to win political and military allies and to perpetuate an environment suitable for private investment in, as well as access to raw materials of, recipient nations.

2

Imperialist Expansion: Accident and Design

Toward the end of the nineteenth century the British Empire was celebrated in a popular history, *The Expansion of England* by J. R. Seeley. While this book is generally ignored by modern scholars, its epigrammatic summation lives on: "We seem, as it were, to have conquered and peopled half the world in a fit of absence of mind."[1] This theme, along with its corollary that the British were reluctant imperialists, has penetrated the literature of empire, providing the kernel of more sophisticated formulations. Not as a witticism but as a summary of sober historical analysis, a modern British specialist puts it this way: "In short, the modern empires lacked rationality and purpose: they were the chance products of complex historical forces operating over several centuries, and more particularly during the period after 1815."[2]

Now that U.S. scholars and publicists are beginning to acknowledge the reality of an American Empire, they too seem to find comfort, or significance, in the elements of chance and reluctance that pervade history. Thus two diplomatic correspondents who have recently published a book

This was originally written as an Introduction to Mark Selden, ed., *Remaking Asia: Essays on the American Uses of Power* (New York: Pantheon, 1974). It also appeared in the January 1974 issue of *Monthly Review*.

tracing, quite superficially, the roots of U.S. interest in Asia back to 1784 entitle their opening chapter, with no hint of satire, "The Reluctant Imperialists." [3] In a more scholarly and penetrating study, *Pax Americana*, Ronald Steel recites the extensive U.S. military involvement around the globe and recalls James Reston's words that these are "commitments the like of which no sovereign nation ever took on in the history of the world." But Steel is quick to point out: "These entanglements happened more by accident than by design. ... We had no intention of virtually annexing Okinawa, of occupying South Korea, of preventing the return of Taiwan to China, of fighting in Indochina, or of remaining in Western Europe. If someone had said in 1947 that twenty years later there would be 225,000 soldiers in Germany, 50,000 in Korea, and a half million Americans fighting in Vietnam, he would have been considered mad." [4]

Both accident and reluctance are, of course, ever present in empire-building. Hitler, and Kaiser Wilhelm before him, must surely have experienced some reluctance: it would have been safer and more efficient to obtain Germany's long-standing goals of empire without the costs and risks of war. And it is equally probable that the U.S. decision-makers are reluctantly bombing Vietnam: they would most likely prefer to exert their will in Southeast Asia without ruining the people and land of Vietnam and without war-induced domestic social and economic problems. As for the influence of chance, it should be obvious that in the absence of omniscience and omnipotence all of history in one sense consists of a series of accidents. Or as Trotsky, a firm believer in the existence of laws in history, observed, "The entire historical process is a refraction of historical law through the accidental." Faced with the reality of empire-building, as with any other recurring phenomenon in history, the analyst needs to discover, or try to understand, why, through the very operations of accident, history moves in one direction rather than another. One might even ask why some countries or social organisms are more accident-prone than others or why at certain times rather than at other times.

While it should go without saying that, given the short-comings of astrology and the flaws in crytal balls, no one in 1947 could have foreseen the specific future configuration of U.S. global involvement, it is nevertheless essential to recognize that the polices and pressures that produced the U.S. drive to global hegemony were far from accidental and were in evidence long before 1947. In fact, the mainsprings of U.S. global strategy during the past quarter century had already taken shape well before World War II was over.[5] But even more important, the striving for empire stretches back to the earliest days of the republic, and even into colonial times.

"Man's character is his fate," said Heraclitus, the ancient Greek philosopher. The same may be said of nations. And the key to the character of the U.S. social organism which had determined its destiny—modified and adapted to be sure, in reaction to chance events and to complex historical forces—has been its persistent urge to expand. Taking the long view, Professor Van Alstyne in *The Rising American Empire* sees this urge as one of "direction and unbroken continuity in the history of the United States":

> The early colonies were no sooner established in the seventeenth century than expansionist impulses began to register in each of them. Imperial patterns took shape, and before the middle of the eighteenth century the concept of an empire that would take in the whole continent was fully formed. A drive south into the Spanish Caribbean was also in progress, with the ultimate goal in view of converting the Caribbean into an American lake. In the Revolution the spirit of conquest was a powerful force, and it took about a century thereafter to satisfy the territorial ambitions of the United States. Except for the internal dissension which was a constant factor during the first half of the nineteenth century, and which finally exploded into a civil war of vast proportions, it seems probable that these ambitions would have been pursued more persistently and energetically, that indeed they would have been pushed to the limit. But by the time of the Mexican War, the controversy between the North and South developed into an obsession; and further conquests became for the time being impossible. On the North American continent American expansion reached its maximum

limits by 1867, the process of advance having been delayed long enough to enable the Canadians to develop the necessary counter-moves. The two related drives, south into the Caribbean and westward to China via Cape Horn, continued to the end of the century, when a burst of energy finished off the process in a war against Spain.[6]

While the focus of attention in U.S. history books is on continental expansion, the conquest of the Indians, and the acquisition of Mexican territory, they often overlook the fact that the so-called frontier was not only on land but on the seas as well, and that the absorption of the Far West was considerably influenced by desire to control the Pacific Ocean and thus to widen trading opportunities in Asia. The early United States was not only an agricultural but also a mercantile and seafaring society. This was especially so of the New England states, where a relative poverty of natural resources meant the lack of suitable agricultural or mineral export products that could be exchanged for European manufactures. The road to prosperity was found in commerce, bringing with it the dominance of a merchant class that spread its interests around the globe: not only in the rum-molasses trade with the West Indies, the marketing of African slaves, and the coastal traffic, but also in whaling, sealing, and trade (including opium) in the Pacific. To facilitate and expand this commerce, U.S. business firms spread to Asia during the earliest days of the Republic: "In the Pacific, Americans established themselves in the Sandwich Islands, 1787; Nootka Sound, 1788; Marquesas, 1791; Fanning, 1797; and Fiji, 1800. American interest in the North Pacific was in whale fisheries, which encouraged the start of an American settlement in Honolulu. The consul to Canton, Major Samuel Shaw, started the firm of Shaw & Randall in that city in 1786, only two years after the Chinese port had been opened to American trade."[7]

These commercial stakes in Asia may seem puny by today's standards, but not if judged in the perspective of the world economy in the eighteenth and early nineteenth centuries. For this spread into the Pacific, in addition to the Caribbean and the slave trade, spurred the emergence of a competitive merchant marine, a supportive navy, and the sort of trade that brought not only wealth to the merchant classes in North Atlantic ports but also nurtured the roots of eventual economic as well as political independence of the nation as a whole.

At the heart of the current economic underdevelopment of most Asian countries, as well as former colonies and semicolonies throughout the world, are the enormous economic and social distortions imposed by Western nations: the transfer of the traditional international trade of these countries into European hands and their eventual adaptation to serve as raw materials and food suppliers for the industrializing nations and as markets for their manufactured products. And it is in this respect that the history of the United States differs so strikingly from that of other colonial or ex-colonial territories. For, instead of becoming a victim of the colonial system, this country emerged at an early stage as an active participant and rival in seeking a share of the profits from the growing world commerce and the forcible opening up of new business opportunities in the non-Western world.

An important ingredient of U.S. ability to compete in the ever-widening sphere of imperialist influence was the attainment, for a variety of reasons, of a high degree of independence as a shipbuilder, trader, and shipper. This was the very opposite of the situation in the colonial areas which, at that time as well as in the future, were transformed into adjuncts of militarily superior powers, an outstanding characteristic of colonial and semicolonial countries being the concentration of import and export shipping in foreign hands. It is noteworthy that the ability of American merchants and shippers to compete with those of the mother country contributed significantly to the tensions and resulting struggle leading up to the final separation. In 1790, U.S.-owned ships already handled 59 percent of its foreign trade. By 1807 this proportion rose to 92 percent. The forward push to economic as well as political independence provided by the American

Revolution was strengthened by the opportunities arising from the subsequent wars between European powers. Thus a large part of the shipping business at the end of the eighteenth century fell to U.S. entrepreneurs during the war years: "... several new routes, on which the profits were very high, developed during the war years. These were the trade in the Dutch East Indies, which first assumed significent proportions in 1797, and the China trade, frequently in conjunction with the fur trade of the American Northwest. The latter route was initiated in 1784, but expanded in the 1790s, when the United States became the major shipper of tea to Europe during the war."[8]

Trade, fishing, and shipping were only the initial nuclei of expansion. Traders became investors; missionaries discovered untold numbers of pagans; and the U.S. navy found steadily increasing duties as the protector of businessmen and missionaries in foreign lands, as explorer of new trade routes, and as opener of additional doors for commerce. (The U.S. Navy Pacific Squadron was organized in 1821, the East India Squadron in 1835. These were in addition to the Mediterranean, West India, and Brazil, or South Atlantic Squadrons during the early nineteenth century.)

There were thus two strands of empire-building: a maritime domain in addition to the better-known acquisition of land across the continent. These were often complementary and mutually supporting, rather than conflicting, movements. Such a complementary relationship manifested itself especially in the struggle for control of the Pacific coast. Jefferson and Adams both saw the Pacific Northwest "as the American window on the Pacific, the corridor across the continent which would give the United States the advantage of a direct route to the great trade routes of Asia."[9] As commercial relations with China grew and rivalry with Britain, Russia, and France for control of Pacific ports and trade routes mounted, ownership of the coastal ports (stretching down to San Francisco, Los Angeles, and San Diego) became an ever more urgent consideration in determining the boundaries the United States sought with Mexico and Canada.[10] Annexation of the coastal ports, however, did not mark the end of western expansion. They became, instead, safe harbors for the growing trade on the long and arduous route around Cape Horn to Asia, and home ports for the U.S. navy operating in the Pacific.

The road to empire in Asia was not built in a continuous and methodical fashion. It proceeded in fits and starts, tempered by competing demands on limited resources (e.g., for the Indian, Mexican, and Civil wars) and by constraints imposed by rival empire-seekers, most especially the British with their dominant navy during the nineteenth century and, beginning at the turn of the twentieth century, the expanding naval power of Japan. Still, the United States didn't miss too many opportunities—for example: taking advantage of Britain's breakthroughs (via the Opium Wars) to obtain treaty ports and extraterritorial rights in China; sending Commodore Perry to force open ports in Japan; pushing for special position in Korea; helping to put down the Boxer Rebellion; stretching U.S. frontiers northward to Alaska and the Aleutians, and westward to Hawaii, Midway, Samoa, Wake, Guam, and the Philippines; imposing the Open Door Policy, and continuing to enforce this policy with the use of the U.S. marines and by patrolling nearly 2,000 miles of the Yangtze River with gunboats.

Seen in this historical context, U.S. imperialist activities in Asia since World War II appear less as the result of a combination of accidents and more as the fruition under favorable circumstances of its long-standing imperial strivings. With Japan, the main Pacific rival, utterly defeated, with Russia, a potential rival, severely weakened, and with Great Britain lacking the resources to create the air force and aircraft carriers needed under modern conditions to dominate the Pacific, it was perfect weather for the United States to spread its sails. Obviously, the contraction of the world imperialist system due to the emergence of socialist systems and the threat of further contraction arising from spreading national liberation movements spurred U.S. interest and active involvement in Asia and other areas of the underdeveloped world. But there is no denying the continuous path of empire-building in Asia and elsewhere throughout U.S. history, independent of the "red menace."

It is important to understand that this expansionism is not the result of some mystical force inherent in the character of the American people. On the contrary, expansion was central to the evolving social system and its remarkable productivity and wealth. Expansion played a major role at each historical stage and helped to mold the resulting economic structure and the cultural environment—both of which reinforced the drive for further expansion. Enterprising capitalists, supported by an energetic state, kept pushing forward in the search for more opportunities for profit; in turn, each new frontier fired the ambition of restless businessmen and spurred the imagination of political leaders dreaming of national wealth and glory.

In interpreting this process of dynamic expansion it is important to recognize that the opportunities for capital formation and accumulation do not make their appearance in the smooth self-generating manner implicitly assumed in the neat mathematical models which economic theorists like to design. While such models may be useful in exploring the mechanisms of coordination which must be present in an anarchic economic system, they overlook certain crucial facts: (1) that such progress as actually does take place is never continuous and orderly, and (2) that unbalanced development is an integral, one might even say necessary, part of capitalist growth.

The most obvious feature of this spasmodic development is the alternating cycle of prosperity and depression. But perhaps more important for understanding the process of expansion are the longer waves in which periods of rapid growth are followed by slow and sluggish growth. Based on evidence for the United States since the 1830s, Professor Moses Abramovitz summarizes this phenomenon as follows:

The economic growth of the United States has taken place in a series of surges during which growth was especially rapid, followed by relapses when growth proceeded much more slowly. In periods of rapid growth, output has increased at rates two, and often three, times as fast as in periods of slow growth. . . . The long waves in the rate of growth reflect similar waves in the rate of growth of resources, both labor and capital; in the rates of growth of productivity; and in the intensity with which resources are utilized.[11]

Underlying these phenomena—both the ordinary boom-bust cycle and the longer swings of alternating galloping and crawling growth—are certain essential characteristics of capitalist development: (1) The speed of growth and even the presence or absence of growth depend in the final analysis on the aggregate investment decisions of businessmen. (2) Capitalist enterprise inevitably entails taking risks, even risks that might end in total loss of invested capital. These risks are generally not incurred unless the odds are right, that is, unless the profit prospects are so encouraging that they far outweigh the danger of loss.

It should go without saying that capitalist societies thrive best when stimulated by exceptionally good profit opportunities, and especially so during waves of speculative fervor and "reasonable" inflation. But these favorable circumstances are not always present. They appear in clusters and are due to various causes, as, for example, a major technological innovation, an upsurge in urbanization, sudden access to new domestic and/or foreign markets, an arms buildup, or war and its aftermath. The impact of any one or a combination of these stimulants can propel the economy forward at a feverish pace. But the factors that induce accelerated growth have an inherent tendency to peter out. It is true that new opportunities for capital investment tend to have a cumulative effect, for they spur related lines of business activity and prolong boom times. But these stimulants are self-limiting. The main canals and railroad lines get completed; areas of settlement are occupied; competing nations encroach on new trade routes; the more independent foreign nations erect tariff walls. And running like a red thread through all the ups and downs of capitalist development is the fundamental paradox: the very process of capital accumulation (the primary engine of growth) generates an imbalance between consumer demand and the output resulting from capital investment; if profits are to be high enough to warrant the risks of enterprise, the flow of income to the mass of consumers must be limited.

So far it has been stressed that capitalist development is characterized both by "normal" business cycles and by longer waves of speedup and slowdown in the rate of growth. But these two kinds of fluctuations are not unrelated. During the longer upswings booms are strong and depressions weak, while the reverse is true during the long downswings. The latter are therefore periods of more or less continuous stagnation which threaten not only the economy but the health of the society as a whole. It is hence not surprising that it is precisely in these periods of stagnation (or slow growth) that new stimuli are sought, and that business and political leaders should be especially receptive to whatever opportunities for foreign expansion may present themselves—or may be created by those with the necessary imagination and daring. This is by no means the exclusive component of the expansionary urge. Other pressures keep coming up, ranging over the centuries—from land speculators promoting acquisition and settlement of new territory; to merchants, farmers, and manufacturers seeking new markets; to monopoly firms desiring control over their sources of raw materials and privileged market conditions. The cause is advanced, and sometimes initiated, by daring, farsighted political and ambitious military chiefs who foster expansion for the sake of their own "personal politics," their notions of patriotism, or their vision of what is needed to increase the power and wealth of their country.

But with all this, it is still important to recognize that these policies are arrived at in a capitalist environment that time and again is faced with the need for stimulants to rev up the engine. The stimulants pounced upon are not always effective; they frequently fail to produce all the hoped-for results. Moreover, domestic political strife may emerge over the choice of strategy and tactics concerning the mode, pace, and geographic concentration of expansion as well as over the preferred method of exercising influence and control—differences that may reflect variations in judgment and/or interpretation of self-interest. But in light of the limited alternatives available for stimulating growth in a profit-oriented society, and the pressure to cope with competing nations also confined to similar limited alternatives and hence pursuing analogous policies, the road to empire becomes well trodden.

It is not uncommon for traditional historians and economists to ridicule the notion that the foreign policies of capitalist powers are strongly influenced by stagnation or the threat of stagnation. Thus, in dealing with the burst of U.S. imperialist expansion at the end of the nineteenth century, they point to the great internal growth of the United States during the twentieth century as proof that there had been plenty of outlets for domestic savings in the last quarter of the nineteenth century. The weakness of this approach is that it interprets history unhistorically. The capitalists and politicians of the 1890s may have dreamed about their country's great and glorious future, but their urgent task was to deal with the present. They may even have made stimulating commencement-day addresses about the country's youth and potential for development, but what faced them the day after commencement was the threat of business failure against the backdrop of repetitive depressions. One of the longest depressions in U.S. business history lasted from October 1873 to March 1879. Indeed, about half the years in the last quarter of the nineteenth century were years of depression.

The point is that theoretical economists and historians do not make decisions about how the nation's savings are to be disposed of. Such decisions are made by practical business people who are very alert to the profit-and-loss potential of opportunities actually available to them. Furthermore, the professorial hindsight that can now identify the enormous investment outlets which materialized in the twentieth century has a way of overlooking the extent to which the Spanish-American War and the subsequent two world wars contributed to the creation of these enlarged domestic investment opportunities.

Just as many economic and other historians are still perplexed by what seems to them the narrow-mindedness and lack of vision of those who masterminded the burst of U.S. imperialist activity in Latin American and Asia at the close of the nineteenth century, so there are now many who have little appreciation of the impact of the depression of the 1930s on the decision-makers before, during, and after World War II. Once again hindsight calls attention to the very substantial growth of the postwar period and casts doubt on the judgment of those in the thirties and forties who had so little faith. It may therefore be worthwhile to review the dimensions of the dilemma of those years. Just to get a sense of what was at stake, let us look at the fluctuations in the production of steel—an indispensable input for the construction, machinery, autos, and other consumer goods, and armaments industries.

Steel Ingots and Castings Produced
(millions of long tons)

Year		Year	
1929	56.4	1944	80.0
1932	13.7	1946	59.5
1937	50.7	1948	79.1
1938	28.3	1949	69.6
1939	47.1	1950	86.5
1941	74.0		

Source: *Historical Statistics of the United States: Colonial Times to 1957* (Washington, D.C.: U.S. Bureau of the Census, 1960), p. 416.

The most striking change, of course, is the drastic drop from 1929 to 1932, with production in 1932 less than one-fourth the previous high. This decline reflects the extent of the crisis in the users of steel. Not all production went down so precipitously, but this kind of contraction was typical of the machinery and construction industries. Thus, residential construction, measured in 1947–1949 prices, slid from $11.6 billion in its peak year of 1926 to $1.7 billion in 1932. Despite the efforts of the New Deal, the recovery reached in 1937 still did not create a demand for steel as high as that of 1929. And this recovery, as can be seen in the figure for 1938, was at best a shaky one. Ten years of depression, during which population and labor productivity kept increasing, left steel production still considerably below 1929. The so-called domestic outlets for savings were surely there, but only on paper. As far as the business community was concerned, there was no point in speculating on the profitability of these theoretical domestic outlets. It was only in 1941 that steel output shot ahead—in response to the war needs of Europe and the heavy armaments program under-taken by the United States in view of the probability that it would soon participate in World War II.

There is no intention here to draw the inference that the United States went to war, or encouraged others to go to war, as a crisis-remedy; the issues are much more complex. But what is important and too often neglected is that the depth and persistence of depression, the apparent inability of the system to snap out of its illness either through a so-called normal recovery or acceptable government measures, domi-nated all policy-making in those years.

Opinions differed strongly on the proper road to eventual full recovery, but the range of policy recommendations was necessarily limited, since the choice had to remain within the conditions imposed by capitalist economics. For example, only when mobilization for war, and more especially the war itself, imposed its priorities on the system did the American people get fed more or less properly and the agricultural surpluses disappear. Surplus food and the potential for producing even more food were both present throughout the depression. But it took the mobilization of twelve million men and women into the armed forces, led by the government, and full employment of the remaining civilian population, made possible by a war-directed economy, to generate the income flows and effective demand that wiped out plaguing agricultural surpluses. Short of war, the policy alternatives had been limited to methods of restimulating market demand. But, since domestic markets proved time and again to be too sluggish either to feed the population or to stimulate business enterprise growth, the capture of foreign markets (including the issue of how to handle the closing down of market opportunities by aggressive rival powers) necessarily rose on the list of policy priorities.

Despite the lift to the U.S. economy given by the war, the experience of the depression and fear of recurrence of stagnation weighed heavily on postwar policy-making. It was clear at the end of the war that the economy was ripe for a new and significant upturn. This optimism was, however, moderated by uncertainty over how long the recovery would last, along with grave doubts about the ability of the private economy to generate enough jobs for the vast number of returning servicemen. The way the war had been financed created large reserves of cash throughout the economy; workers, perhaps for the first time in history, had substantial savings accounts, and veterans' benefits added additional temporary stimuli. At the same time, the backlog of consumer demand was extraordinary, piled up after a long drought of housing construction and some five years of almost no new civilian passenger-car production. Yet, despite the omens of a new wave of prosperity, the economy began to turn down only three years after the war. As can be seen in the above table, steel production in 1949 fell back to below the 1941 prewar high. While the first postwar decline was short lived, and the recovery reinforced on the way up by the Korean War and a new wave of military spending, the experience nevertheless reconfirmed the dangers of stagnation.

It was against the still vivid background of a prolonged

depression and an accompanying breakdown of world financial and commercial markets that the United States sought to reconstitute a postwar world order. To reap the potential profits made possible by the war-created deferred demand, industrialists would need to invest vast sums to quickly create new capacity. The temptations (and the competitive pressure) for such expansion were great, but so was the fear, supported by the recollection of the recent 1930s, that the mouth-watering profit prospects might be transformed into devastating losses just as soon as the effects of the proposed demand wore off. Added assurance of long-term growth was needed to justify the risk of spiraling new investment. This was in the cards if the potential foreign markets could also be tapped. But in order to convert the potential into effective and sustained demand it was necessary to restore the health of traditional trading partners, to overcome the limitations imposed by the dollar and gold shortage outside the United States, and to replace the complex national trade, exchange, and investment barriers that had been erected in self-defense during the depression. The methods adopted to solve these problems fitted in admirably with the long-run striving for hegemony in the capitalist world, reaching fruition as the U.S. dollar became the key currency in foreign trade and New York the hub of world banking and the international money market. The components of the new capitalist world order, built on the ruins of war and the disruption of the preceding protracted economic crisis, fell into place like the pieces of a jigsaw puzzle, influenced by the long history of U.S. empire-building, the ever-present threat of stagnation, the U.S. emergence from the war as the unquestioned dominant military and economic power, and the revolutionary upsurge in the colonial world.

The postwar world economic, financial, and political system erected after World War II is under special stress these days as the United States, its designer and leader, exposes its feet of clay. The inability to suppress the revolution in South Vietnam, the quaking of the world financial system, originally based on the inviolability of the dollar, and the thrust of rival powers, notably Japan and Germany, to attain more competitive and independent positions vis-à-vis the United States—these are all signs of a transition to a new stage. These changes, however, do not as yet portend an alteration of fundamentals: both the struggle for hegemony in Asia and the basic social problems of the underdeveloped countries are still with us and will continue to be for the visible future.

To understand developments in the American Empire and, looming on the horizon, the Japanese Empire in Asia, one must comprehend the basic contradictions in the opportunities for development of the subordinate countries, whether or not they formerly had the status of colonies. Neither the transfer of advanced technology nor injections of foreign aid has succeeded in shaking them out of the morass of poverty, persistent mass unemployment, and misery. They are stuck on the capitalist road, but the options that had been available to the successful capitalist countries in past centuries— options which helped pull them out of impending, recurrent periods of stagnation—are out of the question. Conquest of territory, providing new surges of investment, is impossible. Nor is there, as in the past, the opportunity to dispose, in new areas of settlement, of surplus populations generated by the agricultural and industrial revolutions. At the same time, the economic and financial structure shaped by a long and continuing history of dependence on the more advanced capitalisms, imposes additional limits on the possibility of bootstrap-lifting via the route of profit-seeking capital investment.

It is hard to avoid the conclusion that, more and more, the only real alternative facing these peoples is whether to accept their lot of misery and its accompanying wastage of human lives or to revolutionize their societies so that labor can be fully utilized to begin to meet the real needs of the people.

Notes

1. J. R. Seeley, *The Expansion of England* (London: Macmillan, 1883), p. 8.

2. D. K. Fieldhouse, *The Colonial Empires: A Comparative Survey, from the Eighteenth Century* (London: Weidenfeld & Nicolson, 1966), p. 239.

3. Marvin Kalb and Elie Abel, *Roots of Involvement: The U.S. in Asia 1784-1971* (New York: W. W. Norton, 1971). The theme of reluctance is one of the most pervasive explanations found in histories of colonialism. A characteristic example, in this case referring to South Africa, is the following:

> The border . . . remained too thinly settled to provide real protection; the area instead became an irresistible attraction to Bantu cattle rustlers with grievances against the newcomers. Settlers and tribesmen could not be kept apart; both moved to and fro across the boundary. Governments then tried to enforce security by more advanced lines of demarcation, but each new boundary further compressed the territory of the indigenous tribes and ultimately led to further conflicts, with the result that the imperial power, regardless of its original intentions, reluctantly kept adding to its commitments.

(L. H. Gann and Peter Duignan, *Burden of Empire: An Appraisal of Western Colonialism in Africa South of the Sahara* [New York: Praeger, 1967], p. 19)

4. Ronald Steel, *Pax Americana* (New York: Viking Press, 1968), pp. 10-11.

5. This theme is thoroughly explored in two valuable studies: Gabriel Kolko, *The Politics of War: The World and United States Foreign Policy, 1943-1945* (New York: Random House, 1969), and Joyce and Gabriel Kolko, *The Limits of Power: The World and United States Foreign Policy, 1945-1954* (New York: Harper & Row, 1972).

6. R. W. Van Alstyne, *The Rising American Empire* (Chicago: Quadrangle Books, 1965), p. v.

7. Mira Wilkins, *The Emergence of Multinational Enterprise: American Business Abroad from the Colonial Era to 1914* (Cambridge, Mass.: Harvard University Press, 1970), p. 7.

8. The quotation as well as the preceding percentages are from Douglas C. North, *The Economic Growth of the United States, 1790-1860* (Englewood Cliffs, New Jersey: Prentice-Hall, 1961), pp. 41-42.

9. Van Alstyne, *The Rising American Empire*, p. 93.

10. Professor Graebner puts the case forcefully:

> What [the] traditional approaches overlook is the essential fact that the expansion of the United States was a unified, purposeful, precise movement that was ever limited to specific maritime objectives. It was the Pacific Ocean that determined the territorial goals of all American presidents from John Quincy Adams to Polk. From the beginning, travelers, traders, and officials who concerned themselves with the coastal regions had their eyes trained on ports. The goal of American policy was to control the great harbors of San Francisco, San Diego, and Juan de Fuca Strait. . . . But mercantile interests in the Pacific proved more than a contributing motive to American expansionism. They determined the course of empire. Maritime calculations first defined the objectives of American statesmen on the distant shore. Next, they augmented the srong inclination of British and American officials to seek a peaceful solution to the Oregon controversy. And, finally, they fused Oregon and California into one irreducible issue and created a vision of empire that encompassed both regions. The sea made the settlement of the Oregon question contingent upon the acquisition of California in the fulfillment of the American purpose.

(Norman A. Graebner, *Empire on the Pacific: A Study in American Continental Expansion* [New York: Ronald Press, 1955], p. vi)

11. *Hearings before the Joint Economic Committee, Congress of the United States, Employment, Growth and Price Levels*, Part 2, April 7-10, 1959 (Washington, D.C.: Government Printing Office, 1959), p. 412.

3

Imperialism:
A Historical Survey

Significant as Lenin's analysis of imperialism was—and still is, more than a half century later—we nevertheless should recognize that he was focusing primarily on certain aspects of imperialism: on the rivalry among capitalist nations in the age of monopoly capitalism, on the nature of World War I, and on the revolutionary opportunities of that period. There are, however, other important facets to imperialism, touched on by Lenin but not central to the questions he was trying to answer. Outstanding among these are the questions about the political, economic, and social effects of domination by imperialist powers on colonies, semicolonies, and spheres of influence. There is no incompatibility between the questions Lenin tried to answer and these additional questions. But there is, in my opinion, an important analytical difference. The historical periodization which Lenin insists on, quite properly, when dealing with the intensification of colonialism (and more specifically, the interimperialist rivalry for redivision of the world) does not apply with equal validity to the other issues. To be sure, changes occur over time in both the metropoles and in the periphery, and these changes

This paper was prepared for a seminar on imperialism held in New Delhi, India, in March 1972. It subsequently appeared in the May 1972 issue of *Monthly Review*.

should be studied historically. But the fundamental questions about the forces of production, production relations, and class structures in the peripheral countries can best be analyzed against the entire panorama of colonialism, economic expansionism, and the rivalry among colonial powers, beginning with the earliest distortions introduced by the West into the colonial world.

An attempt to stretch the Leninist theory to fit both topics—the "new" imperialism of monopoly capitalism and the "old" imperialism of early and adolescent capitalism—leads to confusion. One cannot really understand the problems of the colonial world and of neocolonialism if one concentrates exclusively on the new features stressed by Lenin. And this is also why so many of the pedantic discussions (on the Left as well as in academic circles) contrasting Marx's and Lenin's theories of imperialism have little meaning. Marx and Lenin were dealing with different questions: Marx with the growth of a world capitalism that created an international division of labor between the industrialized and colonial worlds, a process essential to the growth of capitalism as a system; Lenin with the special international features of monopoly capitalism.

A second obstacle to the development of a satisfactory modern theory of imperialism derives from the opposite tendency: the compression of Lenin's theory (or a hodgepodge from Lenin, Luxemburg, and Hobson) into a rigid model, not too different in form, even if different in content, from the kind bourgeois economists delight in. The purpose of such compression is to find the key to the necessity of imperialism, a magic "secret" formula, as for example: the drive to export capital pressured by a surplus of capital; or the declining rate of profit; or the inability to realize surplus value within existing capitalist markets; or imperialist expansion as the way out of crisis. It is true enough that each of these factors has been involved, to a greater or lesser extent, in different situations and at different times. But the selection of any one of them as the prime mover of the new imperialism, or of the old imperialism for that matter, results in a mechanical formula that proves quite incapable of encompassing or explaining the facts of history.

It should not be necessary to point out, except for the all too frequent distortions both by academic critics and sympathetic expounders, that Lenin himself never engaged in such formula-construction games. For example, he mentions at least three reasons for the colonial drive in the period of monopoly capitalism:

> The more capitalism is developed, the more the need for raw materials is felt, the more bitter the competition becomes, and the more feverishly the hunt for raw materials proceeds throughout the whole world, the more desperate becomes the struggle for the acquisition of colonies. . . . Finance capital is not only interested in the already known sources of raw materials; it is also interested in potential sources of raw materials. . . .
>
> The necessity of exporting capital also gives an impetus to the conquest of colonies, for in the colonial market it is easier to eliminate competition, to make sure of orders, to strengthen the necessary "connections," etc. by monopolist methods (and sometimes it is the only possible way). [Quite a different kettle of fish from the surplus capital/declining-rate-of-profit formula. Note, in addition, the "also"—a far cry from the common explanation of capital export as the major factor in imperialism.]
>
> The non-economic superstructure which grows up on the basis of finance capital, its politics and its ideology, stimulates the striving for colonial conquest.[1]

The fact is that Lenin's analysis is concerned with a whole complex of forces (political, sociological, and economic) that reach a special degree of urgency—sufficient to define a significantly new and distinctive era—when (1) giant firms, operating within an environment of finance capital, can and must seek greater monopolistic control (including division of markets among the giant firms) in both the advanced and underdeveloped countries, and (2) several leading nations are in a position to compete for monopoly-type control through division (and redivision) of spheres of influence and territory over the whole globe.

If this characterization of the highest stage of capitalism is to be fully understood, however, it has to be viewed in the context of the essential nature of capitalism as such (not merely of its latest stage) and its evolution from its very roots. A full-bodied theory of the onset and persistence of the new imperialism, let alone the old imperialism, must be based on the more fundamental propositions listed below. (Some of these are implicit in Lenin's theory. To the extent that they may not be, it is because Lenin was concerned primarily with the interimperialist rivalry, and only to a much lesser extent with metropolis-periphery relations.)

1. Restless expansion—the accumulation of capital—is the driving force and the very essence of capitalism. The desire and need to utilize the resources of other nations for this accumulation process are present at all stages of capitalist development; how far and how deep this extranational accumulation can go depends upon its feasibility under concrete historical situations.

2. The origin of capitalism as a world system determined its structure and strongly influenced its entire course of development.

3. The more powerful capitalist nations grafted their mode of production on the rest of the world.[2] They thus went beyond the traditional looting and tribute-gathering of former empires, arrangements which merely drained off the surplus of often relatively stagnant colonial production systems. The imposition of capitalist relations, by force and overwhelming economic power, created sources of expanding production and surplus value of continuous benefit to the leading capitalist nations.

4. The world capitalist system which evolved in the process of forcibly transforming noncapitalist societies and adapting the weaker to the needs of the stronger nations, had two historically new features: (a) the institution of an international division of labor between manufacturing nations and those that mainly supplied raw materials and food, and (b) the creation of a hierarchy in which the overwhelming majority of nations and people were, to a greater or lesser degree, economically and financially dependent on a few centers of industry and banking.

5. The economic laws and institutions of capitalism (its

market, price, and financial mechanisms) continuously reproduce the international division of labor and the hierarchy of economic and financial dependency.

It is also important to recognize that a primary active agency throughout the history of capitalism's global expansion has been rivalry among nation states. Indeed, the contradictions inherent in the origin and development of nation states were themselves major propelling forces for expansion. A successful capitalist society needs a strong and centralized state to provide the conditions for unimpeded trade within a good-sized national market: to eliminate the tolls, customs duties, and other restrictions of regional feudal domains; to establish a reliable coinage system; to inaugurate standard weights and measures, etc. But while the nascent capitalist states were needed to establish, and if possible enlarge, inner markets, they were, by the same token, needed to protect these national markets from outside competition and to help develop external trade opportunities. Elimination of domestic rivalry was therefore the counterpart of the generation of international conflict.

Moreover, given the relatively low productivity and hence the comparatively small economic surplus at the time, the centralizing monarchies which created the nation states were under constant pressure to locate adequate sources of wealth to finance their incessant armed struggle against independent feudal lords. This need spurred the alliance between royalty and merchants, bankers, and shippers. And the various partners in these alliances egged each other on in the pursuit of the most profitable undertakings open to them under the prevailing conditions—overseas expansion, the creation of forts and trading posts abroad as bases to take over the trade of other nations, to loot the accumulated wealth or resources of other peoples, and to pirate the merchandise carried on ships of other countries.

In the beginning the alliances formed between the state and commercial interests, although sustained by mutual advantage, were tentative and shaky: competing pressures by other influential groups in society enabled the newly centralized states to have a degree of independence. However, the growth of the resulting world commerce (under the direction of leading European nations), the gold and silver flowing in from foreign conquest, the consequent stimulation of manufactures—all contributed to the breakdown of feudalism, the restructuring of economic life, and the intensification of conflict between the leading interest groups. In turn, the resolution of these conflicts and the adaptation of the state to meet the needs of the victors set the stage for new and intensified overseas expansion and gave further impetus to rivalry between states.

It is this general pattern of expansion which can be detected in the successive stages of colonialism and imperialism. But alterations in economic structure and in the dominant ruling groups of the leading capitalist nations—from commercial to industrial and finally to monopoly capital—called for different strategies of colonial acquisition and for new policies of colonial administration.[3] The underpinnings of these internal changes were strikingly new technologies and economic institutions suited to the new technology. Technical advances also influenced external behavior, the degree to which foreign territories could be acquired and digested. Here, the most important consideration was the advance in armament technology;[4] but even the most pacific of innovations—such as the railroad—became instruments of colonial "pacification." Finally, the concrete forms of empire took shape in the course of wars and other forms of conflict among rival powers.

Definitions of unique stages in history must obviously be approached with caution, since history does not proceed in as orderly a fashion as the abstractions we design. Extensive overlapping between stages and the influence of accidental factors (adding to the richness of history) tend to controvert the neat packaging of distinct periods. Nevertheless, with all due qualifications, enough significant differences exist in the patterns of capitalist expansionism so that periodization can be analytically useful. In taking a stab at it, I would suggest five stages: (1) from the end of the fifteenth century to the middle of the seventeenth century: the rise of commercial capital and the rapid growth of world commerce; (2) from the middle of the seventeenth century to the latter part of the eighteenth century: commercial capital ripens into a dominant economic force; (3) from the late eighteenth century to the 1870s: the rise and eventual victory of the industrial capital, under the spur of the Industrial Revolution; (4) from roughly 1880 to the end of World War I: the rise and victory of monopoly capital, the territorial division of the globe, and the first global struggle for redivision; and (5) since the end of World War I: the beginning of socialism as a rival social system, eventual decolonization, and the rise of the multinational corporation. Space limits allow only a brief overview which will devote relatively more space to the first three stages, and touch only lightly on the last two. My reasons for this procedure are that the penultimate stage was so fully covered by Lenin's *Imperialism* and the last stage will be extensively discussed in other papers at this seminar.

1. European Commerce Enters the World Stage: From the End of the Fifteenth Century to Mid-Seventeenth Century

The outward thrust of European commerce at the end of the fifteenth century had to overcome two obstacles: the blockade (and counterpressure) of the Ottoman Empire, and the fact that trade with and between countries outside Europe was controlled by Asians and Africans. The blockade stimulated the ocean voyages which opened up the Americas, where the inferiority of Indian weapons and the susceptibility of the population to European diseases facilitated European conquest. However, in striving for trade opportunities in other parts of the world, the Europeans came up against well-entrenched commercial systems, as for example in the Indian Ocean:

> After journeying through the inhospitable seas of Southern Africa the Portuguese ships had come into regions where there was a complex of shipping, trade and authority as highly devel-

oped as the European: forms of political capitalism at least as large in dimensions as those of Southern Europe, and probably larger; shipping in bottoms many of them carrying more than those used in European merchant shipping; a trade in every conceivable valuable high quality product carried on by a great multitude of traders; merchant gentlemen and harbor princes wielding as great financial power as did the merchants and princes of Europe.[5]

Here the Europeans had nothing to offer in superiority of goods, finance, or trading ability which would enable them to break into the traditional trade. They did have one decisive advantage, however, the great superiority of European ships of war. Sailing ships strong enough to mount cannon provided sufficient destructive power to force the issue: to cripple the ships of other nations, transfer the trade into European hands, and establish forts for control of the seas.

The main features of this period of expansion—conquest of South America, exploitation of the gold and silver resources found there, and the diversion of established trade—reflect the state of the arts of the period. The relatively undeveloped means of production and the consequently small currently produced economic surplus left direct robbery, whenever practical, as one of the most effective means of accumulating wealth. Hence looting, plunder, and piracy were primary agents of redistribution and new concentrations of wealth. This redistribution took two forms: (1) skimming off by the Europeans of as much as possible of the accumulated surplus of the rest of the world, and (2) conflict among leading European nations—Spain, Portugal, Holland, France, and England—for access to the wealth of other continents, including what they could pirate from each other on the high seas. As one economic historian described the foreign commerce of those days: "The prize in distant commerce went not to the best producers and merchants, but to the group of the best fighters; not size and resources, but ability to organize and willingness to risk resources in conflict, determined the question of success."[6]

In the long run, the flood of new products from the East,

the huge flow of precious metals from America, the opening of new markets, and the demand generated by the several states in the pursuit and establishment of colonies enormously stimulated the expansion of Western manufactures and the ascendancy of the European bourgeoisies—in short, paved the way for the global triumph of capitalism. But there was a limit to the profitability of this first wave of overseas expansion: the wealth obtained by plunder of hoards amassed over years can only be taken once.

There were, moreover, further contradictions contributing to the drying up of the benefits from the first wave of overseas expansion: (1) The handsome profits derived from taking over the trade routes of others do not grow unless the trade itself keeps on expanding, and this did not occur as long as the old modes of production remained intact. (2) Profits from the spice trade dropped, squeezed by restricted supplies on the one side and increasing costs of defending monopolistic control against rival nations on the other. The flow of precious metals from South America declined as the richest mines became exhausted, given the backward techniques then in use, and as the labor force of the superexploited Indians dried up. These were among the reasons why, as Eric Hobsbawm put it, "the 'old colonial system' passed through a profound crisis. . . . Old colonialism did not grow over into new colonialism; it collapsed and was replaced by it." [7]

2. Commercial Capital Dominant: Mid-Seventeenth Century to Late Eighteenth Century

The political and military conditions that set off and distinguish this period are: (1) the waning of Spain's preeminence; (2) the shift in Portugal's dependence on France to dependence on England; (3) the end of a virtual Dutch monopoly of shipping; (4) the growth of colonial rivalry between France and England, and the emergence of Britain's preeminence on the sea and in international commerce. Central to these changes was the triumph of commercial interests in the class struggles that ripened in the English revolution of the seventeenth century. This development puts its stamp on the whole era, conditioning the rise of Britain's leading role in empire, finance, and trade.[8]

In contrast with the vacillation of Britain in earlier decades, the political triumph of commercial capital is reflected in the adoption of clear-cut policies to assure Britain's commercial supremacy. Under Cromwell, Britain set out to build for the first time a national and professional navy. But while a strong navy was needed to back up ocean commerce,[9] the shipping trade itself needed special promotion, in part to compete for commerce, and in part to train a reserve of competent seamen for the growing navy. These considerations, aimed at overcoming Dutch ocean-trade dominance, were behind the Navigation Acts of 1650–1651. These acts not only created a monopoly for Britain's ships in its trade with Asia, Africa, and America, but also created the basis for a whole set of restrictions on its colonies which gave an important boost to the demand for British manufactures. The aim of colonial policy became crystal clear: to create a self-sufficient empire, producing as much as possible of the raw materials and food needs of the mother country and providing exclusive markets for its manufactures.

This goal fitted in with the state of productive resources of those times. We are dealing here with the period of rapid growth of manufactures which preceded the Industrial Revolution. Given the fact that domestic markets were weak and that prices could not be drastically slashed, it followed that the demand for manufactures could be most successfully stimulated in a controlled environment. This meant exclusivity both at home and in the colonies, and also a drive for more colonies, involving wars to take away the proven colonies of other powers.

The search for foreign markets had to overcome many hurdles prior to the Industrial Revolution and to the time when Europe had the military and technical resources to penetrate into the interior of foreign continents, thereby creating markets through the breaking up and restructuring of noncapitalist societies. The populated, relatively advanced countries of the East, such as India and China, had little interest in acquiring European manufactures. And in a large part of the Asian world Europe bought more than it sold, until the nineteenth century.[10] Under these conditions, the growth of plantation colonies (with a new emphasis on expanded production to meet growing European demand) and of white-settler colonies was a major contribution to that burst of demand for manufactures to meet the needs of the settlers in both types of colonies which helped stimulate the Industrial Revolution.

At the heart of this wave of expansion was the slave trade. The prosperity of the extremely profitable sugar plantations was based on the import of African slaves. More than that, the slave trade itself was a most lucrative business, as well as an important prop to British exports via the well-known triangular trade. In sum, the Industrial Revolution germinated in this period—in the boom of export markets and the trade in merchandise and slaves, under monopoly conditions secured through war, control of the seas, and political domination.

On the other hand, this source of European prosperity had its own limitations and began to dry up in the latter half of the eighteenth century. This process was pointedly summarized by Hobsbawm:

> The new colonial economies were not capable of permanent expansion. ... their use of land and labor was essentially extensive and inefficient. Moreover, the supply of slaves (who rarely reproduced themselves on a sufficient scale) could not be increased fast enough, as is suggested by the rapidly rising trend of slave prices. Hence, exhaustion of the soil, inefficiencies of management, and labor difficulties led to something like a "crisis of the colonial economy" from the 1750s.[11] This found various forms of expression—for instance, anti-slavery sentiment, and the Home Rule movements of local white settler oligarchies which grew up rapidly in the last third of the eighteenth century in Latin America, in the West Indies, North America and Ireland, and contributed to the revolution in western Europe.[12]

3. Rise of Industrial Capital:
Late Eighteenth Century to the 1870s

The declining profitability of the old colonies on the eve of the Industrial Revolution led to an intensification of the search for new colonies and to renewal of warfare between rival empires for redistribution of existing colonies. In the 1760s, England launched a campaign of exploration for new markets in Asia and Africa (on both of which continents Portugal and Holland had taken the lead) and in South America (via establishment of bases for smuggling through the barriers imposed by Spain around her colonies). At the same time, the intense Seven Years War (1756-1763) led to France's losing nearly the whole of her colonial empire, and to Britain's doubling her possessions in North America and opening a clear road to the takeover of India and the domination of the Indian Ocean.

In the previous stage, the major struggles among colonial powers resulted in the triumph of Britain over Holland and Spain (from which the victor obtained, as one of the rewards, control over the slave trade to the Spanish colonies). In the period now being discussed, the primary struggle was between England and France, finally decided in the Napoleonic Wars. It is these wars which set the stage for Britain's hegemony for most of the nineteenth century. Competition among the industrializing capitalist nations continued, but an era of relative peace prevailed in the years between Waterloo and the rise of the new imperialism. The wars of these years were wars of conquest as the imperial powers proceeded further into continental interiors, rather than wars among the imperial powers themselves. And one of the major reasons for this was Britain's undisputed mastery of the seas. As put by one student of imperial history: "In the nineteenth century, as a consequence of one nation's overwhelming naval supremacy, such phrases as 'the struggle for command of the sea' had lost all meaning." [13]

Another effect of the Napoleonic Wars, which helped stamp the future of imperialism, was the opportunity given to Britain to grab the overseas markets of rival powers—to build up her trade and banking network in South America, Africa, and the Far East. As seen most clearly in her support of the independence of the Spanish and Portuguese colonies in South America and in her subsequent commercial and financial preeminence on that continent, the benefits made possible by the Industrial Revolution (in contrast with the situation prevailing in the previous stage of dominant merchant capital) could be acquired through informal as well as formal empire.

The basic strategy of economic relations between the advanced capitalist nations and the rest of the world necessarily changed with the growth of mass production and the ascendancy of industrial capital. Instead of colonial products (such as sugar and spices) and slaves, the needs of the industrializing nations broadened out to include an ever-mounting hunger for raw materials to be processed (cotton, oilseeds, dyestuffs, jute, metals) and for food for rapidly expanding urban populations. More important, the previous closed markets of the plantation and settlement colonies were small beer in the light of the flood of products pouring out of the new factories. The pressures of the capital accumulation process and of constantly advancing technology propelled an effort to transform the noncapitalist areas into customers, a process entailing the breakup of the noncapitalist societies. This "breakup" was needed both to create markets and to obtain supplies via commercial agriculture and mining. And while the tactics used to reach these goals varied from one colonial power to another, the basic strategy was universal, involving to a lesser or greater extent the disruption of traditional self-sufficient and self-perpetuating communities; introduction of private property in land; extending the use of money and exchange; imposition of forced labor and recruitment of a labor force depending on wages; destroying competitive native industry; creating a new class structure, including fostering of new elite groups as political and economic junior partners of the imperial powers; imposition of the culture of the metropolitan centers, along with racism and other sociopsychological characteristics of minority foreign rule.

Accompanying the changing character of colonial strategy was the enabling technology, civilian (notably railroads) as well as military. For, in contrast with the previous two stages during which the colonies, except for South America, were largely located along coasts or on small islands, the colonial expansion of this period was characterized by the conquest of continental interiors—including the conquest by the United States of its transcontinental empire, and the tsarist absorption of Central Asia.[14]

During the transition from the colonial system based on merchant capital to that based on industrial capital, some of the ideological and political leaders of triumphant capitalism began to question the utility of colonies, but it would be wrong, I believe, to make too much of this tendency. These anti-imperialists were thinking primarily of the white-settler colonies. As a rule they had no objections to, and for the most part supported, among other things, the wars in India, the Opium Wars, and the retention of Ireland as a colony.[15] What is especially striking about this "anti-imperialism" is its negative aspect: it was directed against special-privilege hangovers in the colonies from the days of merchant capitalism. And its positive aspect was that it provided ideological support and justification for the informal empire of trade and finance which rested on Britain's position as master of the seas, center of international finance, leading exporter of capital, and overwhelmingly foremost manufacturer.

Whether by means of informal or formal empire, the epitome of this stage of imperialism, in contrast with all previous history, is the imposition of the conqueror's mode of production on the society of the conquered. This was achieved in two ways: (1) the use of force or threat of force to transform existing societies to meet the raw material, trade, and investment needs of the conqueror, thereby instituting the division of labor most beneficial to the metropolitan centers, along with the mechanisms for reproducing this division of labor; and (2) killing off the indigenous population and/or moving them into reservations in order to create room for the transplantation of the capitalist system by migration of people and capital from the advanced imperialist centers. In this fashion, the European nations spread their control (in Europe itself as well as in the colonies and ex-colonies) from 35 percent of the globe's land surface in 1800 to 67 percent in 1878, when a new major wave of expansion started.[16]

4. Monopoly Capital and the New Imperialism: 1880s to World War I

The near-completion of the territorial division of the world among the leading capitalist nations (from the 67 percent of the earth controlled by Europeans in 1878 to 84.4 percent in 1914)[17] and the struggle for its redivision are but the most glaring aspects of the new imperialism. What needs to be probed are the underlying roots of such a sudden outburst to see whether this was merely the product of a concatenation of accidents or perhaps of an infectious mania which seized the ruling political groups at that time. And here Lenin's analysis is most pertinent in establishing that the roots of transformation are located in (1) structural changes in industry and finance leading to a new stage of monopoly capitalism, and (2) the maturation of centers of monopoly capital which, under the urgency of these structural changes, were assailing Britain's preeminence.

Some of the associated phenomena of this period that seem to me to merit special attention are:

1. The ripening of monopoly capital was stimulated by what has been called the "second Industrial Revolution"; steel, electricity, oil, synthetic chemistry, and the internal combustion engine.

2. While the laws of capitalist motion spurred both the concentration and centralization of capital, the new technology both required a concentration of finance, and in turn pushed its concentration to new heights.

3. The political redirection required by these changes

usually involved a shift in power to the captains of finance and the new industries, and away from the capitalists associated with the manufactures of the first Industrial Revolution.

4. Monopolistic-type control over raw material supplies became increasingly important both as a competitive weapon among giants and as a guarantee for the security of the capital invested in the new industries.

5. The technology of the steamship and of worldwide communication, together with the extension of imperialist control over almost all the globe, completed the process of creating the worldwide network of trade and finance which produced and reproduced the international division of labor most favorable to the centers of industry and finance.

6. Britain lost her advantage at sea when armor-clad steam warships were perfected. Since Britain, in effect, had to start anew to build a modern fleet, other nations with sufficient industrial capacity had the opportunity to build up competitive strength that could challenge Britain's hegemony.

5. Decolonization and the Rise of the Multinational Corporation: Since World War I

This is the period when the imperialist system begins to decline. Quite obviously, decline does not mean death. But the rise of socialism, the inspiration this has given to the colonial world, and the acceleration of national liberation struggles underline the trend of a shrinking imperialist system.

Within the imperialist world, the distinguishing feature of this period is the challenge by the United States to the financial hegemony of Britain, which is resolved hands down in favor of the United States at the end of World War II. But it is a hegemony which is now tottering, a process which began under the strains of the U.S. war against the Vietnamese people.

The basic features of this period, as they matured after World War II, are conditioned by the struggles for national liberation—not merely the process of formal political decolonization, but, more importantly, the tendency towards social revolution in the periphery as the path to real national independence.

The challenge to the centers of imperialism became one of developing and strengthening the methods of keeping the former colonial world within the network of imperialism for control of raw materials and for all available trade and investment opportunities. The forces unleashed by decolonization brought the issue of economic development to the fore. And it soon became clear that if the metropolitan centers were to keep their informal empires, they would have to control and influence the attempts at economic development in the colonial world. This has been facilitated by the method of decolonization itself, whereby the main economic and financial components of dependency have been maintained intact. To this have been added the various so-called foreign-aid programs, and the controls supervised by such organizations as the World Bank, the International Monetary Fund, and the European Economic Community. All of this is, of course, backed up by direct and indirect interference by the United States and other powers in the politics and class conflicts of the ex-colonies, aimed at strengthening those sections of the ruling class which are most sympathetic and reliable, and providing them with needed military assistance and military alliances. Further, the United States, relying on a chain of military bases around the globe, built up a highly mobile air force and navy as instruments of power ready to be used on a moment's notice.[18]

As in previous stages, the imperialism of this period is also associated with changes in the status of key sections of the ruling classes of the metropolitan centers. The most noteworthy features of the new departure in the post-World War II years are:

1. In contrast with the past, when the producers of military goods were pretty much a distinct industrial group, the new military technology and the growth of conglomerates have resulted in the integration of military production with the dominant industrial sectors.

2. The rising importance of the multinational corporation which drives toward worldwide control of the most profitable and newest industries in both the periphery and advanced countries. (The structure and strategy of the multinational corporation generate further penetration of the ex-colonies and strongly influence the course of development—or more accurately of underdevelopment—in these countries.)

3. The priority of the interests of military-multinational industry on the affairs of state.

True, this describes primarily the situation in the United States, but at the same time it outlines the path now being followed in rival imperialist powers—a process that may well be speeded up in view of the weaknesses now being revealed in the internal and external positions of U.S. capitalism.

Notes

1. V. I. Lenin, *Imperialism: The Highest Stage of Capitalism* (New York: International Publishers, 1939), pp. 82-84.

2. Marx, it is interesting to note, classifies three types of conquests by one people over another.

   Conquests may lead to either of three results. The conquering nation may impose its own mode of production upon the conquered people (this was done, for example, by the English in Ireland during this century, and to some extent in India); or it may refrain from interfering in the old mode of production and be content with tribute (e.g., the Turks and Romans); or interaction may take place between the two, giving rise to a new system as a synthesis (this occurred partly in the Germanic conquests). (Karl Marx, *A Contribution to the Critique of Political Economy* [Moscow: Progress Publishers, 1970], first appendix, pp. 202-3)

3. As far as I know, no comparative historical study yet exists of the leading nation states and the changing patterns of ruling elites as they developed through the various phases of imperialism. Clearly such a study would be very useful in furthering understanding of both the capitalist state and of imperialism.

4. This was neatly summarized by Hilaire Belloc:

> Whatever happens, we have got
> The Maxim gun, and they have not!

For a useful review of the role of war technology in the early phases of European expansion, see Carlo M. Cipolla, *Guns, Sails, and Empires* (New York: Pantheon, 1965). It is also noteworthy that many of the advances in armaments were tested, and their effectiveness studied, in wars of conquest of colonial peoples or in suppression of national wars of liberation. The United States has probably the record for such tests, made in the war against the Vietnamese people. But this practice occurred with earlier weapons too, especially the machine gun. On the latter see G. S. Hutchinson, *Machine Guns: Their History and Technical Employment* (London: Macmillan, 1938).

5. A. Toussaint, *Archives of the Indian Ocean*, as quoted in G. S. Graham, *The Politics of Naval Supremacy* (Cambridge: Cambridge University Press, 1965), p. 37.

6. Clive Day, *A History of Commerce* (New York: Longmans Green, 1938), p. 166.

7. E. J. Hobsbawm, "The Crisis of the Seventeenth Century," in Trevor Aston, ed., *Crisis in Europe 1560-1660* (New York: Doubleday [Anchor Books], 1967), p. 24. The entire paragraph is based on Hobsbawm's path-breaking articles (originally appearing in *Past and Present*) in which, among other things, he clearly spells out the historical significance of, and the differences between, the earlier colonies of plunder and the subsequent plantation and settlement colonies.

8. The resolution of the class struggle in England necessarily influenced the direction of movement in other leading powers, even those where the commercial classes were as yet in a subordinate position. The increasing strength of England entailed the weakening of their rivals' commercial position. The impact of such competition obliged the others to play England's game or fall by the wayside. And in the process the status of merchants, shippers, and manufacturers waxed in those competing nations which succeeded in staying in the game. In similar fashion, the subsequent Industrial Revolution in England made it imperative for other nations to industrialize.

9. Some interesting data on the correlation between the ups and downs of British trade and its power at sea are given in J. Holland

Rose, "Sea Power and Expansion 1660-1763," in *The Cambridge History of the British Empire*, vol. 2 (New York: Macmillan, 1929), p. 537.

10. The diversion of trade discussed in the preceding section applied, as far as Asia was concerned, to the displacement of shipping by Asians rather than to any basic changes in the character of Asian trade, which came much later.

11. The "crisis" of the new colonialism does not contradict the previous point about the decisive benefit obtained for the Industrial Revolution from these colonies. Thus, for a long time prior to 1770 the colonies (including Ireland) bought at least 90 percent of Britain's cotton piece-goods exports.

12. E. J. Hobsbawm, "The Crisis of the Seventeenth Century," pp. 55-56.

13. G. S. Graham, *The Politics of Naval Supremacy*, p. 105.

14. The new space conquered by imperial powers provided land and jobs for the unemployed and the dislocated of rampant capitalism, and no doubt contributed somewhat to the abatement of the social-revolutionary potential of the European working classes.

15. On this, see the useful study by Bernard Semmel, *The Rise of Free Trade Imperialism* (Cambridge: Cambridge University Press, 1970).

16. Grover Clark, *The Balance Sheets of Imperialism* (New York: Columbia University Press, 1936), pp. 5-6.

17. Ibid.

18. The contours of imperialist expansion and strategy can be traced, in part, through the evolution of weapons and the arts of war: from the improved sailing vessels and cannon to improved rifles and the inception of a mass infantry, to the machine gun, modern battleship, submarine, airplane, and missile.

THEORY
AND THE THIRD WORLD

4

Imperialism
Without Colonies

The sudden upsurge during the late nineteenth century in the aggressive pursuit of colonies by almost all the great powers is, without doubt, a primary distinguishing trait of the "new imperialism." It is surely the dramatic hallmark of this historic process, and yet it is by no means the essence of the new imperialism. In fact, the customary identification of imperialism with colonialism is an obstacle to the proper study of the subject, since colonialism existed before the modern form of imperialism and the latter has outlived colonialism.

While colonialism itself has an ancient history, the colonialism of the last five centuries is closely associated with the birth and maturation of the capitalist socioeconomic system. The pursuit and acquisition of colonies (including political and economic domination, short of colonial ownership) was a significant attribute of the commercial revolution which contributed to the disintegration of feudalism and the foundation of capitalism. The precapitalist regional trade patterns

This article was originally presented in 1970 at an Oxford University seminar on Theories of Imperialism; it subsequently appeared in Roger Owen and Robert Sutcliffe, eds., *Studies in the Theory of Imperialism* (London: Longman, 1972), copyright © 1972 by E. R. J. Owen and R. B. Sutcliffe.

around the globe were not destroyed by the inexorable forces of the market. Instead, it was superior military power that laid the basis for transforming these traditional trade patterns into a world market centered on the needs and interests of Western Europe. The leap ahead in naval power—based on advances in artillery and in sailing vessels able to carry the artillery—created the bludgeoning force used to annex colonies, open trading ports, enforce new trading relations, and develop mines and plantations. Based on mastery of seapower, this colonialism was mainly confined to coastal areas, except for the Americas where the sparse population had a primitive technology and was highly susceptible to European infectious diseases.[1] Until the nineteenth century, economic relations with these colonies were, from the European standpoint, import-oriented, largely characterized by the desire of the metropolitan countries to obtain the esoteric goods and riches that could be found only in the colonies. For most of those years, in fact, the conquering Europeans had little to offer in exchange for the spices and tropical agricultural products they craved, as well as the precious metals from the Americas.

The metropolitan-colonial relation changed under the impact of the Industrial Revolution and the development of the steam railway. With these, the center of interest shifted from imports to exports, resulting in the ruination of native industry, the penetration of large land areas, a new phase in international banking, and increasing opportunity for the export of capital. Still further changes were introduced with the development of large-scale industry based on new metallurgy, the industrial application of organic chemistry, new sources of power, and new means of communication and of ocean transport.

In the light of geographic and historical disparities among colonies and the different purposes they have served at different times, the conclusion can hardly be avoided that attempts such as have been made by some historians and economists to fit all colonialism into a single model are bound to be unsatisfactory. There is, to be sure, a common factor in the various colonial experiences; namely, the exploitation of the colonies for the benefit of the metropolitan centers.[2] More-over, there is unity in the fact that the considerable changes in the colonial and semicolonial world that did occur were primarily in response to the changing needs of an expanding and technically advancing capitalism. Still, if we want to understand the economics and politics of the colonial world at some point in time, we have to recognize and distinguish the differences associated with the periods of mercantile capitalism, competitive industrial capitalism, and monopoly capitalism, just as we have to distinguish these stages of development in the metropolitan centers themselves if we want to understand the process of capital development.

The identification of imperialism with colonialism obfus-cates not only historical variation in colonial-metropolitan relations, but makes it more difficult to evaluate the latest transformation of the capitalist world system, the imperial-ism of the period of monopoly capitalism. This obfuscation can often be traced to the practice of creating rigid, static, and ahistoric conceptual models to cope with complex, dynamic phenomena. I propose to examine some of the more common misconceptions on which models of this kind are often based in the belief that it will help clarify the theme of imperialism without colonies. Two such misconceptions are particularly common, both of which relate to the vital role played by the export of capital: those based on arguments concerning the export of surplus capital and the falling rate of profit in the advanced capitalist countries.

1. The Pressure of Surplus Capital

A distinguishing feature of the new imperialism associated with the period of monopoly capitalism (that is, when the giant corporation is in the ascendancy and there is a high degree of economic concentration) is a sharp rise in the export of capital. The tie between the export of capital and imperialist expansion is the obvious need on the part of investors of capital for a safe and friendly environment.

But why the upsurge in the migration of capital during the last quarter of the nineteenth century and its continuation to this day? A frequently-met explanation is that the advanced capitalist nations began to be burdened by a superabundance of capital that could not find profitable investment opportunities at home and therefore sought foreign outlets. While a strong case can be made for the proposition that the growth of monopoly leads to increasing investment difficulties, it does not follow that the export of capital was stimulated primarily by the pressure of a surplus of capital.[3]

The key to answering the question lies, in my opinion, in understanding and viewing capitalism as a world system. The existence of strong nation states and the importance of nationalism tend to obscure the concept of a global capitalist system. Yet the nationalism of capitalist societies is the *alter ego* of the system's internationalism. Successful capitalist classes need the power of nation states not only to develop inner markets and to build adequate infrastructures but also, and equally important, to secure and protect opportunities for foreign commerce and investment in a world of rival nation states. Each capitalist nation wants protection for itself, preferential trade channels, and freedom to operate internationally. Protectionism, a strong military posture, and the drive for external markets are all part of the same package.

The desire and need to operate on a world scale is built into the economics of capitalism. Competitive pressures, technical advances, and recurring imbalances between productive capacity and effective demand create continuous pressures for the expansion of markets. The risks and uncertainties of business, interrelated with the unlimited acquisitive drive for wealth, activate the entrepreneur to accumulate ever greater assets and, in the process, to scour every corner of the earth for new opportunities. What stand in the way, in addition to technical limits of transportation and communication, are the recalcitrance of natives and the rivalry of other capitalist nation states.

Viewed in this way, export of capital, like foreign trade, is a normal function of capitalist enterprise. Moreover, the expansion of capital export is closely associated with the geographic expansion of capitalism. Back in the earliest days of mercantile capitalism, capital began to reach out beyond its original borders to finance plantations and mines in the Americas and Asia. With this came the growth of overseas banking to finance trade with Europe as well as to help lubricate foreign investment operations. Even though domestic investment opportunities may have lagged in some places and at some times, the primary drive behind the export of capital was not the pressure of surplus capital but the utilization of capital where profitable opportunities existed, constrained, of course, by the technology of the time, the economic and political conditions in the other countries, and the resources of the home country. For example, since military power was needed to force an entry into many of these profit-making opportunities, shortages of manpower and economic resources that could readily be devoted to such purposes also limited investment opportunities.

As mentioned above, a reversal in trade relations occurs under the impact of the industrial revolution and the upsurge of mass-produced manufactures. Capitalist enterprise desperately searches out export markets, while it is the overseas areas which suffer from a shortage of goods to offer in exchange. As a result, many of the countries which buy from industrialized countries fall into debt, since their imports tend to exceed their exports. Under such conditions opportunities and the need for loan capital from the metropolitan centers expand. Capital exports thus become an important prop to the export of goods. As is well known, the real upsurge in demand for British export capital came with the development of the railway. It was not only British industry that supplied the iron rails and railroad equipment over great stretches of the globe, but also British loan and equity capital that made the financing of these exports possible. In addition, the financial institutions which evolved in the long history of international trade and capital export acquired vested interests in the pursuit of foreign business. Following their own growth imperatives, they sought new opportunities for the use of capital overseas, while energetically collecting and stimulating domestic capital for such investments.

The important point is that capital export has a long history. It is a product of (1) the worldwide operations of the advanced capitalist nations, and (2) the institutions and economic structure that evolved in the ripening of capitalism as a world system. It is not the product of surplus capital as such. This does not mean that there is never a "surplus capital" problem (fed at times by the return flow of interest and profits from abroad), nor that at times capital will not move under the pressure of such surpluses. Once sophisticated international money markets exist, various uses will be made of them. Short-term funds, for instance, will move across borders in response to temporary tightness or ease of money in the several markets. Money will be loaned for more general political and economic purposes, for one country to gain influence and preferential treatment in another. But the main underpinning of the international financial markets is the international network of trade and investment that was generated by the advanced industrial nations in pursuit of their need to operate in world markets. Thus, while surplus domestic capital may at times be a contributing factor to capital movements abroad, the more relevant explanation, in our opinion, is to be found in the interrelations between the domestic economic situation of the advanced capitalist nations and that of their overseas markets.[4]

Why then the sudden upsurge of capital exports associated with modern imperialism? The answer, in my opinion, is consistent with the above analysis as well as with the nature of this later stage of capitalism. First, the onset of the new imperialism is marked by the arrival of several industrial states able to challenge Britain's hegemony over international trade and finance. These other nations expand their capital exports for the same purposes—increased foreign trade and preferential markets. Thus, instead of Britain being the dominant exporter of capital among very few others, a new crop of exporters comes to the fore, with the result that the total flow of capital exports greatly expands. Second, associated with the intensified rivalry of advanced industrial nations is the growth of protective tariff walls: one means of jumping these tariff walls is foreign investment. Third, the new stage of capitalism is based on industries requiring vast new supplies of raw materials, such as oil and ferrous and nonferrous metal ores. This requires not only large sums of capital for exploration and development of foreign sources, but also loan capital to enable foreign countries to construct the needed complementary transportation and public utility facilities. Fourth, the maturation of joint stock companies, the stock market, and other financial institutions provides the means for mobilizing capital more efficiently for use abroad as well as at home. Finally, the development of giant corporations hastens the growth of monopoly. The ability and desire of these corporations to control markets provides another major incentive for the expansion of capital abroad.

The facts on U.S. investment abroad in the present era are quite revealing on the issue of "surplus" capital; they can help us to answer the historical questions as well. One would expect that if a major, if not *the* major, reason for the export of U.S. capital today were the pressure of a superabundance of domestic capital, then as much capital as could be profitably used abroad would be drawn from the United States. But that is not the case. We have the data on the capital structure of U.S. direct investments abroad in the year 1957. (This is the latest year for which such data are available. Another census of foreign investments was taken in 1966, but the results have not yet been published.) What we find is that 60 percent of the direct investment assets of U.S.-based corporations are owned by U.S. residents and 40 percent by non-U.S. residents, mainly local residents, but including overseas European and Canadian capital invested in Latin America, etc. (see Table I.B).

Now there is an interesting twist to these data. If we separate equity and debt assets, we discover that U.S. residents own 86 percent of the equity and only 25 percent of the debt. What this reflects is the practice employed by U.S.

Table I
U.S. Direct-Investment Enterprise in Other Countries in 1957[1]: Assets Owned by U.S. and Local Residents

A. *Percentage of total assets in equity and debt*

	Total Assets		Equity Assets		Debt Assets	
	$ billion	*Percent*	*$ billion*	*Percent*	*$ billion*	*Percent*
Owned by U.S. residents	$24.0	100.0	$19.7	82.3	$ 4.2	17.7
Owned by local residents[2]	15.6	100.0	3.2	20.6	12.4	79.4
Total	$39.6	100.0	$22.9	58.0	$16.6	42.0

B. *Percentage distribution of assets by U.S. and local ownership*

	Total Assets	Equity Assets	Debt Assets
Owned by U.S. residents	60.5	86.0	25.4
Owned by local residents[2]	39.5	14.0	74.6
Total	100.0	100.0	100.0

(Details may not add up to totals because of rounding off of decimals.)
1. Finance and insurance investments are excluded.
2. More accurately, non-U.S. residents. The owners are primarily residents of the areas in which U.S. enterprise is located, though there was probably a flow of funds from Europe and Canada to U.S.-owned enterprise in other areas.

Source: Calculated from *U.S. Business Investments in Foreign Countries* (Washington, D.C.: U.S. Department of Commerce, 1960), Table 20.

firms to assure control over their foreign assets and to capture most of the "perpetual" flow of profits. As for the debt capital (long- and short-term), which in time will be repaid out of the profits of the enterprise, it is just as well to give the native rich a break. The supposedly pressing "surplus" funds of the home country are tapped very little for the debt capital needs of foreign enterprise.

But we should also be aware that the 60-40 share of the capital assets, mentioned above, exaggerates the capital funds supplied from the United States. Here is how a businessman's publication, *Business Abroad*, describes the overseas investment practices of U.S. corporations:

> In calculating the value of capital investment, General Motors, for example, figures the intangibles such as trademarks, patents, and know-how equivalent to twice the actual invested capital. Some corporations calculate know-how, blueprints, and so on as one third of capital investment, and then supply one third in equity by providing machinery and equipment.[5]

Hence, a good share of the 60 percent of the assets owned by U.S. firms does not represent cash investment but a valuation of their knowledge, trademarks, etc., and their own machinery valued at prices set by the home office.[6]

One may ask whether this phenomenon of using local capital is a feature predominantly of investment practices in wealthier foreign countries. The answer is no. It is true that the share supplied by local capital is larger in European countries (54 percent) and lower in Latin American countries (31 percent), but the practice of obtaining debt capital locally is characteristic of all regions in which U.S. capital is invested (see Table II).

The facts on the flow of funds to finance U.S. direct investments abroad are even more striking. We have data on the source of funds used to finance these enterprises for the period 1957 to 1965. While this information is for a limited period, other available evidence indicates that there is no reason to consider this period as atypical.[7]

These data reveal that during the period in question some $84 billion were used to finance the expansion and operations of direct foreign investments. Of this total, only a little more than 15 percent came from the United States. The remaining 85 percent was raised outside the United States: 20 percent from locally raised funds and 65 percent from the cash generated by the foreign enterprise operations themselves (see Table III.A).

Table II
Percentage Distribution of Assets of U.S. Direct-Investment
Enterprises in Other Countries, by Ownership and Area
(in 1957)[1]

Ownership	Total Assets	Equity Assets	Debt Assets
In Canada			
U.S. residents	62.0	78.5	37.2
Local residents[2]	38.0	21.5	62.8
Total	100.0	100.0	100.0
In Europe			
U.S. residents	46.2	83.9	11.1
Local residents[2]	53.8	16.1	88.9
Total	100.0	100.0	100.0
In Latin America			
U.S. residents	69.1	92.9	24.9
Local residents[2]	30.9	7.1	75.1
Total	100.0	100.0	100.0
In Africa			
U.S. residents	51.5	80.7	23.9
Local residents[2]	48.5	19.3	76.1
Total	100.0	100.0	100.0
In Asia			
U.S. residents	62.4	94.1	13.1
Local residents[2]	37.6	5.9	86.9
Total	100.0	100.0	100.0

Notes and source: As Table I.

Table III
Sources of Funds of U.S. Direct-Investment Enterprises
in Other Countries: 1957–1965

A. *Summary of all areas*

Sources of Funds	Funds Obtained	
	$ billion	Percent of total
From United States	$12.8	15.3
Obtained from abroad	16.8	20.1
Obtained from operations of foreign enterprises	54.1	64.6
From net income	33.6	40.1
From depreciation and depletion	20.5	24.5
Total	$83.7	100.0

B. *Percentage distribution, by area*

Area	Percentage of Funds Obtained		
	From U.S.	From outside U.S.[1]	Total
Canada	15.7	84.3	100.0
Europe	20.2	79.8	100.0
Latin America	11.4	88.6	100.0
All other areas	13.6	86.4	100.0

1. Includes funds raised abroad from non-U.S. residents and from operations of foreign enterprises.

Source: 1957 data—same as Table 1; 1958–1965 data from *Survey of Current Business*, September 1961; September 1962; November 1965; January 1967.

Here again the pattern is similar for rich countries and poor countries. If anything, the U.S. capital contribution is less in the poor countries than in the rich ones: the U.S. capital contribution is 16 percent for enterprise in Canada, 20 percent in Europe, 11 percent in Latin America, and 14 percent in all other areas. Too many inferences should not be drawn from these differentials; large funds came from the United States during these years to finance the rapid expansion of enterprises in Europe. However, it is proper to observe that only a small percentage of the supply of funds needed to finance its foreign investments is coming from the United States. And that is hardly what one would expect on the basis of a theory that the main reason for foreign investment is the pressure of a superabundance of capital at home.

2. The Declining Rate of Profit

A second major ground often advanced for the rise in capital exports is the declining rate of profit. The reasoning behind this is that capital accumulation, accompanied by an ever-rising ratio of fixed capital to labor, produces a dominant tendency for the average rate of profit to decline. Such a decline induces domestic capitalists to invest abroad where labor costs are lower and profits higher.

We cannot now, and do not need to for this purpose, examine either the internal theoretical consistency of this theory, whether the facts bear it out, or, if it is true, how this tendency would work under monopoly conditions. This examination is not necessary, in my opinion, because in any case the declining rate of profit would not explain the pattern of international capital movements. In other words, it is not a necessary hypothesis in this connection, whether in itself it is true or not. This point can be substantiated in relation to two types of foreign investment, the purchase of foreign bonds and the development of oil wells and mines. However, before presenting my reasons for saying this, I would like to point out that there are two separate questions. We are concerned here with the *causes* of the export of capital in the period of imperialism. The *effect* of the export of capital on domestic profit rates is a different, though undoubtedly important, question.

To return to the pattern of international capital movements. First, the declining-rate-of-profit hypothesis cannot apply to loan capital. Rates of interest on money lent abroad are generally attractive, but, for relatively safe loans, they are considerably below the industrial rate of profit. Thus, a purchase of foreign bonds by a corporation would not normally be an offsetting action against a declining rate of profit.

We also need to eliminate this hypothesis to explain the extensive direct investment in oil extraction and mining. Investments in these industries are not primarily motivated by comparative profit rates or falling rates of profit at home, but by the facts of geology. The decisive factors are where the minerals were placed by God, and the transportation problems of getting them to the consuming centers. Profit rates are, of course, always involved, and they are usually very high. Also the investor will take advantage of as low wages as he can get away with. However, the profitability of these extractive industries is not based on low wages but on the abundance of the natural resources where they happen to be and on the monopolistic structures through which they are marketed.

It is true that comparative profit rates do enter the picture when, as in the case of iron mining in the United States, formerly rich iron ore reserves become depleted. A rush then ensues to develop iron reserves in Labrador, Venezuela, and Brazil. But here again the decisive factor is not a declining profit rate due to the process of capitalist accumulation: it is rather a declining profit rate due to the state of nature.

It is a third kind of investment, foreign direct investment in manufacturing, which provides the only real test of the thesis. Here, if anywhere, one might expect capital to flow in response to simple profit-rate differentials. What then about direct investments in manufacturing? It should go without saying that the profit rate dominates all investment decisions, and it should also be clear that capital will continuously seek the highest obtainable profit rate. Whether profit rates are rising or declining at home, we should expect capital to flow out as long as higher profit rates are obtainable abroad. But it is not necessary that profit rates obtainable abroad should be higher than average domestic profit rates to sustain this flow.

What concerns the investor is a comparison of the profitability of additional (or marginal) investment in industry at home and industry abroad. Theoretically, the new investment abroad could have a lower return than the average rate of profit at home and still be attractive. For example, assume that a manufacturer of refrigerators is getting a return of 20 percent on his domestic investment. He wants to make a new investment and finds that he will get only 15 percent at home, but that he can get 18 percent if he uses these funds to make refrigerators abroad. He will be prompted to go abroad, with the result that his foreign investments will yield less than his domestic investment. (This is one reason, by the way, why comparisons of data on average manufacturing profit rates at home and abroad are not really meaningful, aside from inadequacies of the statistics themselves.) So it is this gap in marginal profitability which produces the flow of foreign investment; it has no necessary connection with any fall in the average profitability of investment at home.

3. Monopoly and Foreign Investment

A much more useful hypothesis than the falling rate of profit, I believe, is one that traces the main drive for direct investment of capital on a global scale to the imperatives of capital operating under monopoly conditions. Such an analytical framework embraces an explanation of (1) the main body of investment, in extractive as well as manufacturing industries, and (2) the stepup in capital exports during the period of imperialism. Its central purpose is to demonstrate the interrelation between the concomitant rise in capital exports and monopoly as the core of the new imperialism.

Business, in general, can best be understood as a system of power, to use a phrase of Robert Brady's. It is of the essence of business to try to control its own market and to operate, so far as possible, as if the entire globe were its preserve. This was true from the very outset of the capitalist era. As long, however, as there were many competitors in most industries, the opportunities for control were quite limited. With the development of monopoly conditions—i.e., when a handful of companies dominates each of the important markets—the exercise of controlling power becomes not only possible but increasingly essential for the security of the firm and its assets.

The emergence of a significant degree of concentration of power does not mean the end of competition. It does mean that competition has been raised to a new level: temporary arrangements among competitors about production, price, and sales policies are more feasible than before, and business decisions can be arrived at with reasonable anticipation of what the competitive response will be. Since capital operates on a world scale, the business arrangements to divide markets and/or the competitive struggle among the giants for markets stretch over large sections of the globe.

Furthermore, the competitive strategy changes from the period of competition. Price-cutting is no longer the preferred method of acquiring a larger share of the market. Prices are kept high, and the expansion of production is restrained by the limitation of effective demand at high prices or the ability to win a larger share of the high-priced market from a competitor. Nevertheless, the necessity to grow persists and the capital available for growth mounts; hence the constant pressure for rivals to get a larger share of each others' markets wherever they may be. It should be noted that this struggle for larger markets will naturally take place in the more developed countries, where markets for sophisticated products already exist and where it is possible to take advantage of the privileged trade channels of each others' colonial or semicolonial empire. This struggle also takes place in the less developed countries, where new markets, however small, can be entered and where the first firms to get a foothold often have lasting advantage.

The impetus to invest abroad arises out of this competitive struggle among the giants. First, the ownership of raw material supplies is of strategic importance in the push for control over prices, to hold one's own against competitors who also control supplies, and to restrict the growth of competitors who do not have their own sources. Second, the need to control and expand markets is a major spur and incentive for capital export, especially where tariffs or other barriers to trade impede the expansion of commodity exports.

The correlation between monopolistic motives and the spread of foreign investment is supported not only by this analysis but by the actual pattern of investment, at least in the case of the largest foreign investor, the United States. The monopolistic aspects of U.S. (and other) investments in oil and metal ores are too well known to need dwelling on here. In manufacturing, it is clear, overseas investment is a game for the larger firms. Thus, in 1962, 94 percent of the assets of U.S. foreign manufacturing corporations were controlled by firms with assets of $50 million or more.[8] Moreover, a study of the 1957 census of U.S. foreign investment showed that the bulk of manufacturing investments were made by oligopolistic firms in areas where the advantages of monopoly can be carried abroad: operations protected by patents, exclusive or advanced technical knowledge, and/or product differentiation through brand identification and similar techniques.[9]

This argument in no way denies the primacy of the profit motive. The whole purpose of monopoly control is to assure the existence and growth of profits. The profit motive and capitalism are, after all, one and the same. What needs explanation is why, with the profit motive always present, the export of capital in the form of direct investment accelerates with the onset of the imperialist stage. Here I suggest that tracing the answer to the nature and mushrooming of monopoly (or, more accurately, oligopoly) is a more meaningful explanation than that provided by the falling-rate-of-profit theory, or, as discussed above, the pressure-of-surplus-capital theory.

Given a chance to make additional profit abroad at a higher marginal rate, the entrepreneur will grab at it, providing the politics of the foreign country is friendly to foreign investment and to the withdrawal of profits from that country. There are, however, many factors that influence the size of the profit margin. Low wages and cost of raw materials are only two of these elements; transportation expenses, productivity of labor, managerial ability, and overhead costs are also significant. And monopolistic or semimonopolistic influences which protect sales quotas at high prices carry enormous weight. In this context, it should be noted, that the investment decisions may be tempered by additional considerations. The fact that a major company has established a beachhead in foreign markets will spur competitors to follow suit: even when the immediate profit gain may not be clearly favorable the longer-run requirements of assuring one's share of the world market dictates such a strategy. And, as noted above, trade restrictions will motivate a firm to invest abroad to protect its market on the other side of the trade barrier. When the balance of ingredients is favorable to the profit and/or market strategy, the decision to invest abroad follows as a matter of course.

While on this subject it may be worth noting that one of the most common of the oversimplified explanations of the transnational movement of capital is that which assigns the decisive role to wage differentials between the capital-exporting and capital-importing countries. For the United States, where wages are relatively high, *any* export of capital could be interpreted this way. But one should not infer from this that the main current of foreign investment is to substitute foreign-made for domestic-made goods on the U.S. market. At best, one might argue that some of the overseas production takes the place of what would otherwise be exports from the United States. (In this fashion, wage differentials are eliminated as a competitive element in overseas markets.) The facts on the distribution of sales of U.S. manufacturing firms located abroad (from 1962 to 1965) show that, except for Canada, less than 2 percent of U.S. production abroad is sent to the United States (see Table IV). The high percentage for Canada consists largely of manufactures based on Canadian resources (paper, for example).

Table IV
Direction of Sales of U.S. Manufacturing Affiliates
Located Outside United States, 1962–1965

Areas	Total Sales	Local Sales	Exported to U.S.	Exported to Other Countries
			Percentage distribution	
Total	100.0	82.3	4.1	13.6
Canada	100.0	81.1	10.8	8.1
Latin America	100.0	91.5	1.6	6.9
Europe	100.0	77.2	1.0	21.8
Other areas	100.0	93.9	1.4	4.7

Source: 1962—*Survey of Current Business*, November 1965, p. 19; 1963-1965—ibid., November 1966, p. 9.

Although complete data are not yet available, there seems to have been an increase since 1965 in U.S. firms manufacturing parts and assemblies abroad to be sold in U.S. domestic markets. Nevertheless, the relative importance of this activity does not yet support the argument that this is the major determinant of U.S. overseas investment. On the other hand, these low percentages do not mean that there is not a very real and severe impact on the U.S. worker of such shifts in production as do occur. The move to manufacture components and finished products in Japan, Italy, Korea, Hong Kong, etc., has surely been felt by certain sections of U.S. labor.

4. Imperialism and Crisis

Before an account of how these economic relationships have persisted beyond the decline of colonialism, there are two further areas of dispute about the new imperialism which have to be examined. These are the relation of imperialism to crisis and the role of the state.

We turn now to the first of these: imperialism as the

capitalist way out of crisis. Whatever merit there may be to this approach, it can become confusing unless an attempt is made to sort out cause and effect. The depressions of the 1870s and 1880s, the agrarian disruptions as well as the industrial crises of those years, probably speeded up the birth of the new imperialism. But they themselves were not the cause of imperialism. If anything, both the severity of the economic disruptions and the imperialist policies are rooted in the same rapid transformations of the late nineteenth century.

The roots of imperialism go much deeper than any particular crisis or the reaction of any government to the crisis. They are to be found in the factors discussed above: the expansive drive of each advanced capitalist nation to operate on a world scale, the development of monopoly, and the national rivalries associated with the needs of advanced economies with monopolistic structures.

What economic crises frequently accomplish is to make ruling classes and governments acutely aware of the need for vigorous remedial action. They remind laggard governments of their "duty" and prod them into action. Just as the reality of the contradictions of capitalism reveal themselves more frankly during periods of stress, so the reactions of governments become more overt under such pressure. But the policies and practices of economic and political imperialism are as much part of prosperity as of depression. More energetic and farsighted governments will act, or prepare to act, in periods of calm and prosperity. Timid and shortsighted governments will either wake up when the crisis hits them or be toppled by a tougher political group.

A corollary of the argument that imperialism was a way out of depression is the idea that capitalism will collapse as the area for imperialist expansion shrinks. This thesis is based on an unrealistic and rigid view of how capitalism works. Cutting off markets and sources of raw materials creates serious problems for capitalist enterprise but does not necessarily portend collapse.

It should hardly be necessary to point this out after the

many years of experience during which sizable sections of the globe have removed themselves from the imperialist orbit. Yet oversimplified, mechanistic formulations seem to have a life of their own. It is important to understand the degrees of flexibility that exist in capitalist society and which make the system more durable than its opponents have often supposed. Biological organisms show the same quality: the closure of one heart artery may be compensated by the enlargement of another artery to take over its function. To be sure, these organic adjustments are not eternal and they often lead to other and greater complications. But a significant lesson to be learned from the history of capitalism is that great troubles do not lead to automatic collapse.

The post–World War II experience provides a good example of this flexibility. The enlargement of the U.S. military machine became a powerful support to the U.S. economy. In turn, the success achieved by the United States as the organizer of the world imperialist system on the verge of breaking down gave other advanced capitalisms an important boost, creating markets and enlarging international trade. This flexibility, however, is not limitless. Cracks in the most recent imperialist arrangements are clearly evident in the strains on the international money markets as well as in the mounting difficulties of the U.S. economy itself. Further shrinkage of imperialist territory will create more troubles: it might lead to a sharpening of the business cycle, prolonged depression, mass unemployment. Nevertheless, as we know from historical experience, these do not necessarily bring the downfall of the system. In the final analysis, the fate of capitalism will be settled only by vigorous classes within the society, and parties based on these classes, which have the will and ability to replace the existing system.

5. The Role of the Government

Another area of dispute over the meaning of imperialism concerns the role of government either as an initiator of imperialism or as a potential agent for the abolition of imperialism. Here there are two extremes: (1) those who see government as merely the direct servant of large corporations and banks, and (2) those who see government as an independent force that arbitrates conflicting interests and has wide freedom of choice in setting policy.

Neither of these views, in my opinion, is correct. The operations of government in a complex society result in the development of a political structure that takes on the character of a special division of society, with responsibilities and behavior problems adapted to maintaining political power. As such, a government may be more or less responsive to the needs of particular firms or industries. Aside from differences over tactics, the actions of governing groups will be influenced by previous political experience and training, as well as by their own sense of what is best suited to keep themselves in power. Even a political regime responsive to the pressures of a particular industry or firm will, if it is competent and has integrity, withstand such pressure in the overall and long-term interest of the class, or classes, it relies on to remain in power.

On the other hand, the degrees of freedom enjoyed by ruling groups are much more limited than liberals are inclined to believe. To retain power, political regimes must have a successful economy. They therefore must work to improve the economic and financial structure at hand, and cannot pursue idle fancies of the "what might be if" variety. The more farsighted and aggressive political regimes—those which understand the main dynamic levers of the economy—will foster the growth of the economic system: they will build roads, harbors, canals, railroads, a merchant marine, acquire colonies for the stimulation of commerce, struggle for control of sea lanes to protect their commerce, and aggressively expand their territory (as in the United States in the eighteenth and nineteenth centuries). The incompetent regimes, especially those hampered by too much internal conflict among different would-be ruling groups, will rule over a limping economy. As pointed out above, a government often learns what is needed to sustain and advance the economic underpinning of its society the hard way; reminded and spurred by internal depression and/or the forward push of competing nations.

The limited alternatives open to political regimes have become increasingly clear during the history of imperialism. Here we must keep in mind the two strategically significant developments that mark the birth of, or prepared the way for, the new imperialism: (1) The internal conflicts among competing vested interest groups within the Great Powers become resolved in favor of the needs of large-scale industry and the financiers of these industries. Three such examples may be noted: (a) the compromise between the Northern industrialists and Southern bourbons in the United States after the Civil War; (b) the compromise between the landed aristocracy and large industrialists in Germany; and (c) the emphasis of the Meiji Restoration on creating the conditions for the rise of large-scale, heavy industry in Japan. (2) The successful development of large-scale industry is associated with increasing concentration of power.

Once the structure of each society had been successfully adapted to the needs of the major centers of industry, the path of future economic development became fairly narrowly defined. A later government, even one not a party to the previous resolution of conflict, has to pursue the same path: a comfortable environment for the leading industrialists and bankers, an environment that would stretch over as much of the world as these interest groups needed to operate in. The decisions on how best to create this environment, nationally and internationally, are arrived at by political and military officials, influenced by the latter's ambitions and ideologies. However, the ultimate test of government competence—its ability to achieve its political and military aims—is a successful economy: no welfare scheme can replace full and steady employment, operating factories, and smoothly run finance. And that economic success, in turn, rests on the success of big business and big finance. The practices of the reform administration of Franklin Roosevelt offer a good illustration: the stress on foreign trade expansion as the way out of the crisis, and the outright deal with the "economic royalists" (the term used by President Roosevelt in his bitter diatribes against big business) when faced with the needs of war production. It is instructive also to learn from the practices of liberal and "socialist" regimes in capitalist societies. Not having the kind of specific commitments and longstanding ties with particular business interests that conservative parties do, they are often *more* effective in making necessary repairs to the structure of monopoly business. What they do *not* do is undertake reforms which run counter to the basic interests of big business.

6. Imperialism Without Colonies

It would be wrong to say that modern imperialism would have been possible without colonialism. And yet the end of colonialism by no means signifies the end of imperialism. The explanation of this seeming paradox is that colonialism, considered as the direct application of military and political force, was essential to reshape the social and economic institutions of many of the dependent countries to the needs of the metropolitan centers. Once this reshaping had been accomplished economic forces—the international price, marketing, and financial systems—were by themselves sufficient to perpetuate and indeed intensify the relationship of dominance and exploitation between mother country and colony. In these circumstances, the colony could be granted formal political independence without changing anything essential, and without interfering too seriously with the interests which had originally led to the conquest of the colony.

This is not to say that colonialism was abolished gratuitously. Revolutions, mass rebellions, and the threat of revolution, the fear of further enlargement of the socialist world, and the maneuvering of the United States to gain a presence in the colonial preserves of other empires, these all paved the way for the decline of colonialism after World War II. The

important point, though, is that the requisite dissolution of
the colonies was carried out in such a way as to preserve for
the mother country as many of the advantages as possible,
and to prevent social revolutions directed to real independence for the former colonies. As long as the socioeconomic
underpinning for the continuation of the metropolitan-
colony relationship could be maintained, there was still a
fighting chance that the interests that had benefited most
from colonial control would not be endangered.

These observations do not apply to all the relationships of
dominance and dependence which characterize modern
imperialism. Some independent countries already possessing
suitable social and economic institutions have fallen directly
under the economic domination of one of the stronger
powers and have thus become dependencies without ever
going through a colonial phase. Some of these economic
dependencies may even have colonies of their own. Thus
Portugal was for a long time a dependency of Britain, and the
Portuguese Empire was in a real sense an empire within an
empire. It is not surprising therefore that the history of
imperialism shows a wide variety of forms and degrees of
political dependency. Nor is it difficult to understand why,
on the whole, the major aspects of the imperialist design
should exist in the era of declining overt colonialism just as
they existed in the period of outright colonialism, since the
primary determinants of imperialism remain: (1) the monopoly structure of big business in the metropolises; (2) the
imperative for these economic centers to grow and to control
materials sources and markets; (3) the continuation of an
international division of labor which serves the needs of the
metropolitan centers; and (4) national rivalry among industrial powers for export and investment opportunities in each
other's markets and over the rest of the world. To this has
been added a new factor which generates fear in the advanced
capitalist nations and makes the maintenance of the imperialist system more urgent that ever: the inroads made by the
growth of socialist societies and the spread of national libera-

tion movements which seek to remove their countries from the imperialist trade and investment network.

The decline of colonialism has, of course, presented real problems, some old and some new, for the imperialist centers:

1. How best to maintain the economic and financial dependence of subordinate nations, given the aroused expectations accompanying independence and the greater maneuverability available with political independence.

2. For the previous owners of colonies, how to maintain their preferred economic position and ward off the encroachment of rival powers.

3. For the United States, how to extend its influence and control over the privileged preserves of the former colonial powers.

The problem of maintaining economic dependency in the new environment since World War II has been complicated by the rivalry of the Soviet Union and by the straining at the leash by some of the new independent nations (the latter, in part due to the pressure of the masses and in part due to the new elite seeing an opportunity to get a bigger piece of the action). Despite these complications, which called for new tactics by the imperialist powers, the essential structure of economic dependency has persisted in the period of imperialism without colonies. It is not a simple matter to eradicate dependency relations that have ripened and become embedded over a long stretch of history, beginning with the days of mercantilism. In the several developmental stages of the trade and financial ties of the colonial and semicolonial economies, the economic structure of the latter became increasingly adapted to its role as an appendage of the metropolitan center. The composition of prices, the income distribution, and the allocation of resources evolved, with the aid of military power as well as the blind forces of the market, in such a way as to reproduce the dependency continuously.

This point needs special emphasis since economists are

inclined to think of the price-and-market system as an *impartial* regulator of the economy, one that allocates resources in such a fashion as to achieve the maximum efficiency in their use. This in turn, is based on the assumption that there is such a thing as an absolute, objective efficiency which is equally applicable to all places and at all times. In reality matters are very different. The allocation of resources is the result of many historic forces. To name only a few: wars; colonialism; the way states have exercised their fiscal and other powers; the manipulations (at different times) of influential merchants, industrialists, and financiers; the management of international financial arrangements. In due course, wages, prices, and trade relations become efficient tools for the *reproduction* of the *attained* allocation of economic resources. And in the case of the former colonial world, this means reproduction of the economic relations of dependency.

To become masters of their own destiny, these countries have to overhaul the existing international trade patterns and transform their industrial and financial structure. Short of such basic changes, the economic and financial framework remains, with or without colonies. Even vigorous protectionist policies, adopted by many of the semicolonies, have been unable to break the ties of dependency. True, to some extent, they did encourage development of domestic manufactures. But in many of the more profitable areas, foreign manufacturers opened up factories inside the tariff walls and thus actually expanded foreign economic influence.

The state of dependency is not supported and reproduced by the evolved market relations alone. It is also sustained by the dependent country's political and social power structure. In the most general terms, there are three constituents of the ruling class in these countries: large landowners, business groups whose affairs are interrelated with foreign business interests, and businessmen with few or no ties to the foreign business community.[10] While the nationalist spirit may pervade, more or less, all three of these groups, none of them has a strong motive to sponsor the kind of structural economic changes that would be required for an independent economy. The interests of the first two groups listed above would be severely impaired by decisive moves for independence. The one group that could visualize a gain from economic independence would be the native capitalists, that is, those whose prosperity does not depend on foreign ties and for whom new opportunities would open up as a result of independence. But this group is usually small and weak and to succeed, it would have to break the grip of the other two sectors and destroy the economic base of the latter's power. Success in such a struggle would require an ability to keep power throughout the disruptions involved in the transformation; and it would depend on mobilizing the support of the workers and peasants, a hazardous undertaking in an era when the masses are seeking redress of their own grievances and when socialist revolution can quickly appear on the agenda.

Thus both the economic and political structures of the former colonies are well suited to the perpetuation of economic dependence along with political independence. And the needs of imperialism in the new situation could be met, except for one weakness: the instability of the power structure of the former colonies. This instability has its roots in the colonial system itself. In many colonies, the dominant power had in the past disrupted the traditional ruling groups and destroyed their political power. In addition, the mother countries created and sponsored elites which were psychologically and economically dependent on the foreign rulers. At the time, this was an effective and relatively inexpensive way to keep an annexed nation within the empire. Its weakness was that it prevented the emergence of the self-reliance and strength needed by any one sector to take power in its own name and reshape the economy for its own purposes. On top of this, the alliances that did develop to take over internal political rule were temporary and necessarily unstable. Finally, the changeover to political independence, especially in those countries where the masses were involved in the independence struggle, led to greater expectations of improvement in the conditions of life than could be met by weak postcolonial regimes. The people of the colonies identified colonialism not only with foreign despotism but also with exploitation by those who had adapted themselves to, and cooperated with, the colonial powers.

The retention of influence and control by the metropolitan centers in the postcolonial period has therefore required special attention. The techniques stressed, some old and some new, fell into several categories:

1. Where possible, formal economic and political arrangements to maintain former economic ties. These include preferential trade agreements and maintenance of currency blocs.

2. Manipulation and support of the local ruling groups with a view to keeping the special influence of the metropolitan centers and to preventing internal social revolution. Included here, in addition to CIA-type operations, are military assistance, training the officer corps, and economic aid for roads, airports and the like needed by the local military.

3. Establishing influence and control over the direction of economic development and, as much as possible, over government decisions affecting the allocation of resources. Under this heading fall bilateral economic aid arrangements and the policies and practices of the World Bank and the International Monetary Fund. These activities, in addition to influencing the direction of economic development, tend to intensify the financial dependence of aid recipients on the metropolitan money markets.

Central to the period of imperialism without colonies is the new role of the United States. The disruption of other imperialist centers following World War II and the concomitant growth of strong revolutionary movements generated both the urgency for the United States to reestablish the stability of the imperialist system and the opportunity to make inroads for its own advantage. Perhaps the greatest gain accruing to the United States as a result of the economic disruption of the war and early postwar years was the triumph of the U.S. dollar as the dominant international currency and the establishment of New York as the main international banking center. Thus was created the financial mechanism for enlarging the economic base of U.S. business interests through expansion of exports and enlargement of capital investment and international banking both in the home bases of advanced capitalist nations and in the Third World.

In addition to using its new economic and financial strength, the United States stepped up its efforts to enter the preserves of the former colonial powers by (1) becoming the main provider of military and economic aid, and (2) constructing a global network of military bases and staging areas. The extensive system of military bases is designed to threaten the socialist countries and to prevent the breaking-off of components of the remaining imperialist system. By the same token, the U.S. global military presence (in conjunction with the military forces of its allies) and its predisposition to actively engage these forces (as in Vietnam) provides the substance of the political force which maintains the imperialist system in the absence of colonies.

Notes

1. Carlo M. Cipolla, *Guns, Sails and Empires: Technological Innovation and Early Phases of European Expansion, 1400-1700* (New York: Pantheon, 1965), "Epilogue."
2. Obviously, the immediate objectives in the acquisition of colonies were not uniform; some colonies were pursued because of their strategic military value in building and maintaining an empire, others were pursued to prevent the enlargement of competitive empires, etc. The common factor referred to is in the colonial experience itself. Regardless of the planned or accidental features of the acquisition process, the administration of the colonies (and the manipulation of the semicolonial areas) was aimed at, or led to, the adaptation of the periphery areas to serve the economic advantage of the metropolitan centers.
3. The analysis of the surplus question is well developed in Paul A. Baran and Paul M. Sweezy, *Monopoly Capital* (New York: Monthly Review Press, 1966). A distinction needs to be made, however, between the question posed by Baran and Sweezy and the one we

are examining here. In fact, they deal with the concept of "economic surplus" and not "surplus capital." The term "economic surplus" does not necessarily imply "too-muchness" of capital. It is simply a surplus over necessary costs of production; whether any of it is also surplus in the sense of the theories which relate surplus capital to capital export is a totally different and even unrelated question. In *Monopoly Capital*, Baran and Sweezy deal with the basic dynamics of investment and employment in relation to the stagnation-inducing tendencies of monopoly. They argue that the export of capital does not offset the stagnation tendency since the income returning home is greater than the outflow of investment. Hence, the export of capital intensifies the surplus problem of investment outlets rather than alleviating it. It should be noted that Baran and Sweezy are dealing with the *effect* of capital export, not the *cause*. And, in dealing with the effect of this export, they do not attempt to analyze it in all its ramifications. They are concerned solely with its effect on the disposal of the economic surplus in the home country. This is quite a different question from the one we are posing: What is the cause of the rise in the export of capital.

4. On the interrelation between British capital export and export of goods, see A. G. Ford, "Overseas Lending and Internal Fluctuations, 1870-1914," and A. J. Brown, "Britain in the World Economy, 1820-1914," both in the *Yorkshire Bulletin of Economic and Social Research*, May 1965. On the question of capital surplus and/or scarcity, note the interesting observation by A. J. Brown in the above article:

> . . . Professor Tinbergen, in his remarkable econometric study of the United Kingdom in this period (*Business Cycles in the United Kingdom, 1870-1914*, Amsterdam, 1951), finds a positive association between net capital exports and the short term interest rate, suggesting that money became scarce because it was lent abroad rather than that it was lent abroad because it was plentiful. (p. 51)

5. *Business Abroad*, July 11, 1966, p. 31.

6. It is difficult to untangle all the factors to get a more realistic picture. First, not all the equity capital represents the original investment; some of it is reinvested surplus. The *Business Abroad* observation would apply only to the original investment. Also, there is a counter tendency which leads to an understatement of U.S. investment. In some industries, especially in the extractive

ones, firms have written off assets which are still being productively used.

7. Note the more recent growth of U.S. direct investments abroad despite government restriction on the outflow of investment capital to reduce the balance-of-payments deficit. *Business Week* comments:

> More important, though, is the growing ease with which U.S. companies can borrow abroad. This year . . . companies will finance 91 percent of their planned overseas spending from sources outside the U.S., up from 84 percent last year. . . . Financing abroad has become so easy, in fact, that the federal controls on dollar movements from the U.S. have been only a minor obstacle to foreign spending plans. (August 9, 1969, p. 38)

8. *Foreign Income Taxes Reported on Corporation Income Tax Returns* (Washington D.C.: U.S. Treasury Department, 1969).

9. Stephen Hymer, "The Theory of Direct Investment," Ph.D. dissertation, Massachusetts Institute of Technology, 1960, since published in book form as *The International Operations of National Firms: A Study of Direct Foreign Investment* (Cambridge, Mass.: MIT Press, 1976).

10. This generalization is obviously too broad to be useful in the analysis of any specific country. The class and social composition of a given country will be much more complex than indicated by the three large groupings outlined in the text; special country-by-country analysis is required if the dynamics of any particular area are to be understood. Thus, in some countries, attention must be paid to the role of small landowners, rich peasants, and rural moneylenders and traders. Urban business groups are also frequently more stratified than indicated in the text, with insignificant distinctions between commercial and industrial interest groups, and within each of these categories, different degrees of dependence on the industrial and financial affairs of the metropolitan centers.

5

Economic Myths
and Imperialism

As a rule, polite academic scholars prefer not to use the term "imperialism." They find it distasteful and unscientific. Thus, Professor Thornton of Toronto University writes, "Imperialism ... is no word for scholars. It has been analyzed too often, given too many shades of meaning. In our time it has become a football, a war cry, a labelled card in a sociological laboratory."[1] Similarly, "exploitation" is not a nice word. One of today's leading academic specialists on colonialism, David K. Fieldhouse, Beit Lecturer in the History of the Commonwealth at Oxford University, in a paper on economic exploitation of Africa explains, "Exploitation, like imperialism, is no word for scholars because it has long been confused by ideological concepts."[2]

Scholars generally have had no trouble with emotionally laden words—such, for example, as murder, rape, or syphilis—even when the existing mores frowned on such usage in polite society.[3] It is only a certain class of words, significantly enough, that over the years has raised the hackles of scholars. Thus, not only "imperialism" and "imperialist exploitation,"

This originally appeared in a Foreword to the American edition of Pierre Jalée, *Imperialism in the Seventies* (New York: Third Press, 1972). It also appeared in the December 1971 issue of *Monthly Review*.

but even such an important term in the socioeconomic lexicon as "capitalism" is treated by academics with great circumspection.

To be sure, academics are becoming somewhat desensitized to the use of the term "capitalism." Among other things, the growth of socialist societies enforces some sort of taxonomy of social systems, although many, if not most, academics still prefer some such euphemism as "free" or "private" enterprise. However, even those bourgeois economists who bravely adopt the term "capitalism" still balk at the combination of "capitalist" and "exploitation," since their system of thought excludes the very possibility of capitalist exploitation, other than as a rare and temporary aberration.

Desensitization to the use of the word "imperialism" is also coming along, but at an exceptionally slow pace. On the whole, scholars as well as publicists find it easier to attach the label of imperialism to another country, not to one's own, or to a past period of history, not to the present. Thus, one may find in the United States considerable agreement that French occupation of Indochina, and the French war against the revolutionary war of independence of the Indochinese people, should be identified as imperialism. Similarly, the Spanish-American War can today be labeled, even in polite U.S. society, as imperialism, although the nature of that war as one waged against the peoples of the Philippines, Cuba, and Puerto Rico is not as generally acknowledged. Nevertheless, the underlying continuity of U.S. imperialism—including the similarities between the U.S. attempt to reap the fruit of the final dissolution of Spain's empire in the Western Hemisphere and in the Pacific and the current attempt to fill the imperialist vacuum created by the dissolution of France's empire in Asia—is as yet barely recognized. But it is also true that the ferocity and tenacity of the U.S. war against the peoples of South Vietnam, Laos, and Cambodia are opening more and more eyes: an experience which is stimulating the more advanced and critical minds in the United States to learn more about the history and practices of imperialism, including that of the United States in the present epoch.

The major obstacle to such enlightenment is the pervasiveness of the ideological rationalization for imperialism. The extent of this pervasiveness is not easy to perceive because such rationalization is deep-seated. Its roots are intertwined with the accepted, conventional modes of thought and the consciousness of a people. Thus, they are located in the false patriotism and the racism that sink deeply and imperceptibly into the individual's subconscious; in the traditions, values, and even aesthetics of the cultural environment—an environment evolved over centuries, during which self-designated "superior" cultures assumed the right to penetrate and dominate "inferior" cultures. These roots are also buried in the sophisticated theorems of both liberal and conservative economics, sociology, political science, anthropology, and history. For these reasons, citizens of an imperialist country who wish to understand imperialism must first emancipate themselves from the seemingly endless web of threads that bind them emotionally and intellectually to the imperialist condition.

It is, of course, easier to identify the preconceptions of past generations than to recognize one's own blinders. For this reason it is instructive to look back at the way imperialist thinking has permeated the consciousness of even many socialists and advanced reformers. Such a retrospective view should alert us to the need for critical exploration of our own accepted doctrine. We cite here only one example from English history, though there are plenty of cases of "social imperialism" in other periods of English history and in other imperialist centers to choose from.

At the time of the Boer War an intense debate took place in Britain's Fabian Society over whether the Society should criticize Great Britain's militarism and imperialism.[4] The pro-imperialists won; and to consolidate the victory, George Bernard Shaw wrote a pamphlet called *Fabianism and the Empire*. In it that committed socialist and independent thinker, who so often dissected the hypocrisy of the existing culture with a sharp scalpel, explained:

Great Powers, consciously or unconsciously, must govern in the interests of civilization as a whole; and it is not in those interests that such mighty forces as gold-fields, and the formidable armaments that can be built upon them, should be wielded irresponsibly by small communities of frontiersmen. Theoretically, they should be internationalized, not British-imperialized, but until the Federation of the World becomes an accomplished fact we must accept the most responsible Imperial Federation available as a substitute for it.[5]

By "the most responsible Imperial Federation" Shaw obviously meant Great Britain. What else would a typical Englishman think, be he socialist, Tory, or Whig? But what is especially significant here is that Shaw's argument is but a variation of the dominant imperialist theme of his times and of his country: Great Britain's responsibility for empire arose from its obvious superiority in political administration; its manifest destiny was to civilize the heathens by teaching them the art of government.

With the progress of formal decolonization, the manifest destiny of the imperialist centers has changed. The new manifest destiny—the manifest destiny of our times—is the responsibility to teach the heathens the art of economics, so that these poor people can also become healthy, wealthy, and wise. Accordingly, the rationalization of contemporary imperialism leans heavily on bourgeois economic theory. This is not meant to imply that the imperialist centers are aloof from the politics of the former colonial areas and current spheres of influence. Waging wars, fomenting counter-revolution, bribing officials—these and other means of direct and indirect intervention are very much part of the game. But the longer-run imperialist strategy for the Third World falls into two main categories: first, stabilization of those political arrangements which most reliably, under the given conditions, guarantee continuation of the capitalist property system; and second, control and influence over economic development with a view to assuring dependency upon, and integration with, the trade and investment network of the imperialist sector of the world.

The accepted ideas of the advanced capitalist societies

provide a rich breeding ground for the ideology of this new phase of imperialism—imperialism without colonies. The equation of freedom of the individual with freedom of enterprise is a useful formula to justify the political programs of the imperialist centers. Over and above this is the implicit assumption that freedom of trade along with freedom of enterprise will inevitably foster the most advantageous path of economic development.

According to the conventional wisdom, all that is needed to get the underdeveloped countries moving is a healthy push; freedom of trade and investment will take care of the rest. Not unlike an inert mass in Newton's laws of motion, the underdeveloped countries will roll endlessly along, gaining momentum from an occasional further push, if only an initiating source of new energy is applied. Such an initial push, liberals and conservatives agree, can only come from an adequate injection of technically advanced capital via private investment, and, if that is not enough, by public foreign aid.

Comforted by this universal dogma of the Western world, liberals and progressives with their humanitarian instincts can find themselves in substantial agreement with the programs devised in the imperialist centers for control and influence of the periphery. Liberals worry about the insufficiency of foreign aid, and they criticize the crass use of such aid to obtain special political privilege or to prop up reactionary governments. They therefore press for more and "purer" foreign aid, and they pray for honest and intelligent governments in the underprivileged nations which will use the aid to best advantage. Not unlike G. B. Shaw at the time of the Boer War, they are practical realists. Sensible enough to believe that reform must occur in the real world in which great and rich powers dominate the scene, they are thereby caught in today's imperialist ideological trap.

The more theoretically inclined of the liberals go so far as to speculate about the consistency of their policies with the true, long-term interests of the dominating monopoly corporations. They see a global harmony of interests in the rapid economic development of the underdeveloped countries.

Since such economic development will presumably mean higher standards of living for the starving masses, it will also mean larger markets and higher profits for the international business community. All that remains, therefore, is for these corporations and foreign offices of the imperialist states to see the light.

Such liberals unfortunately do not understand that capitalists live in the actual present and not in the uncertain future. Of course capitalists want ever larger markets yielding ever larger profits. But these must be sought in the here and now, not in some hypothetical promised land. As a rule, corporations judge the feasibility of a foreign investment on its ability to return the initial outlay from the profits of the first three to five years. The capitalist imperative to concentrate on the present reality at home and abroad does not stem from psychological weakness or physical shortsightedness, but from the practical necessity of operating in a world of giant rivals and under the restraint of inherent financial limitations. If history delivers to them larger markets, they will eagerly exploit their new-found opportunities. But their decisions and actions have to be decided in terms of the concrete alternatives confronting them, always keeping in mind the imperative need to protect their assets and to raise their profits to the greatest possible extent. Imperialist governments, it is true, can afford to base their practices on a somewhat longer perspective; but they too have to touch base from time to time with the practical necessities of their business community, in view of the ineluctable fact that under capitalism the economic health of the social body rests on the economic health of the large corporations.[6]

The distorted bourgeois vision of economic development possibilities in the underdeveloped nations is traceable in large part to a special kind of myopia: the inability to focus on the fact that (1) the lopsided array of a few rich alongside many poor capitalist countries is the result of (and is still influenced by) the history of colonialism and semicolonialism, and (2) the normal economics of free and equal trade continuously reproduces and perpetuates the international

maldistribution of wealth. In short, the conscious and un-
conscious defenders of the imperialist world system have
not yet grasped, or are simply unwilling or unable to grasp,
the heart of the question, as summarized in Marx's observation: "If the free-traders cannot understand how one nation
can grow rich at the expense of another, we need not
wonder, since these same gentlemen also refuse to understand
how in the same country one class can enrich itself at the
expense of another."[7]

A major source of mystification about the causes of unequal income and wealth is faith in the efficacy of the
marketplace. Left alone, markets will presumably iron out all
artificial or unjustified inequities. They are the objective and
impersonal regulators which achieve the most efficient allocation of resources: in the long run they make sure that every
one gets what's coming to him. It follows, conversely, that
everyone's "getting what's coming to him"—and the inequality of incomes implied in this formula of distribution—is
the product of hard facts, of objective and necessary economic laws. (When efficiency and economic necessity enter
the door, morality and social justice fly out the window.)

The reality is different. In practice the market is merely an
instrument of existing institutions. And these institutions are
as much, if not more, the products of politics and the way
power is exercised as of economics. This becomes especially
apparent when we examine the "law of markets" as it per-
tains to foreign trade.

The accepted doctrine here is the one worked out by
David Ricardo, a doctrine drummed into every student who
takes an economics course in the United States. We are
referring, of course, to what is known in economic literature
as the theory of comparative advantage. According to this
theory, when the impersonal marketplace is the master, each
country will concentrate on making those goods for which it
is best suited and will buy from other countries products for
which they are best suited. In this way, each country gets the
maximum benefit from foreign trade.

To make his point, Ricardo used the following example:

(1) Portugal and England as trading partners, and (2) wine and cloth as the items of trade. Since England produces cloth more efficiently than it could make wine, it pays for England to concentrate on the production of cloth and to exchange its cloth surplus for foreign wine. Portugal, on the other hand, is a relatively more efficient producer of wine than cloth. Hence Portugal specializes in wine and exchanges its wine surplus for cloth.

According to Ricardo's theory, Portugal ought to specialize in wine even if it were able to make cloth more efficiently than England. What is decisive is that each country should use its resources in such a way as to get the greatest possible amount of both wine and cloth. Thus, if Portugal could get more wine *and* more cloth by putting all its capital into wine and then importing cloth, the best course for Portugal's prosperity would be to concentrate on wine even if, hypothetically, Portugal could produce cloth more efficiently than England. It follows that each country is better off under the banner of free trade, for with free trade each country will make maximum use of its comparative advantages—comparative advantages arising from the quality of the soil, the skills of labor, the experience of capitalists, etc.

This comparative advantage doctrine has, as noted above, become almost universal dogma in Western culture, to the point of becoming accepted as the common sense of our times. Not only is the doctrine itself treated as absolute truth in economics textbooks, but Ricardo's very illustration is repeated over and over again.[8] The frequent recurrence of this illustration is easy to understand, since it is plausible, and the facts seem to be consistent with the theoretical model. Indeed, at the time Ricardo wrote, and perhaps up to this day, he was absolutely right: England did have a comparative advantage in making cloth and Portugal in making wine. But the rub is that he was equally wrong in thinking that this was the inevitable result of "pure" economics or that it proved the inevitable superiority of free trade.

Here what is needed is not a knowledge of abstract economic laws but of history. And what a study of history reveals is that the comparative advantages of England and Portugal had their origin not so much in *economics* as in *politics*. The comparative advantage that mattered was rooted not in soil or labor productivity, but in the superiority of British seapower and in Portugal's inability to hold on to its overseas empire without the protection of the British navy.

These remarks on Portugal and England, and what follows on this subject, are based on, and abstracted from, a recent, most illuminating, and useful book by Sandro Sideri, *Trade and Power.*[9] The close ties between England and Portugual go back to the fourteenth century. In the early stages of the "friendly" relationship between the two countries, Portugal was the dominant power, due to its strong navy and the use of that navy to obtain vast and rich colonial possessions. But Portugal had a small population and was unable to stand alone against the inroads of neighboring Spain. Conquered by Spain in 1580, Portugal required sixty years to regain its independence.

The many years of foreign control and the struggle for independence greatly weakened Portugal. To maintain its independence and to keep control over its far-flung colonial empire, it needed English help—support that became increasingly meaningful as a result of the rising strength of the English fleet. England, in turn, could make good use of Portuguese harbors in its own striving for empire and for command of the sea lanes of the South Atlantic Ocean and the Mediterranean Sea. But a simple *quid pro quo* was not enough for England, given the great disparity of power between the two countries. In a series of four commercial treaties, beginning with the Treaty of 1642 and ending with the Methuen Treaty of 1703, England imposed the conditions which established and enforced the "ideal" international division of labor celebrated to this day as a prime example of the virtues of objective and independent economic laws. The terms of the several treaties increasingly fostered Portugal's economic dependence on England—a price Portugal had to pay for maintaining a colonial empire without adequate military resources.

The earlier treaties (1) opened the door to English ships in

Portugal and in Portugal's African and Indian territories; (2) gave special privileges to English traders in Portugal; and (3) required that Portugal buy all its ships from England. Each subsequent treaty broadened England's advantages, including the right to trade with all the Portuguese colonies (except for some trade monopolies Portugal retained in Brazil), the setting of limits to duties on imported British goods, and the exclusive right to rent ships to Portugal. The privileges thus obtained by England gave it access to the profitable African slave trade and the trade with Portugal's American colonies, boosted the British ship-building industry, and opened up markets for British manufactures.

All this, however, was merely the setting for the definitive international division of labor imposed by the Methuen Treaty of 1703.[10] In barest outline, the background to this treaty can thus be summarized: (1) A series of economic problems in Portugal had led to the development of a protectionist policy. Since commercial treaties inhibited the raising of tariff barriers, Portugal practiced protection by forbidding its people to wear foreign cloth. In addition, it took various steps to stimulate successfully the domestic manufacture of cloth. A lucrative market for British manufacturers and merchants was thus cut off. (2) While the British people preferred the lighter French clarets to the heavier Portuguese wines, wars with France and France's own protectionist policies induced Britain to look for alternative sources of wine. (3) Gold had been discovered in Brazil, and over the years productive gold mines had been developed there.

Against this background, the provisions of the commercial Methuen Treaty were few, but they hit directly at the crux of Britain's problem: Portuguese restrictions on English woolen cloth and wool manufactures were lifted; in return, Britain guaranteed a lesser duty on Portuguese wine relative to French wine. The results were likewise clear and simple: Portuguese cloth manufacture was smothered in its infancy; instead of developing a dynamic manufacturing industry, Portuguese capital flowed into viticulture and wine-making—to such an extent that investment in these fields replaced not only manufactures but even such investment as was needed to expand production of corn and other foodstuffs. As for England, the Methuen Treaty contributed substantially to expansion of English cloth production and the resulting larger-scale production helped reduce manufacturing costs and thus strengthened English ability to penetrate other foreign markets.

On top of all this, the gold obtainable in Portugal's Brazilian colony came to play a strategic role in these new trade arrangements, as well as in Britain's subsequent great economic development. Consequent to the treaty, Portugal's economy—with its concentration on wine, and in the absence of a manufacturing industry which would have given greater economic flexibility—became increasingly dependent on the British economy. While trade between the two countries flourished, Portugal's imports of goods from England far exceeded exports to England.[11] A large portion of the ocean trade between the two nations was carried in English bottoms, thereby intensifying Portugal's unfavorable balance of payments. The solution: the gold mined in Brazil was used to settle the bulk of Portugal's accounts with England. Portugal thus became a transmission belt, actually more like a sieve. Brazil's gold was shipped to Portugal and was then in large measure transshipped to England. Thus, Christopher Hill observes, "Especially after the Methuen Treaty of 1703, Portuguese trade, and particularly the gold of Brazil, contributed to the establishment of London as the bullion market of the world."[12] It would take us too far afield to explore the significance of London's becoming the world's bullion market. Suffice it to say, for the present, that this development was a valuable stimulus to England's evolution as world banker and foremost capitalist nation.

Those who are not economists, and perhaps some who are, may well wonder why so much space has been devoted here to the commercial treaties between Portugal and England. Our hope is that this will provide a beneficial illustration of the need to shake loose from the preconceptions of accepted "knowledge." For what is generally believed to have been natural and efficient when treated abstractly as a "pure" problem of international trade turns out to be historically created—created in the context of colonialism, war, nationalist rivalries, and military power. Moreover, this is but a mild example of the origins of the international division of labor: it occurred, after all, between two Christian, colonizing powers. This illustration barely touches upon the kind of international division of labor imposed by the practices of outright colonialism, including the changes in these countries where production ability previously had been superior to that of the colonizers. As the noted economic historian Carlo Cippola wryly comments, it was fortunate for England that India had no Ricardo of its own:

> The story of the East India silks and calicoes that were imported into England and caused difficulty for the English textile industry is so well known that it does not need to be told here. It was fortunate for England that no Indian Ricardo arose to convince the English people that, according to the law of comparative costs, it would be advantageous for them to turn into shepherds and to import from India all the textiles that were needed. Instead, England passed a series of acts designed to prevent importation of Indian textiles and some "good results" were achieved.[13]

One of the chief hindrances to a full understanding of imperialism, and especially of imperialism without colonies, is the lack of appreciation of the extent to which international economic relations are the result of the social transformations imposed by colonialism and the whole complex history of imperialism. Such social transformations concern not only production and trade, but also the class structure, the politics, and (last but not least) the social psychology of peoples with a long history of subjugation under direct and indirect foreign rule.

The economic aspect of such social transformations is especially obscure because of what one might call, to use Marx's term, the fetishism of commodities. The dictionary defines a fetish as "a material, commonly an inanimate object regarded with awe as being the embodiment or habitation of a potent spirit, or as having magical potency because of the materials and methods used in compounding it." Conditioned as we are by living in a society operating with commodities

and money prices, we endow the market with magical potency and regard the price system with equal awe. And in the
process we forget, or never realize, that markets and prices
are not the ultimate controllers of our lives. To the extent
that they do control our lives, it is only because we accept,
and live under, our existing class structure and political
system. The underlying reality is to be found in the social
relations of our time, in the relations among people. It is this
reality which is masked by the worship of the impersonal
magical powers of the price system.

If one has the presumption to talk about, or even hint at,
unequal exchange between industrially advanced and industrially backward nations, the professor of economics cries out
in rage, or explains patiently: "That is a contradiction in
terms. There can be no inequality of exchange, since the
market adjusts all inequities. All prices must, under the force
of economic laws, represent exchange between equivalents."
Up to a certain point, the professor is absolutely right. For
once the price system is in existence, the system cannot
continue unless each price at the very least covers the cost of
what is needed to produce the commodity. If the price of a
given commodity does not cover these costs, the commodity
cannot for very long continue to be produced. It is in this
sense that prices govern the use of productive resources.

But what are costs? In the final analysis all costs are
reduced to labor, mental and physical, and the way labor is
used. The other components of the production process—raw
materials and machinery—are also the products of labor, and
the way labor was used in the recent or distant past.

But where does this labor come from? How does it happen
to shift from one job to another? What determines the cost
of labor? These are far from easy questions, and we surely
don't pretend to know all the answers. However, it is clear
that any reliable set of answers must take into account two
propositions: (1) the creation and maintenance of a labor
force are far from "pure" economic phenomena, and (2)
there is no absolute "correct" or "equal" cost of labor, other
than the rock-bottom biological minimum for keeping body
and soul together. Labor as a cost in the production process

varies from country to country, from region to region within a country, and from occupation to occupation.

Entering into these differences are elements of force, politics, class struggle, and a long history of economic manipulation by those who hold the economic reins. Lurking behind, and incorporated into, today's wages and wage differentials is the history of slavery and semislavery, and the exploitation of ethnic, national, racial, and interregional disparities. This may not be easily discerned in the advanced capitalist nations where the creation of a wage-seeking labor force, along with its inner incongruities, evolved over centuries. But it should be more obvious as far as the areas of Western penetration are concerned, where a good deal of their capitalist history occurred in the last hundred years. Here, quite clearly, superior military power was the ultimate determining factor in obtaining the labor to dig the mines and harvest the plantation crops, as well as in creating the kind of money economy which prevails in these areas to this day. Whatever equality of exchange one may assume exists between the products of the metropolises and the periphery, one thing is obvious: it contains within it an inequality in wages that congeals a long and bitter history of force and oppression.

The costs that enter into prices are determined not only by the costs of living labor but also by the exertion of past, dead labor—the way labor was used to create harbors, canals, railroads, irrigation trenches, dams, factories, machinery, and equipment. On this score, striking disparities also obtain between, on the one hand, the kind of investments made in the imperialist centers, and, on the other hand, those made in the colonial periphery designed to serve the interests of the metropolises. The interests of the metropolises, it should be noted, included not only the means of transportation and communication needed to extract and export the resources of the periphery, but also those needed to effectuate the military occupation by an alien power. Furthermore, these and other so-called external economies were created to meet the particular needs of countries whose boundaries were artificially created in the foreign offices of London, Paris, and Berlin. Notably in Africa, the setting of boundaries and the resulting trade routes were the product of secret trade-offs and deals by the great powers—resembling, if anything, a parlor game of Monopoly, with complete indifference to either economic efficiency or the well-being of the people of the colonies.

Prices, of course, include profits as well as the costs of past and present labor: the profits of industrialists, landowners, bankers, and merchants. Here too, obviously, the power relations between, on the one hand, capital and labor in each country, and, on the other hand, capital in the metropolis and in the periphery are of decisive significance. Thus, from whichever angle we approach the cost-price relations, we find that prices and costs are themselves the products of the social system and the current as well as the congealed past power relations of that system. The technical parameters which economists study are those that, at best, condition the manner in which the arrived-at social system behaves. That is why, if one wants to come to grips with the essentials of capitalism and imperialism, the investigation must be able to penetrate the screen created by the fetishism of commodities and commodity exchange. In one sense, prices and wages undoubtedly do reflect the exchange of equivalents. But these equivalents are the products of a specific historical process. They are far from God-given, eternal, and immutable; and by no means are they objectively necessary—except within the given historical and technological framework.

The equivalents of our time—created, as noted, by a social system and its particular history—are instruments which facilitate the efficient reproduction of the *existing* allocation of resources and of the *existing* property arrangements. In this context, prices and markets are impartial: they repeatedly reproduce the existing class structure of a society, the existing income distribution within a country, and the existing income differentials among countries. They are the impartial regulators of the attained capitalist institutions, and of the economic dependency of the periphery on the metropolis.

Tinkering with and reforming backward capitalisms will have little effect on basic social inequities, internal or external. For even honest provision of foreign aid, technical assistance, education for the elites, and peace corps devices can— in the absence of a breakaway from the imperialist network— at best only help make the imperialist system more efficient and perhaps extend its life somewhat. Reforms and "improvements" of this type cannot accomplish more, for the simple but profound reason that the historically arrived-at property, exchange, and wage system will continue relentlessly to reassert the imperialist relations of dependency. And this is why the primary task of the peoples of the Third World, as they struggle to throw off the shackles of imperialism and to achieve a humanitarian economic development, is the abolition of the capitalist system itself, with all that it implies with respect to price and wage relationships. This is an absolutely necessary condition—although in itself no guarantee of ultimate success—for entrance on the road to independence and development.

No wonder, then, that the academics have their troubles with such words as imperialism and capitalism, for it is around these concepts and the phenomena they define that the mass upheavals of our times are erupting. Bourgeois scholars naturally have difficulty facing up to either the fundamentals of revolutionary change or the processes whereby imperialism and capitalism will meet their doom.

Notes

1. A. P. Thornton, *The Imperial Idea and Its Enemies* (London: Macmillan & Co., 1959), p. x.
2. David K. Fieldhouse, *The Economic Exploitation of Africa: Some British and French Comparisons* (mimeographed, no date), p. 1.
3. As to social taboos, one need only recall how London's respectable mid-Victorian critics venomously attacked Ibsen's *Ghosts* because it dealt openly with venereal disease.
4. The background to this debate can be found in Bernard Semmel, *Imperialism and Social Reform* (London: George Allen & Unwin, 1960), pp. 66-72.
5. G. B. Shaw, *Fabians and the Empire* (1900), as quoted in Annette T. Rubinstein, *The Great Tradition in English Literature: From*

Shakespeare to Shaw, vol. 2 (New York: Monthly Review Press, 1969), p. 908.

6. To appreciate just some of the limitations in the real life of the corporate world, in contrast with the fantasies about the omnipotence and possible farsightedness of the corporation, observe the nature of the cash liquidity crisis of 1970. For this, see "The Long-Run Decline in Liquidity," *Monthly Review* (September 1970). An example of the limitations of the potential farsightedness of the imperialist state can be seen in its inflation and dollar crisis. For this, see "The End of U.S. Hegemony," *Monthly Review* (October 1971).

7. Karl Marx, *On the Question of Free Trade*, an address delivered in 1848 and reprinted as an appendix to Marx, *The Poverty of Philosophy* (New York: International Publishers, 1969), p. 223.

8. It should be noted that in what Keynes would probably have included in his "underground of economics," some unorthodox liberal economists, disturbed by the too-flagrant contradiction between facts and theory, are questioning the validity of the comparative advantage doctrine as applied to the case of the underdeveloped nations.

9. S. Sideri, *Trade and Power: Informal Colonialism in Anglo-Portuguese Relations* (Rotterdam: Rotterdam University Press, 1970).

10. The treaty is named after John Methuen, who negotiated it for England. The full text of the treaty is given in Adam Smith, *The Wealth of Nations*, bk. 4, chap. 6, "Of Treaties of Commerce" (New York: Modern Library, 1937), pp. 512-13.

11. "According to the official figures, England achieved a surplus in her visible trade with Portugal in every year between 1700 and 1760." H. E. S. Fisher, *The Portugal Trade: A Study of Anglo-Portuguese Commerce, 1700-1770* (London: Methuen & Co., 1971), p. 19.

12. Christopher Hill, *Reformation to Industrial Revolution* (New York: Pantheon Books, 1967), p. 187.

13. Carlo M. Cippola, *European Culture and European Expansion* (Baltimore: Penguin Books, 1970), p. 152.

6

The Multinational Corporation and Development—A Contradiction?

Among current ideas about the importance of the multinational corporation for the future of society and the nation state are quite a few flights of fancy indulged in by conservatives and radicals alike. It is time that some of these be brought down to earth, and there is no better way to do this than to examine the roots of this phenomenon historically. As we see it, the multinational corporation can best be understood as a logical stage in the evolution of capitalist enterprise, a stage during which innate tendencies of the capitalist firm come into full flower. This can be recognized most clearly if we begin by taking special note of what Marx considered the mainsprings of capitalist behavior.

Since Marx's central focus was the study of economic institutions as part of a historical process, he separated out of the multitude of operations of capitalist enterprises those features which he considered decisive in determining historical development, or, as he put it, the laws of motion of capitalism. Among the governing principles he selected are

This article was originally presented in 1974 at a conference on the multinational corporation at Yale University; it subsequently appeared in David E. Apter and Louis Wolf Goodman, eds., *The Multinational Corporation and Social Change* (New York: Praeger Publishers, 1976), copyright © 1976 by Praeger Publishers.

those which are also found at the heart of today's multi-national firm:

1. The conditions of capitalist enterprise impose on the individual firm the necessity to expand continuously. As Marx wrote in *Capital:*

> The development of capitalist production makes it constantly necessary to keep increasing the amount of capital laid out in a given industrial undertaking, and competition makes the imma-nent laws of capitalist production to be felt by each individual capitalist, as external coercive laws. It compels him to keep constantly extending his capital in order to preserve it, but extend it he cannot, except by means of progressive accumu-lation.[1]

This growth imperative is graphically summarized in Marx's much quoted epitomization: "Accumulate, Accumulate! That is Moses and the prophets! . . . Therefore . . . reconvert the greatest possible portion of surplus product, into capital!"[2]

2. The process of accumulation of capital generates, and is in turn further advanced by a growing concentration of capital in fewer and fewer hands. This process of concentra-tion takes two interrelated forms: the spread of large-scale production and the combination of firms through mergers and acquisitions. The organizational instrument most useful for this persistent tendency of capitalist development is the corporation, more often called in Marx's day a joint-stock company.[3]

3. The world market provides "the basis and vital element of capitalist production."[4] In fact, capitalism was born in the commercial revolution of the sixteenth and early seventeenth centuries—a revolution which produced a global market cen-tered on the needs and desires of the nations of Western Europe. The expansion of international trade stimulated the spread of capitalist enterprise, furthered the transition from feudalism to capitalism, and led necessarily to a continuous deepening and widening of the world market.[5]

These three cardinal attributes of business enterprise—investment expansion, concentration of corporate power, and growth of the world market—are eventually uniquely fulfilled in the multinational corporation, but the latter cannot take shape until the concentration of capital reaches the stage conveniently called monopoly capitalism (as distinguished from competitive capitalism), in which competition among only a few giant corporations is the typical pattern in each of the leading industries.[6]

Foreign investment played a relatively subordinate role in the international economy of competitive capitalism, and that role was to aid and support what was of primary concern in that period: the promotion of markets for rapidly expanding domestic industries, and the procurement of raw materials for industry and food for burgeoning urban populations. (This is not to deny the growing importance of foreign investment to the British economy during the period of competitive capitalism: as a most useful component in the maturation of its money markets, and its international financial ascendancy; and as a spur to its metals and machinery industries. Loans and direct investments were useful aids in the acquisition of railway-building concessions, and thus they supported the rising exports of iron and steel, railway equipment, and allied capital goods. Capital went abroad, and the resulting profits were reinvested overseas, for a variety of political and economic reasons. Nevertheless, the central integrative factor was the expansion of foreign trade.) In contrast, the economies and politics of the monopoly stage entailed a heightened attention to the spread of ownership, control, and influence over productive activities in foreign lands. The expansion and deepening of the world market was no longer correlated primarily with exports of commodities; to an increasing extent it took the form of transnational migration of capital. This new interest in foreign investment was grounded in the distinguishing features of this new phase of development in the advanced capitalist countries which began to shape up towards the end of the nineteenth century:

1. A host of new industries based on major technological breakthroughs appeared on the scene. Examples are steel,

electric power, oil refining, synthetic chemicals, aluminum, and automobiles. Most of these new industries required an unusually large scale of production (along with enlarged, more complex capital markets to mobilize the needed finance)—thus accelerating the trend towards further concentration and centralization of capital.

2. Industrial processes relied more and more on the conscious application of science. This, along with the pressure of competition among giant firms and the urgency to protect large capital investments, encouraged growing attention to research and development for product innovation and improvement in production methods.

3. The new industries created a demand for a wide variety of raw materials, often entailing the discovery and development of new sources of supply in distant lands. At the same time the corporate giants felt an increasing need to own or otherwise control these sources of supply as a form of insurance against being squeezed by rivals, as a means of protecting the huge amounts of capital sunk in the extraction and processing of the needed materials, and in order that the profits of the extractive industries accrue to themselves.

4. Under the impact of the new industries and advances in transportation associated with the new technologies, the world market reached a new high in integration: the remaining self-contained areas were transformed into adjuncts of international markets; a single multilateral system of international payments evolved; and more or less uniform world prices came into effect for the more common commodities of world trade.

5. The state assumed an increasingly important role in stimulating, influencing, and resolving conflicts among the emerging giant corporations. Protective tariffs and other trade barriers—no longer for the protection of infant industries but for the benefit of more advanced, export-oriented manufactures—became the order of the day. Above all, the evolving monopoly phase was tied to the mushrooming of militarism, with the latter performing two indispensable services: (a) a vital and rapidly growing market for the heavy

industries, for which government funds were readily available, and (b) assistance, via direct military action or the threat of force, in obtaining privileged trade and investment opportunities.

These and related developments both reflected and intensified the pressures on large capitalist enterprises to expand their international operations. While most involvement abroad was at first based largely on loans to governments and industry,[7] equity investment before long began to take a prominent place as the modus operandi of the giant firm in the world market, evolving eventually into the flowering of the multinationals. This evolution proceeded at an uneven pace, influenced by international conditions, the state of the domestic economy, and the organizational strength of the corporations themselves. But the thrust was always toward the expansion of control over production and marketing on a global scale. And from its very beginning, the burgeoning of foreign investment in the late nineteenth and twentieth centuries was closely linked with the maturation of monopoly-type firms and their social and political alter ego, the new imperialism. Capital flowed abroad to gain exclusive control of raw material supplies needed for the new industries, to acquire maximum leverage from technological and other monopolistic advantages, to make the most use of regions with exceptional market opportunities, and to profit from the low wages and favored locations of colonies, semi-colonies, and spheres of influence. Moreover, the very obstacles erected in this period to restrict imports and protect domestic industry gave added impetus to the spread of foreign investment as a means of jumping trade barriers.

Another important development of this period was the dramatic shifts in the national sources of capital moving into foreign operations: these changes reflect not only the fluctuating fortunes of the advanced capitalist nations but the essential nature of the internationalization of capital as part of a continuous struggle for power and ascendancy by nations and their industries. Great Britain's headstart in the area of capital exports, stemming from its initiating role in the industrial revolution, its huge empire and dominant navy, and its being the headquarters of the international money market, led quite naturally to its becoming the foremost owner of foreign productive assets. France and Germany, however, were fast on the same trail. Together, the three nations accounted for almost 90 percent of foreign investment at the outbreak of World War I, Britain owning 50 percent, Germany and France 40 percent.

Despite the debtor status of the United States, a number of U.S. firms participated in the new wave, with substantial investments moving abroad before the turn of the century. On the whole, though, the position of the United States was relatively minor compared to the big three, representing only some 6 percent of the total in 1914. All this changed radically as a result of the dislocations of World War I and the subsequent readjustments in power relations among the advanced industrial nations: the loss of Russia as a host to foreign investors; the drastic reduction in Britain's investments in the United States as a result of the liquidation of assets to pay for U.S. exports of munitions; and the decline in Germany's and France's roles. Thus, the 40 percent held by Germany and France in 1914 dropped to 11 percent by 1930. At the other extreme was the expansionism of U.S. industry and finance striving to realize its "manifest destiny" in world affairs. Along with other political and military realignments on the international scene between World War I and the Great Depression, including a U.S. bid to take over paramount position, came the marked rise in the absolute and relative status of U.S. investment activities abroad: the 6 percent of 1914 became 35 percent by 1930.

The impressive forward movement by the United States was speeded up and consolidated in the new world situation arising out of World War II and the postwar arrangements. By the early 1970s, 52 percent of the world's foreign investments were in the hands of U.S. corporations, the result of an unprecedented eightfold growth in this type of capital accumulation by U.S. firms since 1945. Once the Western European and Japanese economies got back on their feet, the reach of their corporate giants also began to extend to capital accumulation across national boundaries. British firms ran a weak second and French firms a much poorer third to the United States; the two combined accounting for a little over 20 percent of total foreign investment in the early 1970s. Germany and Japan, for obvious reasons, were laggards (in 1971 they represented 4 and 3 percent of the total, respectively), but their rates of growth hint at probable major changes ahead in their foreign production role. Between 1966 and 1971, Germany's foreign investment increased by 190 percent, and Japan's by 280 percent.[8]

The Rise of the Multinational Corporation

The groundwork of the clear-cut dominance of U.S. foreign investment that took shape in the post-World War II years was grounded on the overwhelming U.S. military and economic power and the *Pax Americana* which this power sought to establish. As part of the coalescence of these interrelated developments, the multinational firm appeared on the stage as the quintessential embodiment of the innate logic of capitalist enterprise: relentless accumulation of capital on a world scale, aided and abetted by ever greater concentration and centralization of enterprise. As we see it, the main contributing factors to the explosive acceleration of U.S. foreign enterprise and the emergence of a qualitatively new form of international capitalist operation, pioneered by U.S. firms, were as follows:

1. The system of international payments, once focused in the London money market during the British Empire's hegemonic heyday and the predominance of British foreign investment, was reconstituted under U.S. leadership by the Bretton Woods agreements. The enshrinement of the U.S. dollar at Bretton Woods provided the financial framework for the great leap forward of U.S. corporate investment abroad. The international payments created the unique, prolonged deficit in the U.S. balance of payments, made possible the deficit financing not only of the far-flung military bases and

military operations of the U.S. government, but also the sprouting of foreign affiliates of multinational firms. The breakdown of the Bretton Woods system in 1971 proved to be no serious obstacle, for by then the huge float of U.S. dollar liabilities outside the country, the financial assets accumulated in the interim by multinational subsidiaries, and the resulting Euro-dollar market provided the practical financial media for still further international business growth by U.S. firms. (The World Bank—the second institution created at Bretton Woods—also contributed to the spread of foreign investment by, among other things, financing the needed infrastructure.)

2. The prosperity and type of economic development spurred by the Marshall Plan, which had been undertaken largely to rebuild and strengthen European capitalism as a political and military ally, led to an intensification of the kind of monopolistic competition that characterizes the multinational firm. The Marshall Plan, financed and steered by the United States, stimulated the rehabilitation and growth of native giant firms and at the same time prepared a fertile seedbed for the sprouting of U.S. corporate enterprise in Western European countries and their dependencies. In addition, the NATO arrangements, the continuous presence of U.S. military power in Western Europe, and the latter's reliance on the U.S. nuclear umbrella reinforced the special relations within the so-called Atlantic Alliance, which among other things sustained a favorable environment for U.S. business expansion across the Atlantic.

3. Designed to influence and control "safe" and allied nations, the postwar U.S. program of military and economic aid also helped create and support many new investment opportunities. Japan was the notable exception; the Japanese consciously and far-sightedly managed to retain their home market and to limit the encroachment of U.S. foreign investment. Their ability to get the U.S. government to go along with this obstinacy, despite the U.S. military occupation, was perhaps due to the special role assigned to Japan as the primary bastion of capitalism in the Far East and as the

major ally of the United States in that area. Not only was the protection of foreign private investment a prerequisite for the receipt of such aid, but energetic encouragement of an inflow of foreign investment was fundamental to the economic development programs designed in response to the advice and pressure of the loan and grant administrators. Perhaps even more important was the proliferation of experts among business, professional, and military personnel engaged in distributing this aid. Increased knowledge of local industrial and financial practices; better acquaintance with indigenous geography, language, laws, customs, and markets; and, above all, close contacts with the "right people" in government and elite circles—all this was, and continues to be, of invaluable assistance to capitalists seeking avenues abroad for the piling up of further investments.

4. World War II and its aftermath introduced and galvanized business and technological changes that primed the rapid growth, and helped develop the distinguishing features, of the multinational firm. War production requirements fattened the industrial giants of the U.S. economy and gave a push to further concentration of economic power. Enlivened by strong direct and indirect government demand for military goods during the war and ever since, the giant firms turned into supergiants. The technological underpinning for the new earth-girdling enterprise was also intimately associated with the militarization of the economy. The heavy expenditure of funds and personnel on weapon development achieved significant breakthroughs in the fields of communication, transport, and computers, which in turn opened up new opportunities for the business community. The technological edge achieved during the war has been further sharpened with the help of continuing subsidies: at least since the mid-fifties, between 50 and 60 percent of research and development in the United States has been financed by the federal government,[9] an indeterminate additional share is paid for by private industry in anticipation of new products or new technologies that will eventuate in still larger defense contracts. The changes that contributed most to facilitating networks

of global industry closely coordinated from a few metropolitan centers were: (a) speeded-up and expanded air transport; (b) vastly improved modes of communication; and (c) sophisticated computers for the amassing and analysis of data needed to plan for global maximization of profit.

The developments outlined in the above four points help to explain what is distinctively new in the latest phase of international capitalist affairs. Previously, foreign investment activities consisted to a great extent in acquiring control of raw material sources, establishment of manufacturing subsidiaries for particular locational advantages, and the spread of international banking largely in colonial and semicolonial nations. These were, as noted above, products of the striving for monopolistic advantage and manipulation by the most powerful firms to divide world markets. While foreign investment as an integral constituent of monopoly capitalism moved ahead energetically, several features of the years prior to World War II limited its rate of growth. Apart from the effect of the Great Depression on the rate of investment, the major restraints were the following: 1) World markets became divided by cartel-like arrangements in a large number of important industries, manufacturing as well as raw material extraction. Spheres of influence were parceled out. Poaching on each other's territory was prohibited, including curbs on where foreign investment could be located. 2) Nations with colonial empires attempted insofar as possible to keep their colonial possessions as exclusive investment preserves for themselves. This limitation was especially onerous for U.S. business in the light of the small share of the colonial world occupied by the United States. 3) Despite the steadily increasing power of giant firms, few had the financial resources and managerial strength for truly worldwide operations. The typical international enterprise ran to only two, three, or four foreign branch plants. The noteworthy exceptions were the early multinational organizations in the oil industry.

One after another of these inhibitions faded away during and after World War II. Many cartel agreements evaporated during the war. Decolonization created new opportunities for trade and investment competition from metropolitan centers which formerly were excluded or were disinclined to attempt to climb over expensive barriers. The pervasive military presence of the United States around the globe, the strength of this military power, and the design of the imperial world order under U.S. leadership not only opened doors in advanced as well as underdeveloped countries but also inspired confidence in foreign investors—most especially, of course, in U.S. business interests—about the security of their overseas assets. (This is in addition to the influence of U.S. power on the readiness of ruling elites of weaker nations to create an attractive environment for outside capital.) Finally, as discussed earlier, the accelerated concentration of power increased the number of firms able to operate internationally; more and more supergiants, assisted by the new technologies, were capable of exercising central control over a large and geographically widespread number of affiliates.

This extended scope for accumulation on a global scale developed a momentum of its own, especially as the resulting terms of monopolistic rivalry changed. While cartel deals did not entirely disappear, and some new cartels came on the scene, the struggle for markets among giant firms in many industries shifted to producing goods in each other's territory and in the dependencies of the various metropolitan centers. In the very nature of monopolistic competition, as one or more of the giant firms in a particular industry spread its tentacles abroad, competitors were eventually impelled to do likewise. The changeover in the strategy of competition, and the experience gained in the process of running a business on an international scale, kept on strengthening the impulse for, and widening the geographic range of, new foreign locations yielding lower costs of production and/or improved market control. The path, once opened up, became a well-trodden one.

The upshot was an explosion of U.S. foreign production activity, a quickening of the global spread of competing giants from other advanced industrial nations, and the advent of the age of the multinational firm. Thus, within the short span of a quarter of a century, the multinationals reached such a level in the international accumulation of capital that their output away from home base began to outdistance trade as the main vehicle of international economic exchange. The combined sales of foreign affiliates of multinational corporations in 1971 is estimated to have been $330 billion, while total exports of all capitalist economies in that year amounted to $312 billion. It should be noted though that this has come about because of the very substantial excess of output abroad over exports in the United States and Great Britain. Except for Switzerland, and the fast-approaching Sweden, the other capitalist nations still show a substantial excess of exports over their foreign production.[10] (This is aside from the fact that a substantial portion of foreign trade is now conducted between multinationals and their subsidiaries.) As in the past, the modern upsurge in transnational production is also concentrated in the hands of a relatively small number of companies. But in contrast with the former pattern, the leading firms are no longer operating in only one or two foreign countries but have truly spread their wings: for example, two hundred of these companies, among the largest in the world, now have affiliates in twenty or more countries.[11] Moreover, the multinationals, or their prototypes, were formerly for the most part in raw material extraction and to a limited extent in banking. Today's global firms have invaded manufacturing and services, and taken a major leap into international banking. (Note that deposits in foreign branches of the larger New York-based banks compared with their domestic deposits have increased from 8½ to 65½ percent between 1960 and 1972.[12])

Speculation about Supermultinationals

Such rapid and striking changes naturally cry out for new interpretations. Similarly, analyses of international economic events that ignore, or do not adequately reflect, the effects of the multinationals are bound to come a cropper. At the same time, however, it is especially important not to fall victim to oversimplified projections and conjectures or great sounding theories based on speculation rather than fact. For it is in the nature of transitional periods for many sprouts to emerge, some to wither while others mature and become dominant. Simple linear projections, without weighing countertendencies, are therefore unreliable guides. Thus, a frequently met expectation is that the process of concentration and centralization of capital will before long end up with a handful of global companies owning and operating the preponderant part of the capitalist world's enterprise. This is hardly a novel theme. Reading the death of competition into the decline of competition has recurred time and again, ever since the giant corporations loomed on the scene almost a hundred years ago. The onset of the multinational age has quite naturally precipitated a blossoming of such expectations. It is important, however, to distinguish clearly between a steady pressure within capitalism towards more concentration of power on the one hand and the virtual elimination of all competition on the other. While the direction may be persistently towards the ultimate in monopoly, the logical end of this process is never reached because of obstacles arising from the nature of the very forces which propel it forward.

What needs to be understood is that the very process of concentration and centralization of capital is spurred by competition and results in intensifying the struggle among separate aggregates of capital, albeit on a different scale and with altered strategies. As a rule, above average growth of an enterprise, or a merger of two or more firms, occurs in more than one sector of an industry in a given period: the emergence of one focus of power stimulates, by example or by the threat of extinction, reflex convergencies of capital. In addition, contending focuses of financial power generated within the rapidly inflating capital markets associated with the process of concentration, interindustry as well as intraindustry rivalry, technical innovations and new industries induced by competition, and state intervention to forestall or ameliorate a crisis—all serve to create conflicting blocs of power, no one of which has the strength to win a battle for absolute control or the will to risk the loss of accumulated assets in such intensified economic warfare.

This being the case, as each giant firm holds on to its attained share of the market, the potential for further accumulation of capital within an industry is generally restricted to the growth of demand for that industry's products. Under the impetus of the growth imperative, then, the search for new worlds to conquer generally narrows down to two main channels for accumulation: diversification (development of new products and new consumer "needs" as well as buying into other industries) and conquest of foreign markets. While the entry into the international scene produces new strains and tensions, the underlying reality is still competitive struggle among industrial and financial power groups. In addition, we frequently find state intervention contributing to the perpetuation of monopolistic competition within and between industries. Faced with foreign economic penetration, the advanced industrial states tend to strengthen their own giant firms, and, if necessary, step right into the act themselves through ownership and operation of industry. (Of the leading 211 manufacturing companies in capitalist nations with sales of over $1 billion, at least twelve are state owned.)[13] Struggle for markets on a world scale will of course encourage, and necessitate, further mergers and alliances, but these are for the purpose of more effective competition and not its elimination. In this connection, the rise and decline of U.S. hegemony is a useful illustration. American economic dominance was a natural outgrowth of the great disparity of economic strength between the United States and the war-devastated nations. Viewed abstractly and in terms of straight-line projections, many expected this hegemony to grow until the world's productive capacity would be in the hands of a few U.S. firms. But the requirements and side effects of this dominance (the global military stance, the military adventures, the rebuilding of its allies, the European Common Market, the related unsettling of international financial arrangements) produced its own countereffects, leading to increasing challenges to U.S. dominance from other capitalist nations.

On the international as on the domestic scene, the means and intensity of conflict will vary over time, depending on political and military conditions, particular circumstances in a given industry, and the general state of the market (whether the latter is experiencing stagnation, growth, or decline). Alliances and truces in a particular industry may produce temporary calm, but these generally last only until a new crisis rekindles the flames of competition. For the essential nature of modern monopoly capitalism is restless struggle on the world stage by giants and supergiants which, despite their accumulation of power, are far from omnipotent; indeed, the dialectical interrelation between coalescence and competition of capitals is one of the most important contributors to the dynamics of the economic system.

Multinationals vs. the Nation State

A second popular line of theoretical projections in the multinational age holds that internationalization requires, and eventually will result in, the decline of the nation state. In part, this type of speculation is prompted by the search of big business for the ultimate in freedom for the international movement of capital, profits, and goods. However, this theory has more objective roots in the supposed contradiction between the evolving global structure and strategy of the multinationals and the restrictions inherent in the nation state. The typical foreign manufacturing subsidiary in the premultinational years was either a plant that merely assembled components sent from the home country or a more integrated duplicate of the parent company adapted to the host country's markets and standing pretty much on its own feet. The strategic difference between such forms of organization and the typical multinational manufacturing organization—in fact, that which gives the latter its uniqueness and novelty—is the high degree of interdependence among the subsidiaries and the kind of coordination needed in the central offices of the parent company in the pursuit of global profit maximization. A classic example of the new level of integration is provided by a former head of General Motors:

> If the South African assembly operation and its recently added manufacturing facilities are to function smoothly and efficiently, they must today receive a carefully controlled and coordinated flow of vehicle parts and components from West Germany, England, Canada, the United States, and even Australia. These must reach General Motors South Africa in the right volume and at the right time to allow an orderly scheduling of assembly without accumulation of excessive inventories. This is a challenging assignment which must be made to work if the investment is to be a profitable one.[14]

We see here not only the shape of the foreign operations of General Motors in today's world but also get a glimpse of the model for which many multinational manufacturing firms are striving. Their ideal would be to maximize overall profits by the highest degree of flexibility in the global movement of capacity and of goods at lowest production and distribution costs—all to be finally planned, coordinated, and directed from one financial center. The realization of such a dream quite clearly would imply the complete removal of all national barriers. And it is therefore not surprising to find that the advanced thinkers and publicists of the business community have sounded the tocsin: the old-fashioned nation state is standing in the way of progress. Reverberations of this theme are heard in both orthodox academic and radical circles, by those who see the free sway of international capital as the wave of the future as well as by those alarmed over its implications.

Implicit in much of this thinking is an oversimplified technological determinism. The assumption is made that the multinational method of integrated global production represents a higher and more progressive stage of industrial organization—one that reaches a new level of large-scale efficiency and is realistically based on the interdependency of the various regions of the earth. It is then inferred that what is rational will prevail: since the system of nation states interferes with an advanced global technology of production and management, the nation state will tend to fade away, with many of its functions being replaced by formal or informal international institutions.

This line of thought has two weaknesses: the assumptions, implicit and explicit, are wrong; and what is most relevant is disregarded. The multinational firm may indeed be a more efficient organism, but the issue is: efficient for what? Its superiority is in the realm of profit-making by oligopolistic organizations designed to exploit to the hilt the existing hierarchy of nations; in other words, the imperialist world order. Decisions on location and integration of plants are, of course, influenced by such technical factors as transportation costs and proximity to raw materials. These are, more often than not, minor inducements compared to more pressing economic and political considerations, which have nothing to do with the design of a superior form of international production: the political climate for foreign investment, the wage rates, tax advantages, and imperatives of monopolistic competition. Nor is the large scale of corporate enterprise in and of itself evidence of greater efficiency. The scale of organization is not arrived at by purely technical criteria (even if there were such a thing, independent of social values) but with concern for greater effectiveness in the exercise of economic power to protect and control markets.

Furthermore, it is hypocrisy or obfuscation to see any resemblance between the transnational integration brought about by the multinationals and the growing interdependence of the earth's regions. The latter arises from the problems of limited natural resources and the effects of environmental changes in one region on the life-supporting possibilities of other regions. On such matters, the global corporations are the culprits and not the saviors: far from being organisms that have grown out of the *necessary* interdependence of all parts of the world, they have been built to obtain the maximum-profit advantage out of the artificial interdependence imposed by the long history of colonialism and imperialism.

In sum, from the viewpoint of either technology or management, the multinationals are hardly the prototypes of a superior international mode of production, certainly not the mode of production that will cope with the world's problems of hunger, disease, scarcity of resources, and environmental pollution. The multinationals are not basically out of harmony with the system of nation states and the interwoven imperialist network; in fact, these firms—and their so-called global technology and administrative structures—evolved in a system of nation states in a fashion best adapted to struggle for profits and control in precisely that environment.

In addition to speculation about the fate of nations based on technological determinism, there is another trend of thought tending to the same conclusion but based on an oversimplified concept of the relations between the state and big business. One finds, especially among radical critics, the anticipation of a coalition or conspiracy of multinationals which will settle international matters among themselves and then force the nation states to conform to their will. In other words, as the multinationals grow in strength, their common interests will prevail over and hence weaken the nation states. In a certain sense, there has always been a community of interest among capitalists who viewed the world as their playground. This has been the common cause of a class whose success depends upon antagonism against workers and other subordinate classes throughout all capitalist nations, including most assuredly a united front against national liberation and proletarian revolutions aimed at overthrowing capitalist rule. In addition, the interference by foreign capitalists in the affairs of weaker dependent states is central to the whole history of capitalism (the most recent well-documented and publicized example being, of course, ITT's activities in Chile). But these aspects of capital's unified world spirit are a far cry from the rule, by an international committee of business firms, over the advanced capitalist nations. Such a notion overlooks the essence of the international firms as participants in economic warfare among themselves, in which the gains of one are the losses of another. Even more important, this type of prognostication ignores the underlying symbiosis of monopoly capital and its home state, as for example:

1. Above all, the multinational corporations need social stability in the countries where they operate or expect to operate. For internal stability, a police force is needed; for external law and order, an army, navy, and air force. Business firms will, when necessary, invest in private armies to guard their property and repress trade unions. They will also devote resources to assure a friendly environment and have a voice in security matters. Thus they will spend money to bribe officials, influence newspapers, radio, television, and other forms of "public relations" and in general on activities that will sustain friendly governments or get rid of unfriendly ones. This type of investment, however, is minuscule compared with the huge sums needed to finance and direct national police and military forces (for example, to finance a navy and air force in the Mediterranean Sea and Persian Gulf). Even the supergiants are not rich or willing enough to use their profits on such activities on the global scale on which their businesses are spread. Nor is it reasonable to expect competing financial groups (conflicted between the need to support a common interest and the perpetual pressure to get an advantage over rivals) to reach agreement on how to maintain security and stability in the absence of a state to knock heads together. The dependence on force as the bedrock of business enterprise acts to strengthen, not weaken, the nation state.

2. It is important to keep in mind that almost all the multinationals are in fact *national* organizations operating on a global scale. We are in no way denying that capitalism is, and has from its very beginning been, a world system, or that this system has been further integrated by the multinationals. But just as it is essential to understand, and analyze, capitalism as a world system, it is equally necessary to recognize that each capitalist firm relates to the world system through, and must eventually rely on, the nation state. Thus, the decisive owners and the headquarters of the multinationals are located in one of the metropolitan centers, and dividends are paid in the currency of that center. No matter how

profitable the widespread and integrated foreign affiliates are, their profits have little meaning to owners unless these profits are more or less freely convertible at an advantageous rate in the home country's money. And this assurance can hardly be provided by a council of international firms, for these matters are the product of a multitude of economic activities over which the corporations can have little control. Moreover, there is little reason to expect that the leaders of the multinationals of different countries could reach an amicable agreement on exchange rates, since there is no objective standard of equity. Quite the contrary, an exchange rate that will benefit one nation's economy and its business community will likewise disadvantage another. Foreign monetary exchange relations are therefore focal points of power struggle; and because of the complexity and diversity of international money transactions they require the active participation of states. Having conflicting interests among themselves in domestic as well as overseas economics, the multinationals are in no position to dictate the terms of the battle over foreign exchange. In fact, neither is there a state that can now dictate in the area of foreign exchange. What the multinationals of each nation expect, and demand, is that the state operate as effectively as possible to represent their common interests in protecting the currency in which their profits are ultimately distributed.

3. The more multinationals struggle among themselves for market control, the more they need and rely on active support of the state. As noted above, funds and direct intervention of the state are called for to back up domestic corporations whose stability is threatened by entrance of larger and stronger foreign competitors. Furthermore, rich as these giants are, they nevertheless depend extensively on government support through subsidies for research and development, government purchases of goods and services (notably for the military), and so on. Finally, the giants are far from all-powerful financially. They are subject to the vicissitudes of the market, the perils of speculation, overextension of credit, and other business risks. Even the seemingly strong-

est of the banks, manufacturers, and public utilities must face the possibility of bankruptcy in critical circumstances. Here again, in the final analysis, they count on the rescue operations by the state, not only because of their influence on the state, but also because the state needs them to keep the economy on an even keel. (The above reasons apply equally to joint ventures and other alliances by firms of different nations. In these situations each participating firm still expects to be paid eventually, in its own national currency, and to rely on its nation state in the event of extreme difficulties.)

Nation State Sovereignty

If, as we maintain, the nation states of the advanced capitalist areas are becoming more rather than less important for the well-being of the multinationals, what are we to make of the widespread claims that these firms are whittling away the sovereignty of the state? Obviously, this question needs to be put separately for the advanced and underdeveloped capitalist nations. With regard to the advanced countries, the argument is made that the operations of the multinationals in parent as well as host country are harmful to the national interests of both insofar as these activities limit each state's ability to keep employment high, maintain a sound currency, and otherwise control the economy for the common good. There are two aspects to this proposition: the definition of national interest, and the ability of the state to contol the economy.

What is meant by the national interest? The concept is more or less identifiable when a nation is occupied or indirectly oppressed by a foreign power. In the absence of a palpable common enemy, however, the delineation of the national interest is not so clear-cut. This is especially so if the interests of different classes or sectors of a nation's population are antagonistic to each other. And antagonistic they must be except in an egalitarian society or one working towards such a goal. For when resources are limited, the more one sector of the population gets in the way of assets and income, the less will go to the others. (This fundamental conflict of interest exists at all times, even when the distributable pie is growing.) How resources are distributed depends ultimately on the socioeconomic structure and accordingly on which class owns and controls the bulk of the nation's resources. Under such circumstances, the national interest, no matter how clothed in the ideology of the times, boils down to providing the best environment for the arrived-at socioeconomic structure. Various types of compromise are reached among the classes and among diverse groups within the dominant class, but how far such compromises can go is itself limited by the constraints of the economic structure and limited resources. Because of these constraints, the national interest becomes equated with the interests of those individuals and institutions who, by virtue of their ownership of the decisive wealth of the community, direct and regulate the allocation of economic resources. From this angle, as the multinationals become the dominant form of business enterprise, the national interest, as long as the capitalist system is operative, is to protect these organizations. As Professor Robert B. Stobaugh of the Harvard Business School put it: "To an important extent, the economic health of the United States depends upon the economic health of its multinational enterprises."[15] Since the success of the state rests on the success of its economy, there is at bottom no contradiction between the national interest and the multinationals: the global corporations need the support of their state and the state needs prosperous multinationals.

The above point may seem to apply only to the parent country and not necessarily to a host country, such as a Western European nation, where key industries are in danger of being dominated by foreign enterprise. But here too the national interest assumes the form of supporting an environment best suited to the needs of an economic structure whose engine is fueled by expanding giant enterprises. The struggle among these giants, whether of foreign or domestic origin, must be conducted in accord with the rules of the game. Even in the face of setbacks, it is still in the interests of the host states whose economies are based on monopoly capital to maintain an environment where such battles can take place. Two other factors help keep the door open in Western Europe for U.S. enterprise: (1) the role of the U.S. military in stabilizing the Third World and the trade and investment activities of enterprises based in all the advanced capitalist nations, and (2) the huge float of U.S. dollar liabilities in European markets, the product of U.S. hegemony during the first two postwar decades. There are, to be sure, many sources of friction in these pressure areas just as there are in the competitive struggles of the multinationals. The road is far from smooth and contains many detours, as for example in the recent energy crisis and in the threat of a future world economic depression. But the tensions are best understood within the context of the laws of motion of imperialism rather than in terms of a mystifying abstraction like the national interest.

We come now to the second component of the argument over the decline of state sovereignty: the weakening of the state's capacity to control its interest rates, fiscal policies, and money supply for the commonwealth. Underlying this train of thought is a model of a self-contained economy which can be regulated to keep the economy going at full employment and at a steady rate of growth. Neither of the two aspects of this model is realistic. First, the advanced capitalist nations were never self-contained; they were always part of a world economy, and their strengths and weaknesses were always tied to the financial and industrial problems of operating in world markets. As we have seen, the growth of the multinational corporations is merely the latest emanation of the restless accumulation of capital and the innate drift towards greater concentration and centralization of capital. Second, much of the thinking about the self-regulating potential of government economic intervention is illusory. Whatever limited use the Keynesian tool kit may have, it should surely be evident in these inflationary times that the tools are self-limiting; their effectiveness tends to peter out. Moreover, whatever success government policies do have comes from maintaining or restoring the health of the economy via promoting the power of the giant firms, for without the prosperity of these firms the economy can only go downhill. The basic reasons for the impotence of governments to maintain their economies on an even keel are to be found in the limits and contradictions of monopoly capitalism. In other words, the problems arise not from the evils of the multinationals or the presumed diminution of the sovereignty of the advanced industrial nation states; the problems are inherent in the nature of a capitalist society.

Multinationals in the Third World

Where the issue of state sovereignty does assume significance is in the underdeveloped nations. Typically, the balance of economic and financial power in most of the Third World is unequivocally in favor of the multinational firms. So much so that an adverse action of the latter, whether deliberate or arising out of impersonal market forces, can critically affect the whole economy, reducing employment levels, living standards, and export volume, as well as necessitating currency devaluations. But even though in today's environment the multinationals embody the essence of foreign domination, they are not, in our opinion, the only or even the most important determinant of underdevelopment in the Third World. The problem of state sovereignty goes deeper and involves not only countries where the influence of foreign investment is overwhelming, but also those underdeveloped areas where the operations of foreign investment are not necessarily decisive. What really makes the difference in the Third World is that these countries, under the sway of a long history of colonialism and semicolonialism, have evolved a mode of production, a class structure, and a social, psychological, and cultural milieu that are subservient to the metropolitan centers. So long as these conditions prevail, even the removal of the multinationals would not basically change either the sovereignty or the underdevelopment question. In the absence of a fundamental change in economic and class structure, the dependency of these economies, and hence their states also, would sooner or later reassert itself after the nationalization or withdrawal of the multinationals. The reason is that their economic structure, the nature of their international trade, and their wage-and-price relations are all geared to reproduce, through the ordinary processes of the market place, the subordinate condition of these societies.

In marked contrast with this view, the mainstream of Western thought is concerned with how the underdeveloped world can get out of its rut while more or less maintaining the existing socioeconomic structure. In this context, there is much talk about social reforms, accompanied by imaginative economic analysis and advice. But common to all orthodox economic thinking—indeed the kernel of its prescriptions—is reliance on a sufficient injection of just two ingredients: capital (money) and technology. It is therefore argued that even if the multinationals have many undesirable features (repression of sovereignty, distortion of resource allocation, and so forth), they are a necessary evil, for they are the bearers of the money and the Promethean fire that will ultimately set the Third World free.

If there is any validity to this doctrine, it could only be with respect to technology. It is time that the myth about the money-capital contributions of foreign enterprise is put to rest. For the facts on this are crystal clear. First, a substantial portion of the financing of multinationals in the Third World is raised in the host country itself, by loans from local sources and by using part of the profits and depreciation reserves generated within the host country. Second, the aggregate flow of capital *out of* the host country to pay dividends, interest, royalties, and management fees (even forgetting hidden transfers due to overpricing of goods shipped from the parent companies to their affiliates) is in excess of the flow of capital *into* the host countries. In other words the operations of the multinationals, whatever other benefits they may bring, result in a new flow of capital from the underdeveloped to the developed nations.

It is true that the activities of the multinationals, especially those engaged in extractive industries, often contribute to a significant expansion of exports by Third World countries. However, these rising exports are generally offset by (1) rising imports needed to operate and expand the new enterprises and to supply the higher consumption standards of foreign technicians and those nationals who get some of the gravy, and (2) the outflow of foreign exchange reserves for the payment of profits, and so on, to foreign investors. These offsets to rising exports usually limit the ability of the host country to import capital goods, and they thus become even more dependent on foreign investment for their capital goods demand. This condition changes, of course, when host countries take over foreign-owned industry, or, as in the case of the oil-exporting nations, are able to exercise control over the price of their exports.

The question of technology transfer, on the other hand, does touch a vital spot. While real development presumes a wide variety of social and economic changes, there is no doubt that the *sine qua non* of any meaningful progress is a major increase in the output of goods and services. And the extent to which production can advance depends on bringing as much of the population as possible into useful productive activity on the one hand, and increasing the productivity of the employed on the other. The latter requires a stepped-up increase in the use of science and machinery (including improved methods of organization of production).

Taking account of these elementary truths, the advocates of the need for foreign investment build their case on the following assumptions: (1) the science and technology of the industrialized nations can only—or, if not only, most efficiently—be transferred by foreign investors who have a profit incentive to do so, and (2) the multinationals are best suited to bring in the needed technology. The first assumption has been proven false by history. Japan, the Soviet Union, North Korea, and China have all demonstrated that an underdeveloped country can speedily (as compared with the most successful industrial nations) obtain, exploit, and adapt modern science and technology without dependence on foreign investment. (To the extent that these countries obtained limited foreign technical assistance from foreign capitalists, it was done with contracts for a specific planned undertaking initiated by the host country, and it excluded long-term or perpetual ownership and profit-taking by foreign entrepreneurs.)

Subsumed in the second assumption is again a crude technological determinism, with overtones of vulgar and distorted Marxism: the belief that technological progress as such is the most powerful driving force of social development, plus a corollary that the most modern technology will inevitably produce the most modern and progressive society. One need not dispute the crucial role of technology to find fault with these oversimplifications. First, it should be recognized that new science and technology will not automatically produce conforming social changes. A social agent is needed for social change: specifically, a class that has both a vital interest in pursuing and utilizing a particular type of innovation, and the will and power to implement this interest. In the absence of such an agent and the proper environment in which it can flex its muscles, the best of science and technology may lie fallow. Second, a distinction needs to be made between past technological change and the fruits of capitalism. In general, the state of the technical arts at each stage of social development determines both the potential and the limits of production. Looking broadly at the long stretch of history prior to capitalism, the "limits" were more important than the "potential." Thus the standard of living of the vast majority of the world's population through almost all of human history was necessarily severely restricted despite the many revolutionary advances in production and transportation. While one can speculate on how much better past societies might have been with better organization of economic activity or with a more equitable distribution of output, the basic reality remains that even with the best will and the most altruistic of rulers, the people's living conditions would not have been altered significantly: the constraints on the production potential imposed by the available knowledge and tools were too severe.

With the industrial revolutions of capitalism, however, the situation changed dramatically. A body of scientific and technological information (not to mention tools and the ability to reproduce the tools on an expanding scale) has been generated which opens up entirely new horizons for the living standards of the people of the world. Limits are clearly and most decidedly present, as no doubt there always will be. The difference today is that the "potential" carries more weight than the "limits": the room for choice has been vastly enlarged. In contrast with the past, when certain types of social development were circumscribed by barriers of knowledge, the limits imposed by the prevailing technical arts are of lesser importance. Society can, if it wishes, select from a wide variety of technologies, with many more degrees of freedom in the choice of priorities. Thus, even though technology still imposes certain limits and restricts the range of choice, what is most important today—in fact, decisive—is the agent of change: who is in charge and for what purpose?

This is the context in which the role of the multinationals as the bearers of modern technology should, in our opinion, be viewed. If the existing class structures in the Third World are to be more or less maintained, if production is to be geared to meeting the effective demand of the top income groups, and if the trickle-down doctrine of economic orthodoxy is to be the reigning rationale—then by all means, the multinationals are doing a necessary and useful job. One might insist, as do so many liberals, that the claws of the multinationals be trimmed and their greed curbed somewhat. But if what is wanted is a technology that will meet the consumer needs of the upper strata, then it is reasonable to expect that on the whole the multinationals will supply in the speediest and most efficacious fashion what the existing host society and its entrepreneurs find impossible to do by themselves. In thus meeting the needs of such Third World countries, the multinationals will select the most suitable way of producing the required goods at the lowest cost (consistent with the special outlays the oligopolists must make to maintain their management and marketing structures). Moreover, this transfer of technology will also multiply opportunities for local elites to enrich themselves. If this gravy is insufficient for the native ruling classes, new sources of profit and capital accumulation can be stimulated by enlarging participation in international trade. And for this the multinationals are also the best bet: their knowledge and influence are invaluable. To widen the scope of international trade for the Third World and its profit-taking classes, the multinationals can be relied on to choose and introduce the best technology and industrial organization for the most effective use of a valuable Third World "asset": its depressed living standards and the accompanying exceedingly low wages. But while recognizing the real and potential contributions of the multinationals in transferring modern technology for these purposes, it should equally be understood that the sectors of advanced industry thereby created will coexist with the traditional miserable living conditions of the bulk of the Third World's population.

Let us suppose, on the other hand, that there is a totally different class structure in the Third World, that the property-owning classes who obstruct social progress have been removed from power, and that the new ruling class (or alliance of classes) insists on an opposite set of priorities, as for example giving first and absolute precedence to improving the lot of the impoverished majority by eliminating hunger and epidemic diseases, raising housing and clothing standards, bringing medical services to the poor and dispersed, introducing education and cultural opportunities for the masses, and so on. The science and technology to achieve these goals exist. This, however, is not the technology that the multinationals have to offer; these firms are not suited to select the most appropriate technology.

The multinationals do, of course, have a great store of talent and experience which could be put to use in countries operating with a relatively primitive technology. Thus, a few of the large corporations have been experimenting with the mass production of items that are especially adapted for wide use in the less technically advanced countries. However, flexible as these firms may be, their ingenuity and enterprise are necessarily confined to production and marketing items that meet each company's profit objective. And the profit goal is precisely what stands in the way of the multinational devoting itself to the most urgent priorities: the basic needs of the most impoverished masses in the Third World—the poor peasants, the rural and urban unemployed, and the working class.

Before considering the sort of industrial arts needed, we should recall that there are two components of the task of increasing national output: full and nonwasteful use of the labor supply, and increasing labor productivity. Under the first heading the multinationals, to say the least, have nothing to offer. What is needed, if the most urgent priorities are heeded, is a mobilization of the people to lay the groundwork for improving agriculture and health: to undertake water conservancy projects, provide irrigation networks, dig latrines and sewer systems, create roads and canals, innoculate the population against epidemic diseases, install rural electrification, and so on. It is true that modern earth-moving and other machinery could be very helpful, and surely more efficient than hand tools and crude equipment in completing most of these tasks. But the jobs won't get done by waiting and hoping for the best technology, for poor countries haven't the resources to pay for or to manufacture enough of the needed equipment for the amount of work involved in laying the basis for eliminating hunger and reducing disease.

When it comes to the most urgent technologies needed to raise labor productivity and increase agricultural yields, again we find that the multinationals have little to offer. What is most urgently required is not sophisticated electronics or mass production of automobiles or washing machines. Much more pressing is a need for carts, wheelbarrows, and bicycles in vast numbers to replace the movement of goods on head or shoulder; enough cement to waterproof linings of irrigation works, drainage, and silos; pumps, pipes, and sprinkling apparatus for irrigation; supplying the farm population with simple hand and mechanical devices for plowing, weeding, and threshing; and so on. In addition, the standards of industrial organization and efficiency would differ radically from those of the multinationals. Thus the remedy for rural unemployment requires small-sized and diversified manufacturing plants which would be anathema to the cost and profit calculations of big business.

It is not our purpose to outline a plan of development or to deny the desirability and necessity to learn from and borrow the most modern technology available. The intention is simply to insist that the order of precedence in the choice of technologies, their adaptation and mix, will differ depending on the social goals and on which classes have the power to determine priorities. And outstanding among the priorities of a society seeking to solve the most urgent problems of poverty and technical backwardness is for *themselves* to become masters of the industrial and agricultural arts so that they, and not others, may choose and adapt the technology they deem most important, including, when needed, the most complex modern industries. For this, a complete change in social power and social psychology is called for: to throw off the yoke of subservience to Western technology and culture; to develop self-confidence; to spread respect for, and education in, science, mathematics, and engineering; and to generate in the lowliest peasant the urge to experiment. Such a transformation cannot be ordained from above, it cannot be imported. It can only come through the experience gained in the process of becoming self-reliant, as the mass of the working people in field and factory learn—by doing—to care for and repair machinery, as large numbers of workers and farmers become master mechanics, and as indigenous design and engineering capabilities are aimed for and attained. If ever an adage made sense, it certainly does for the underdeveloped nations: "God helps those who help themselves."

Notes

1. Karl Marx, *Capital* (Moscow: Progress Publishers, 1957), vol. 1, p. 555.
2. Ibid., vol. I, p. 558.
3. Ibid., vol. I, pp. 585-88.
4. Ibid., vol. III, p. 110.
5. Ibid., vol. III, pp. 332-33. Note also Marx's evaluation of the inner drive to world operation in capitalism (*Grundrisse* [New York: Vintage, 1973], pp. 308-408), as he explains why "The tendency to create the *world market* is directly given in the concept of capital itself."
6. While this monopoly phase came into full blossom after Marx's time, he sensed the significance of its early sprouts. An interesting example is found in his discussion of the impact of price fluctuations in the process of circulation:

   > ... the greater disturbances the greater the money-capital which the industrial capitalist must possess to tide over the period of readjustment; and as the scale of each individual process of production and with it the minimum size of the capital to be advanced increases in the process of capitalist production, we have here another circumstance to be added to those others which transform the function of the industrial capitalist more and more into a monopoly of big money-capitalists, who may operate singly or in association. (Karl Marx, *Capital*, vol. II [Moscow: Progress Publishers, 1956], p. 110)

7. It should be noted that loans to industries (and portfolio investments) at times were as effective as direct investment, in so far as the lenders influenced and controlled production and marketing operations. And there was, of course, a growing amount of direct investment in extractive and manufacturing industries. But on the whole, the composition of transnational capital migration differed significantly before and after the age of the multinationals. For earlier patterns of capital exports, see Herbert Feis, *Europe, the World's Banker, 1870-1914* (New Haven: Yale University Press, 1931). And for still earlier developments, see Leland H. Jenks, *The Migration of British Capital to 1875* (New York: Alfred A. Knopf, 1927).
8. The estimates of foreign investments in 1910 and 1930, given in the preceding paragraphs, are from Williams Woodruff, *Impact of Western Man* (London: Macmillan, 1966), p. 150. The data on

1970 and changes since 1966 are from United Nations, *Multinational Corporations in World Development* (New York: United Nations, 1973), pp. 139, 146.

9. U.S. Bureau of the Census, *Statistical Abstract of the United States: 1973* (Washington, D.C.: U.S. Supt. of Documents, 1973), pp. 522-23.

10. United Nations, *Multinational Corporations in World Development* p. 159.

11. Ibid., p. 7.

12. Ibid., p. 12.

13. Ibid., p. 190.

14. F. G. Donner, *The World-Wide Industrial Enterprise* (New York: McGraw Hill, 1967), pp. 35-36.

15. *Wall Street Journal*, June 6, 1973. Prof. Stobaugh conducted the U.S. Department of Commerce Study, "Multinational Enterprises and the U.S. Economy."

7

Militarism
and Imperialism

Peace reigns supreme in the realm of neoclassical economics. War, militarism, and the pacification of natives are treated as merely elements which disturb the harmonious equilibrium models which are to supply us with the universal truths about the allocation of scarce resources.

One of the distinguishing features of Marxist thought, on the other hand, is the conviction that economic processes must be understood as part of a social organism in which political force plays a leading role and in which war is at least as typical as peace. In this context, militarism and imperialism are seen as major determinants of the form and direction of technological change, of the allocation of resources within a country, and of the allocation of resources between countries (notably, between rich and poor countries). Accordingly, price and income relations, treated as the ultimate yardsticks of economic efficiency and social justice in neoclassical economics, are viewed, in the Marxist context, as evolutionary products of capitalist institutions in which polit-

This was originally a paper delivered at a session on the Economics of Imperialism at the annual meeting of the American Economic Association, December 30, 1969. It subsequently appeared in the February 1970 issue of *Monthly Review*.

ical force and "pure" economics are intertwined. Rosa Luxemburg put the Marxist case this way:

> Bourgeois liberal theory takes into account only [one aspect of economic development]: the realm of "peaceful competition," the marvels of technology and pure commodity exchange; it separates it strictly from the other aspect: the realm of capital's blustering violence which is regarded as more or less incidental to foreign policy and quite independent of the economic sphere of capital.
>
> In reality, political power is nothing but a vehicle for the economic process. The conditions for the reproduction of capital provide the organic link between these two aspects of the accumulation of capital. The historical career of capitalism can be appreciated only by taking them together.[1]

The facts of U.S. history provide eloquent testimony to the accuracy of this diagnosis. Thus, Professor Quincy Wright, who directed a major study of war under the auspices of Chicago University, observed in 1942: "The United States, which has, perhaps somewhat unjustifiably, prided itself on its peacefulness, has had only twenty years during its entire history when its army or navy has not been in active operation some days, somewhere."[2]

Professor Wright identifies years of peace as those in which no action of any sort occurred. A more revealing picture is obtained if we measure months of war against months of peace and bring the information up to the present. Adding up the months during which U.S. military forces were engaged in action—starting from the Revolutionary War and including wars against the Indians, punitive expeditions to Latin America and Asia, as well as major wars—we find that the United States was engaged in warlike activity during three-fourths of its history, in 1,782 of the last 2,340 months.[3] In other words, on the average, there have been three full years in which our armed forces have been engaged in action for every full year of peace. This comparison does not indicate the full extent of the use of military power by the United States to enforce its will. For example, it does not include activities such as those formerly conducted by U.S. gunboats in a "constant patrol in the Yangtze River ... from the mouth of the river up nearly 2,000 miles into the very heart of China."[4]

It should therefore come as no surprise to discover that war-related expenditures have constituted the dominant sector of the federal budget throughout our history. Omitting the years of World War II and the postwar period, where the record is so well known, a tabulation of federal expenditures by decade, from 1800 to 1939, for army, navy, veterans' compensation and pensions, and interest on the debt (prior to the New Deal federal debt incurred was primarily a result of war spending) shows that except for one decade, at least 54 percent of federal expenditures were for military activities or preparations during the decade or to meet obligations arising from previous military activity.[5] The one exception was the decade of the Great Depression (1930-1939) when the percentage dropped to somewhat below 40 percent. In seven of the fourteen decades the war-related share of the federal budget was 70 percent or more.

This almost continuous preoccupation with military affairs was clearly not inspired by fears of invading barbarians. Of course, the competing colonial and commercial interests of France, England, Spain, and Russia were part of the reality in which the infant and adolescent United States had to operate. At times, self-defense had to be considered. Moreover, resolution of internal tensions, as in the Civil War, exercised a major influence on military aspects of U.S. life. All of this, however, occurred within a context of empire-building. For there has been a continuous thread in U.S. history, beginning with colonial and revolutionary days, of economic, political, and military expansionism directed towards the creation and growth of an American empire. The original expansionism, for which military investment was needed, concentrated on three main thrusts: (1) consolidation of a transcontinental nation; (2) obtaining control of the Caribbean area; and (3) achieving a major position in the Pacific Ocean.[6] It should be noted that this expansionism was not confined to what is now considered the continental territory of the United

States: striving for control of the seas, as a shield and pro-
moter of international commerce, has been an ingredient of
U.S. policy from its earliest days. In fact, the struggle to
incorporate the West Coast into the United States was,
among other things, prompted by the desire to control
Pacific Ocean ports for the Asian trade.[7]

The experience thus gained in the early stages of empire-
building turned out to be most useful when the leading
nations of the world entered the stage of imperialism. Several
decisive and coinciding developments in the late nineteenth
and early twentieth centuries mark off this new stage:

1. The onset of significant concentration of economic
power in the hands of a relatively small number of industrial
and financial giants in advanced nations. Competing interest-
groups continued to exist, but now the success or failure of
the advanced economies became closely identified with the
prosperity of the new giant corporations whose modus operandi required control over international sources of supply
and markets.

2. The decline of Great Britain's monopoly position as
world trader and world banker. The burgeoning competitive
industrial powers—notably, Germany, France, the United
States, and Japan—pressed for a reshuffle of established trade
relations and a redistribution of world markets.

3. Industrialization and new naval technology enabled
competitive nations to build up their own naval strength to
the point where Great Britain could no longer maintain
unilateral control over the major sea lanes. As Quincy Wright
put it in the study already referred to, "Naval inventions and
the spread of industrialization had ended the *pax Britannica.*"[8] Control over sea routes also involved establishing
military bases where naval units could be refueled and repaired. The availability of decisive mobile military power
on the one hand required acquisition of strategic foreign
territory to support bases, and on the other hand provided
the means for aggressive pursuit of colonial possessions.

4. The earliest stage of the new imperialism engendered a
race by the major powers for control of available foreign real

estate. According to Theodore Ropp, after 1880 "every great power except Austria-Hungary . . . became involved in . . . active, conscious colonial expansionism. . . ."[9] Of the traditional colonial powers—the Netherlands, Portugal, Spain, Britain, France, and Russia—the last four continued to add to their holdings. (Spain, after losing Cuba and the Philippines, proceeded to conquer Spanish Morocco.) And, at the same time, five new powers entered the race for colonial territory: Germany, Italy, Belgium, Japan, and the United States. As for the United States, it was the Spanish-American War, of course, that placed it with both feet in the imperialist camp. And it was success in this war, plus the subsequent pacification of the Cuban and Philippine "natives," which satisfied two long-term U.S. expansionist ambitions: a leading position in the Caribbean, broadening the highway to the rest of Latin America, and a solid base in the Pacific for a greater stake in Asian affairs.

As far as the United States is concerned, there have been three distinct stages in the drive to empire: (1) the period when the United States was the supplier of food and raw materials to the rest of the world, when it was an importer of capital, and when maritime commercial interests were relatively very strong; (2) the period when the United States began to compete with other industrialized nations as an exporter of manufactured goods and an exporter of capital—a time when a small number of industrial and financial gaints began to dominate the economic scene; and (3) the period when the United States becomes the major, dominant capitalist economy, the largest manufacturer, foreign investor, trader, the world's banker, and the dollar becomes the key international currency.

The energy and determination with which the expansionist strategy is pursued change from time to time. In the transition from one period to another, and because of internal as well as external conditions, it appears at times as if the United States is "isolationist" and uninterested in further extension of its influence and control.[10] Yet it is especially noteworthy that the drive for business opportunities on a world scale is ever present. Even when, as in New Deal days, domestic solutions were sought for crises, the development of foreign business was high on the agenda of government and private enterprise. Given the structure of the economy, the major operating levers work in such a way as to repeatedly reassert expansionism as the dominant strategy. In this perspective, the history of the years since the end of World War II is far from a new departure; instead, it is a culmination of long-term tendencies which profited by, and matured most readily in, the environment created by the course of the last major war.

The postwar leap forward in empire-building and the transition of U.S. society to rampant militarism are associated with two phenomena: (1) the desire to resist and repress socialist nations and to defeat national liberation movements designed to release underdeveloped countries from dependence on the imperialist network, and (2) the extension of U.S. power to fill "vacuums" created by the decline of Western European and Japanese influence in Asia, Africa, and Latin America.

Combating the rise of socialism is, of course, not a new objective. The destruction of the Russian Revolution was a top priority of the imperialist powers beginning in 1917. In this connection, Thorstein Veblen's observations on the Versailles Treaty in his 1920 review of Keynes's *The Economic Consequences of the Peace* are most pertinent:

> The events of the past months go to show that the central and most binding provision of the Treaty (and of the League) is an unrecorded clause by which the governments of the Great Powers are banded together for the suppression of Soviet Russia— unrecorded unless record of it is to be found somewhere among the secret archives of the League or of the Great Powers. Apart from this unacknowledged compact there appears to be nothing in the Treaty that has any character of stability or binding force. Of course, this compact for the reduction of Soviet Russia was not written into the text of the Treaty; it may rather be said to have been the parchment upon which the text was written.[11]

The failure of the United States to join the League of

Nations reflected no slackness in its efforts to contain anti-imperialist revolutions: in Russia, these efforts took the form of armed intervention and support of anti-Bolshevik forces with food and other economic supplies; in Hungary, the manipulation of food supplies to help defeat the Bela Kun government. Surely the issue at that time was not fear of aggressive Russian or Hungarian militarism. Nor can much credit be given to political or religious idealism. The relevant motive, clearly, was recovery of territory lost to free enterprise and prevention of the spread of the contagious revolutionary disease to Western Europe and the colonies. Any such spread, it was recognized, would severly affect the stability and prosperity of the remaining capitalist nations.

Capitalism as an economic system was never confined to one nation. It was born, developed, and prospered as part of a world system. Karl Marx went so far as to claim, "The specific task of bourgeois society is the establishment of a world market, at least in outline, and of production based upon this world market."[12] One might add that it has been the specific task of imperialism to fill out this outline and establish a complex international network of trade, finance, and investment. Given this network, it follows that limitation of opportunity to trade and invest in one part of the world restricts to a greater or lesser extent the freedom of action of private enterprise in other parts of the world. The dimensions of the defense of free enterprise therefore become worldwide.

The United States had long ago accepted its destiny to open and keep open the door for trade and investment in other parts of the world. The obstacles were not only the heathens who wanted to be left alone, but the preference systems established in the colonies of the older nations. The decline of political colonialism and the weakness of the other great powers thus placed upon the United States a primary responsibility for the defense of the capitalist system and at the same time afforded golden opportunities to obtain special beachheads and open doors for U.S. enterprise.

With a task of this magnitude, it is little wonder that the

United States now has a larger "peacetime" war machine, covering a greater part of the globe, than has any other nation in all of past history. Imperialism necessarily involves militarism. Indeed, they are twins that have fed on each other in the past, as they do now. Yet not even at the peak of the struggle for colonies did any of the imperialist powers, or combination of powers, maintain a war machine of such size and such dispersion as does the United States today. In 1937, when the arms race in preparation for World War II was already under way, the per capita military expenditures of all the great powers combined—the United States, the British Empire, France, Japan, Germany, Italy, and the Soviet Union—was $25. (Germany's per capita of $58.82 was then the largest.)[13] In 1968, the per capita military expenditures of the United States alone, in 1937 prices, was $132. This was only in part due to the Vietnam War: in 1964, our most recent "peace" year, the per capita military expenditures in 1937 prices was $103.[14]

One of the reasons for this huge increase in military outlays is no doubt the greater sophistication of weaponry. (By the same token, it is the advanced airplane and missile technology which makes feasible the U.S. globe-straddling military posture.) An additional reason, of course, is the military strength of the socialist camp. I would like to suggest a third reason: that a substantial portion of the huge military machine, including that of the Western European nations, is the price being paid to maintain the imperialist network of trade and investment *in the absence of colonialism.* The achievement of political independence by former colonies has stimulated internal class struggles in the new states for economic as well as political independence. Continuing the economic dependence of these nations on the metropolitan centers within the framework of political independence calls for, among other things, the worldwide dispersion of U.S. military forces and the direct military support of the local ruling classes.

Precise information on the dispersion of U.S. forces is kept an official secret. However, retired General David M. Shoup, former head of the marine corps, who should be in a position to make a realistic estimate, stated in a recent article in *The Atlantic:* "We maintain more than 1,517,000 Americans in uniform overseas in 119 countries. We have 8 treaties to help defend 48 nations if they ask us to or if we choose to intervene in their affairs."[15] The main substance of U.S. overseas power, aside from its present application in Vietnam, is spread out over 429 major and 2,972 minor military bases. These bases cover 4,000 square miles in 30 foreign countries, as well as Hawaii and Alaska.[16] Backing this up, and acting as a coordinator of the lesser imperialist powers and the Third World incorporated in the imperialist network, is a massive program of military assistance. According to a recent study,

> U.S. military aid ... since 1945 has averaged more than $2 billion per year. It rose to as much as $5 billion in fiscal year (FY) 1952 and fell to as low as $831 million in FY 1956. The number of recipient countries rose from 14 in 1950 to a peak so far of 69 in 1963. In all, some 80 countries have received a total of $50 billion in American military aid since World War II. Except for 11 hard-core communist countries and certain nations tied closely to either Britain or France, very few nations have never received military aid of one kind or another from the United States.[17]

The above factual recital by no means exhausts the international functions of U.S. militarism. Space considerations permit no more than passing reference to (1) the active promotion of commercial armament sales abroad (contributing a sizable portion of the merchandise export surplus in recent years); (2) the extensive training of foreign military personnel; and (3) the use of economic-aid funds to train local police forces for "handling mob demonstrations and counterintelligence work."[18] These are, in the main, additional instruments for maintaining adherence and loyalty of the nonsocialist world to the free-enterprise system in general, and to the United States in particular.

The military forces of the politically independent underdeveloped countries frequently perform a very special function. This arises from the relative weaknesses of the competitive elite power groups: large landowners, merchants, industrialists, and financiers—each with varying degrees of alliance to interest groups in the metropolitan center. When none of these ruling-class groups has the strength and resources to take the political reins in its hands and assert its hegemony over the others, the social order is operated by means of temporary and unstable alliances. Under such circumstances, and especially when the existing order is threatened by social revolution, the military organizations become increasingly important as a focal point for the power struggle within the ruling classes and/or as the organizer of political arrangements. Space limitations do not permit a review of this special role of militarism in the underdeveloped world as, one might say, the skeletal framework of the imperialist system in the absence of colonies. It is this framework that is supported and nurtured by the practices mentioned above: military training and advisory services, the widespread military assistance programs, and the stimulus given to commercial sales of U.S. armaments.

This militarism which is working to control the rest of the world is at the same time helping to shape the nature of U.S. society. Some sense of the immensity of this impact can be obtained by noting the relevance of military spending on the employment/unemployment situation. In the first three quarters of 1969, approximately 8.3 million persons were employed as a result of the military program: 3.5 million in the armed services, 1.3 million Defense Department civilian employees, and 3.5 million engaged in producing and moving the goods purchased for the military services.[19] At the same time, there are at least 3.7 million unemployed.[20]

Consider for a moment what it would mean if 8.3 million were not engaged in military affairs. Without substitute employment, this could mean a total of over 12 million unemployed, or a 14.3 percent rate of unemployment. The last time the United States had such a rate of unemployment was 1937. The percentage of the labor force unemployed in 1931, the second full year of the Great Depression, was less than 2 points higher, 15.9 percent.[21]

So far we have not taken into account the multiplier effect. It has been estimated that for every $1 spent on national defense, another $1 to $1.40 of national product is stimulated.[22] If we accept only the lower estimate, and assume for the sake of the argument equivalent labor productivity in the military and civilian sectors, we reach a measure of unemployment in the neighborhood of 24.3 percent, in the absence of the military budget. Compare this with the unemployment rate of 24.9 percent at the depth of the depression in 1932.

A counter argument can, of course, be made to these broad generalizations. Unemployment insurance, for example, would to a limited extent, and for a very limited time, act as an offset. Conceivably, a sharp decline in military spending, if there were no financial collapse accompanying it, would reduce interest rates and thus perhaps stimulate construction and some types of state and municipal investment. A reduction in taxes would generate consumer demand. A rise in the federal social welfare program would have its effect. But it is by no means obvious that these counteractions would have anywhere near the same impact on the economy as defense spending.

Economists are to a large measure captives of the neat models they create, and they consequently ignore strategic dynamic elements which keep the economy going. For example, they tend to underestimate, if not ignore, the special effects of persistent inflation on business practices regarding inventory accumulation and investment in plant and equipment. Even more important is the almost total neglect of the influence of stock market and real estate speculation on (1) business investment decisions, and (2) the buoyancy of the especially important luxury trades. Inflation and speculation —partners of militarism have been key triggers of our postwar prosperity, and they are too easily ignored as economists blandly transfer a block of GNP from one category to another, as if such transfers are made in the economy as simply as one keeps accounts.

The experience of the last depression still remains a challenge to economists to come up with an explanation of the way in which the economy operates in reality. For example, consider where we stood in 1939 after ten years of depression. Personal consumption expenditures had finally climbed to a new high—6 percent above 1929 in constant prices. Yet, at the same time, nonresidential fixed investment expenditures were 42 percent below the level of 1929, and residential construction was 20 percent below.[23] Despite six years of rising consumer spending, and the start of orders flowing in from France and England for rearming, the investment community was still in a state of depression, and over 17 percent of the labor force was unemployed.

In this connection, it is important to recognize that one of the major attributes of the huge military spending in the postwar years is its concentration in the producers durable field and the stimulation it gives to the demand for machinery and equipment. If we combine the spending for producers durable goods resulting from the military with private spending for the same type of goods, we find the following: 36 percent of the output of the producers durable goods industries is purchased directly or indirectly by the federal government.[24] (These data are for 1963, before the impact of the Vietnam War.) It is here, I suggest, that we find the unique role of military spending in raising and sustaining production and employment at new highs.

There are, to be sure, other impacts of defense spending that help to explain the magnitude and structure of the postwar economy: the unique role of research stimulated and financed by military and space programs; the special place of defense spending in nurturing the growth and prosperity of key giant industrial and financial enterprises; the support given by U.S. military power to acceptance of the U.S. dollar as an international currency;[25] the ease with which military orders can be fed into the economy in spurts which act as adrenalin injections to the private sector.

At the least, it can be concluded, economic theory and analysis which omit imperialism and militarism from their underlying paradigm are far removed from the reality of today's world. More realistically, it can be said that they operate to obscure the truth about the great problems and dangers of the second half of the twentieth century.

Notes

1. Rosa Luxemburg, *The Accumulation of Capital* (New York: Monthly Review Press, 1964), pp. 452-53.
2. Quincy Wright, *A Study of War*, vol. I (Chicago: University of Chicago Press, 1942), p. 236.
3. Calculated from list in Lawrence Dennis, *Operational Thinking for Survival* (Colorado Springs: R. Myles, 1969), appendix II.
4. Office of Naval Intelligence, *The United States Navy as an Industrial Asset* (Washington, D.C.: Government Printing Office, 1923), p. 4.
5. Calculated from data in *Historical Statistics of the United States, Colonial Times to 1957* (Washington, D.C.: Government Printing Office, 1961), pp. 718-19.
6. Richard W. Van Alstyne, *The Rising American Empire* (New York: Norton, 1974).
7. Ibid., chap. 5, "Manifest Destiny and Empire, 1820-1870."
8. Quincy Wright, *A Study of War*, vol. I, p. 299.
9. Theodore Ropp, *War in the Modern World* (New York: Macmillan, 1962), p. 206.
10. The isolationism was usually more apparent than real. See William Appleman Williams, *The Tragedy of American Diplomacy*, 2nd ed. (New York: Dell, 1972), chap. 4, "The Legend of Isolationism."
11. Thorstein Veblen, "The Economic Consequences of the Peace," in *Essays in Our Changing Order* (New York: Kelley, 1934), p. 464.
12. In a letter from Marx to Engels, October 8, 1858, in Karl Marx and Friedrich Engels, *Correspondence, 1846-1895* (New York: International Publishers, 1934), p. 117.
13. Quincy Wright, *A Study of War*, pp. 670-71.
14. The data on military expenditures are the purchases of goods and services for "national defense" and "space research and technol-

ogy" as used in computing Gross National Product. The 1964 and 1968 data are reported in the *Survey of Current Business*, July 1968 and July 1969. The adjustment for price changes was made by using the implicit price deflators for federal purchases of goods and services, as given in the *Economic Report of the President*, January 1969.

15. General David M. Shoup, "The New American Militarism," *The Atlantic*, April 1969. The figure of 119 countries seems too large. General Shoup was probably including bases on island locations, which he counted as separate countries. Our guess is that U.S. armed forces to man bases, administer military assistance, and train foreign officers are located in seventy to eighty countries.

16. *New York Times*, April 9, 1969.

17. George Thayer, *The War Business: The International Trade in Armaments* (New York: Simon and Schuster, 1969), pp. 37-38. This is a summary of data presented in *Military Assistance Facts*, May 1, 1966, brought up-to-date through fiscal year 1968.

18. For (1), see ibid.; for (2), see John Dunn, *Military Aid and Military Elites: The Political Potential of American Training and Technical Assistance Programs*, unpublished Ph.D. dissertation, Princeton University, 1961; for (3), see Edwin Lieuwen, *The United States and the Challenge to Security in Latin America* (Columbus: Ohio State University Press, 1966), p. 16.

19. Data on armed services and Defense Department civilian employment from *Defense Indicators* (Bureau of the Census), November 1969. The estimate of the number employed by private industry for military production is based on Richard P. Oliver's study, "The Employment Effect of Defense Expenditures," *Monthly Labor Review*, September 1967. Mr. Oliver estimated 2.972 million employed in private industry in the fiscal year ending June 30, 1967, as a result of Defense Department expenditures. We brought this estimate up-to-date by (1) assuming no increase in productivity or major change in the composition of production since fiscal year 1967; (2) using the expenditure data for the first three quarters of 1969, (3) adding space research and technology and one-half of Atomic Energy Commission expenditures, both of which had been excluded in Mr. Oliver's estimates; and (4) adjusting for price increases in the last two years. The resulting figure of 3.5 million is therefore a broad estimate, but the margin of error is not such as in any way to invalidate our analysis.

20. Based on data in *Employment and Earnings* (Bureau of Labor

Statistics), January to November 1969. The 3.7 million estimate represents the full-time unemployed plus the full-time equivalent of those who were working involuntarily less than a full week. This estimate does not take into account the unemployed who are not counted in the government survey.

21. *Economic Report of the President,* January 1969 (Washington, D.C.: Government Printing Office, 1969), p. 252.

22. U.S. Arms Control and Disarmament Agency, *Economic Impacts of Disarmament* (Washington, D.C.: Government Printing Office, 1962).

23. *Economic Report of the President,* January 1969, p. 228.

24. Calculated from tables in "Input-Output Structure of the U.S. Economy: 1963," *Survey of Current Business,* November 1969. The percent of direct and indirect output attributable to (1) gross private fixed capital formation, and (2) federal government purchases were used. These percentages were applied to the gross output of each of the industries manufacturing durable goods. It is generally estimated that 85 percent of federal government purchases are for the military. The figure is probably higher for durable goods manufacturing industries alone.

25. Given the inadequate U.S. gold reserves, the U.S. dollar can serve as an international currency only as long as foreign banks are willing to keep dollar credit balances in the United States as a substitute for gold payments. It is interesting that former Under Secretary of the Treasury for Monetary Affairs Robert Roosa included the military strength of the United States as a factor in maintaining the present international monetary system: "Moreover, the political stability and enormous economic and military strength of the United States have also increased the desirability of keeping balances here rather than in any other country in the world" (Robert V. Roosa, *Monetary Reform for the World Economy* [Mystic, Ct.: Verry, 1965], p.9).

8

The Impact of U.S. Foreign Policy
on Underdeveloped Countries

Compressing an analysis of the impact of U.S. foreign policy on underdeveloped countries into a twenty-minute presentation must necessarily result in what may appear to be a recitation of dogmatic assertions. This will seem especially so when the position taken flies in the face of conventional wisdom and the common currency of academic discourse. Yet even though such compression involves omission of supporting evidence, steps in the reasoning process, and necessary qualifications, a digest of the main argument may nevertheless help clarify the essential differences between the radical and customary views on the subject.

The crux of my position is that there exists a fundamental clash between U.S. foreign policy and the interests of the people in the underdeveloped world. To examine the roots of this clash—of what in effect is a conflict of interest—we need first to be clear about the answers to two questions: (1) what is U.S. foreign policy? and (2) what are the major restraints on the modernization of underdeveloped nations?

The stumbling block to answering the first question is that

This paper was originally presented at a discussion series for students of political economy at American University in the fall of 1970. It subsequently appeared in the March 1971 issue of *Monthly Review*.

U.S. foreign policy may at first blush seem to be but a jumble of diverse, bumbling, and contradictory actions and programs. In fact, learned journals specializing in international affairs will at times publish lengthy articles complaining about the absence of a clear-cut foreign policy consistent, with avowed principles. But these yearners for consistency overlook, on the one hand, the variety of pressures that contribute to day-to-day policy decisions, and, on the other hand, the inevitable contrast between the ideology and ideals of foreign policy around which public opinion is mobilized, and the underlying reality.

Even though the day-to-day policy decisions are the product of numerous, and not necessarily consistent, political, military, and economic variables, and even though these decisions are made by diverse human beings, some competent and some incompetent, a clearly discernible major trend of foreign policy nevertheless does exist. We know from physics and chemistry that elements and compounds will, under certain conditions of volume, pressure, and temperature, assume different phases. But we also know that while water, for example, may under certain conditions appear as steam and under other conditions as ice, its inherent nature remains H_2O. A similar essential nature of U.S. foreign policy can be detected throughout the various phases of hot war, cold war, strident militancy, and moments of hesitation. This major drift of U.S. foreign policy has two closely related components:

1. A drive to maintain as much of this globe as possible free for private trade and private enterprise. Subsumed under this are such considerations as (a) the prevention of competitive empires from acquiring privileged trading and investment preserves to the disadvantage of U.S. business interests, and (b) wherever feasible, the attainment of a preferred trading and investment position for U.S. business.

2. The promotion of counterrevolution. This too is composed of several elements: (a) abortion of incipient social revolutions; (b) suppression of social revolutions in progress;

and (c) counterrevolution against established socialist societies—through war, economic pressure, or corruption of leaders and nations in the socialist fold.

Such a basic foreign policy is not peculiar to the United States, nor is it a policy peculiar to the post-World War II period. The conflict of interest among the advanced capitalist nations for the division and redivision of the world has been an integral part of what the textbooks call "modern history," hammered into the annals by two world wars. Nor is the nervous, military reaction to social revolutions merely a current policy aberration. It is now one hundred years since the conquering German army joined forces with the conquered French army to throttle the Paris Commune. Long before the atom bomb was developed and long before the Soviet Union could be considered an effective expansionist power, the Allied Powers at the Versailles Treaty table were plotting the destruction of the infant Bolshevik revolution. In fact, the United States along with other Allied Powers sent armed forces to join the counterrevolution against the Bolsheviks. It is within this historic context, and the even longer record of expansionism in the growth of our republic, that the consistency of U.S. foreign policy can be traced.

A foreign policy of this sort has special relevance for the underdeveloped nations because it is precisely social revolution—the nemesis of U.S. policy—that is the order of the day in the Third World. To appreciate this clash of interests we need to examine the second question raised above: what holds back modernization of the underdeveloped nations?

The usual textbook approach to the industrial backwardness of the Third World is to list a host of twenty, thirty, or more common characteristics of underdevelopment. The trouble with such an approach is that little distinction is made between symptoms and causes. More often than not, in this seemingly hopeless amassing of difficulties, a way out is sought by focusing on a panacea such as population control—and even that panacea is examined as a technical problem, independent of the social and economic environment which contributes to the pressure of population and remains an obstacle to "gimmicky" solutions.

If these long, eclectic arrays of symptoms of underdevelopment have any virtue, it is to illustrate that the problem has deeper roots than, for example, the popularly held notion that lack of natural resources is a major cause of a nation's poverty and stagnation. In fact, there are advanced countries with poor resources and underdeveloped countries with rich natural resources. More important, the very extensiveness of the number of characteristic features of underdevelopment suggests the potential inadequacy of mere tinkering with reforms of existing social structures, and introduces the issue of a need for wholesale restructuring and redirection of these societies.

The main direction of U.S. academic thought and U.S. foreign policy, however, is to shrink from the dangerous implications of restructuring social and economic systems. Instead, the focus is on simpler, more comfortable, and safer ways out: population control and the spread of modern technology through foreign investment and foreign aid. The more thoughtful advocates of the population-control remedy recognize that it is far from a cure-all. At best, it is a stopgap measure (assuming it can work under the existing socioeconomic conditions) to hold the line against a mounting danger of mass starvation in the face of the slight progress made in increasing food production.

The more basic remedy is usually identified as the transfer of capital and technology from the rich to the poor nations: a consequence of the conventional diagnosis that the underlying causes of backwardness are the lack of modern technology and the shortage of domestic capital. Such a prescription is clearly consistent with the diagnosis; it is also consistent with the ideology under which U.S. foreign policy parades. The trouble is that the diagnosis is wrong.

To many in the advanced nations, and especially to those in the United States, technology looms as a talisman, a type of magic art: just let it loose in foreign lands and all the wonders of prosperity will follow. One needs only to reflect a bit on the U.S. condition to realize how shallow this faith is.

Thus, despite the availability of the most advanced technology and despite the large transfer of funds, the Appalachian region remains a major pocket of poverty and underdevelopment. And how far have technology and a surplus of domestic capital gone in solving the poverty of the ghettos?

The dimensions of the poverty problem are much greater, of course, in the underdeveloped nations. But to understand the question of inadequate technology in those regions, we have to recognize that technology does not stand alone—it needs people to use it. And it is on the latter we have to concentrate for an answer: the willingness and ability of the people inside the country to apply improved technology which will put the unemployed to work and which will raise the output of the people at work. To take advantage of technology, it is necessary, among other things, to have a literate population, a high social evaluation of science and scientific method, and receptivity on a mass scale to technological innovation. This is especially so because the technology most needed is not arcane computers and complex electronic systems in a few key cities, but an extensive spread of technology throughout the agricultural sector—that sector in which the largest part of the population of the underdeveloped countries is to be found.

This does not mean that more advanced technology could not be used to good advantage. We need to understand though that there is no instant magic, no basic solution to the problems of development, in the wonders of modern science and technology. The requirements in the Third World—where an agricultural as well as an industrial revolution is needed—extend to steel plows, wheelbarrows, small pumps, and irrigation systems. The need is not only for equipment, but for selection of seeds and plants and improved techniques in the use of the land. For this, the mass of farmers who till the soil have to be involved. And, for this, the mass of people have to change; more important, the constraints on the development of the people have to be removed.

The crucial obstacles to the needed changes are not to be found in the innate nature of the people, or in special features of their culture, or in their religion. The obstacles, instead, are located in the social institutions under which the people live, in the type of landowning, in the vested interests of the large landowners and businessmen, and in the social priorities imposed by the ruling classes. Let me cite a simple illustration. One of the puzzling aspects of India's economic trials has been the seeming indifference of small farmers to undertake simple work needed to irrigate the land they work. The Indian government spends large sums of money to dig broad canals in order to make more water available for farming. But the farmers failed to take advantage of this potential boost to their output; they did not dig the ditches needed to bring the water from the rivers and canals to their small plots. I once asked a leading U.S. agricultural specialist who had spent a great deal of time in India: What went wrong? Was it laziness? Stupidity? Ignorance? The conservative agronomist laughed at my naive questions. The simplest and most ignorant farmer, he explained patiently, knows the importance of water. But the irrigation ditches had to pass over land owned by big landowners who exacted a tax for the use of the ditches—a tax the farmers could not possibly pay.

Furthermore, given a profit-directed economy along with extensive poverty, there is no percentage in the mass production of improved farm tools, equipment, and chemicals needed for upping farm output. The technology for most of these essential products is not complex, nor are the domestic businessmen stupid. The entrepreneurs do not do what is needed for economic development because there is not enough potential profit in such undertakings, or because they can make more profit in other ventures.

For these reasons, and others, social revolutions are the order of the day for most of the underdeveloped world; revolutions that remove the power of those classes whose interests are in the status quo; revolutions that change the social priorities, open the floodgates of education, arouse the enthusiasm of large masses of the people, and change the production structure to produce what is needed for the advancement of the people and not what brings the most profit to the property owners.

Once the issue of social revolution is introduced, the

capital-shortage factor—a primary canon of economic orthodoxy—assumes a new significance. First, the revolution can
quite quickly halt two major sources of waste of capital: (1)
by severely reducing the consumption of the rich and the
better-heeled middle classes, and (2) by confiscating foreign-
owned investments. Such steps are useful in two ways: (1)
the profits of agriculture, manufacturing, mining, and commerce can be fully utilized for the most important development projects, and (2) scarce foreign exchange can be more
effectively applied to purchase of raw materials and equipment, instead of being drained off for the import of luxuries
and for payment of profits, interest, royalties, and management fees to foreign investors.

The second contribution a social revolution makes to the
tackling of the capital-shortage obstacle is through mobilization of labor to be used to some degree as a substitute for
capital. A great deal of necessary construction, for example,
can be obtained this way. Naturally, it would be better to use
machinery. But if there is no machinery, and the need is
great, idle and underutilized labor can be used, for example,
for road-building, flood control, irrigation works, and housing construction—as was done in the centuries before there
were bulldozers, trucks, cranes, etc. This is not the ideal
solution, but it is a solution that faces up to the reality that
God helps those who help themselves. If you will permit me
another homely illustration, let us consider the question of
rat control. In many of the underdeveloped countries, the rat
population destroys a significant proportion of the annual
farm crop. With adequate capital investment, it is possible to
string around fields electrified low wires that will kill maraud-
ing rats. Since there is little electricity and no money for
wires, the rats get their fill. Ironically, as has been shown by
the revolution in China, the organized effort of masses of
people, devoted to first things first, can get rid of the rats,
without benefit of modern technology.

A third contribution to overcoming the capital-shortage
problem is the revolution's concentration on education and
health for the masses. Aside from humanitarian considerations, improved nutrition and medical care contribute to

raising the productivity of labor. Education quite obviously adds to human capital. For many of these countries, the issue is not only the achievement of universal literacy but redirection of the educational priorities from one of training an elite ruling group (schooled in the humanities, law, and medicine for the urban well-to-do) to one that builds on (1) science and mathematics needed for mastery of technology and greater self-reliance, and (2) politics and economics needed for resourceful and effective economic and social planning. Again, the need is not only for the seemingly esoteric and complex. To advance in scientific farming, farmers who can confidently keep books and do arithmetic are needed. The question we need to ask ourselves is: Why, in the twentieth century, has it taken social revolutions to make the most dramatic leaps in health and education for the vast majority of the population?

From whichever angle we approach the problem of development, we hit against the limits imposed by the established social institutions and the priorities (or values, if you wish) protected by the existing ruling classes. And these are the very ruling classes that are protected and nurtured by the advanced capitalist nations—most particularly in these days, by the military and foreign policy of the United States. The social systems of the underdeveloped countries have a long history, one that is dominated by the colonial and semi-colonial arrangements imposed under the *force majeure* of the successful and rich capitalist nations. Primarily by force, but also by the perpetuation of the resulting economic relations, the Third World was converted primarily into a supplier of raw materials and food for the metropolitan centers, and a buyer, to the extent its resources permitted, of the manufactured goods produced in the industrialized nations. The resulting economic structure created at one and the same time (1) an economy whose resources are bent to supply the needs of the industrialized nations, and (2) ruling classes whose prosperity, whether they like it or not, stems from a perpetuation of this dependency; in short, a subservient component of the imperialist network of trade and investment.

A new departure toward development, instead of underdevelopment, entails a restructuring of these industrially backward economies to obtain greater flexibility and a more effective use of their own resources, a redirection of their societies to meet the needs of the people rather than to foster the prosperity of the wealthy at home and abroad. Necessarily contained in this new departure is, in addition, a release from the psychological dependence on the culture and "superiority" of the advanced nations, along with the blossoming in the population as a whole of self-confidence, self-reliance, and independence in thought and action. By exerting its efforts to contain the revolutionary impulse that seeks to free itself from the material and psychological bonds of imperialism, U.S. foreign policy (including its military posture and action), in effect, is the primary obstacle to the development of the underdeveloped nations.

9

Capital, Technology, and Development

In the mythology of bourgeois social science, capital and technology are the magic that presumably will bring the entire world into the Garden of Eden. Libraries, UN agencies, various economic institutes around the world are bulging with reports and studies telling us how a country can get out of the stage of underdevelopment, how it can lift itself out of the quagmire of poverty and misery. All sorts of ideas and proposals are contained in these publications, but there is one common thread. If you just put in enough capital, if you just introduce enough modern technology, the underdeveloped societies will be vitalized and will start growing on their own.

Now this kind of thinking is not entirely false. Underlying the almost blind faith in the miraculous powers of capital and technology is a sound appreciation of some elementary truths. In order for people to have more food, clothing, medicine, and other necessities, more has to be produced. To produce more, two things are necessary: first, more people have to be engaged in useful productive activity, and I stress the word useful. And second, the labor of the workers and

This is a revised version of a talk given at the convention of the Association of Arab-American University Graduates in Chicago in October 1975. It subsequently appeared in the January 1976 issue of *Monthly Review*.

the peasants has to yield a larger amount of goods than is now the case. For both of these purposes, but especially to increase productivity, more and better equipment is needed. It stands to reason that in order to get more and better equipment, resources (or as some call it, capital) have to be mobilized from either internal or external sources.

The trouble with these simple truths is that when they are abstracted from the concrete, historical circumstances in which they have to be applied, they end up as fetishes— fetishes that tend to obscure the real issues. What these fetishes disguise is the fact that production is a *social activity*. This means that to get at the heart of the problem of production, we must first and foremost focus on people and the social relations into which they enter. Unless we put people, people as producers and people as consumers, at the center of our analysis, we lose sight of what it is all about.

Capital

When we think about capital, we have to understand that there are three aspects to capital, and we should always keep in mind the differences which distinguish them one from another:

1. Capital is a social relationship. It represents relations among divergent classes in society.

2. The material component of capital—equipment, tools, machinery—may, and indeed usually will, be used differently in different sets of social relations.

3. Capital in today's world is clothed in the form of money.

In a capitalist social system—and this is what distinguishes such a system—the material components of capital are owned by a small minority of the community. What kind of material components are used, what products are made from these components, and *for whom* these products are made are all questions which are decided by the owners of capital. Capital in the form of money is the essential medium guiding its use in this kind of economy. But in and of itself money capital has little bearing on the course of events, since everything depends on what the owners and managers of money want to do with it. Money capital can lie in idle hoards. It can be used for land, stock-market, and commodity speculation. It can be misapplied, to set off waves of inflation without a significant increase in production. Or it can be dissipated in lavishly luxurious ways of living by the upper classes. If the owners of money capital decide to use it for the purchase of equipment and the making of goods, they will search out areas of investment that promise maximum profits and inspire confidence in the safety of the resultant operation. Risk and profit are the constant ingredients in all thinking about what to do with money capital and with components of capital in its material form.

A constant flow of profits is not enough. Because of the possibility that capital will be lost, and because of the pressures of competition, there is compulsion for profits to keep on growing. Capitalists have to make more and more profits to protect their investment, to expand the capital base, and thereby make even more profits. It is for this reason that throughout the history of capitalism long waves of prosperity and great technical achievements produce, at the same time, poverty and insecurity not only among workers, farmers, and the unemployed, but also in backward regions within the advanced capitalist nations and in the colonial, semicolonial, and neocolonial countries. These stark contrasts are the natural and necessary results of social relations which dictate that the material components of capital be used to maximize profits and minimize risks.

If we study the history and nature of capitalism we can understand why Third World nations face formidable obstacles when they try to imitate the ways of advanced capitalist countries. For one thing, many, if not most, of the underdeveloped nations currently have significantly lower levels of per capita production and consumption than existed in Western Europe and the United States when these countries began their upward spiral of industrialization. This relatively greater poverty is itself a result of the long history of penetration and exploitation of the rest of the world by the handful of originally successful capitalist countries. The disruption of established precapitalist economies to create new market opportunities; the redirection of the traditional trade of Asia and Africa to serve the purposes of the Western world; the manipulation of natural resources to extract the agricultural and mineral products desired by the metropolitan centers; and the creation of new, or corruption of old, elites for more effective control by the dominant countries—all these changes, imposed by force and violence, contributed to stagnation of strategic economic sectors and impoverishment of vast populations.

Third World societies, furthermore, are held back not only by unusually narrow inner markets but by inferior opportunities in foreign markets as well. The "ideal capitalist models" had unusual assistance in building their industrial base—opportunities which helped overcome the inevitable internal barriers to growth as production capacity outstripped domestic demand, and in addition provided new vistas which stimulated the "animal spirits" of entrepreneurs. When domestic markets faltered in England, France, Germany, the United States, and Japan, these countries (or their representatives) shot out to create and take over new markets abroad. There was a world to conquer, and conquer they did. But such opportunities no longer exist. The successful capitalisms have achieved dominance in the realm of international trade and do not complacently entertain the prospect of competition by upstarts.

In the absence of such safety valves as territorial conquest and easy entry into foreign trade channels, the underdeveloped countries must rely ever more on the help of foreign investors. Not only do the latter have a monopoly on modern technology, they also hold the keys to export possibilities. Dependence on foreign monopolies for industrialization, in turn, means that native capitalist classes remain dependent and insecure. Clipping the claws of foreign investors—whether by more favorable contracts, joint ventures, or similar means—does not change the fundamentals of this dependency, nor does it add much vigor to national entrepreneurs. The latter, in their weakness, are unable to challenge contending elite groups, such as vested agricultural interests. The upshot then is a shifting compromise among various sectors of the ruling class. It is because of this that the underdeveloped countries are so irresolute in carrying out the social reforms and the agricultural revolution needed for a buoyant capitalism.

Since the obstacles to successful capitalist development are today so gigantic, the pursuit of industrialization inevitably involves the accumulation of capital at the expense of keeping the masses down. Agriculture remains backward, investment is insufficient to cure unemployment in urban and rural areas, and wages are kept at pitifully low levels to provide adequate incentives for entrepreneurs. Production decisions are, and must be, made to satisfy the desires of the middle- and upper-income sectors of the population, those that have the money to buy. The technology introduced is the kind most favored by, and closely tied in with, foreign capital, since this is the technology best suited for profit-making and for squeezing into some of the interstices of foreign trade. Brazil is an outstanding example of what I am referring to. Brazil has been successful in taking a significant step forward in industrialization—one in which native capitalists have actively participated, along with foreign investors from a number of advanced capitalist states. With what consequences? The real wages of the working class have declined and the backward agricultural regions have remained stagnant and poverty-stricken.

Technology

Granted, some of you may say, that we should be more conscious of a fetishistic belief in the efficacy of capital, and that we must keep our eye on social relations. But what about the material components? Can the evils of backwardness be eliminated without modern technology? It is precisely this general, and in a sense tautological, way of putting the question which leads to difficulties. For in and of itself technology is no panacea. It too must be examined in terms of the social setting. The decisive questions should be: What kind of technology? For what purpose? By whom will it be chosen and applied?

Thus, if the social purpose, whether guided by individual entrepreneurs or governments, is to meet first the market demands of the people who have money to spend, trusting that with more industrial development and more people at work the benefits of technology will trickle down to the lower classes, then the most modern technology of the Western world is best suited and indeed necessary. But if there is an entirely different social purpose, involving a change in class power, which defines as the first and paramount priority meeting the food, clothing, housing, medical, educational, and cultural needs of *all* the people, then modern technology is no panacea, even though in the longer run various aspects of it will have to be introduced. But a too rapid introduction of modern technology can be harmful, since it may require that important domestic resources be diverted from the most urgent needs of the vast majority of the population.

It is true that there is an aura of magic surrounding the fast-moving automatic machines and advanced chemical production processes that promise miracles of mass production. But these miracles can make only a minor contribution to raising agricultural output to levels necessary to overcome starvation and malnutrition. For this, what is generally needed first are water conservancy projects, irrigation and drainage systems, pipes, pumps, transportation equipment (often of the simplest kind, such as wheelbarrows and bicycles), a variety of improved farm tools and simple machines. Large-scale modern factories could in theory be helpful, but they are not the key to solving the most urgent needs of poor countries. A great deal of what is required can be practically achieved only by the mobilization of labor and its concentration on the most socially urgent projects. Many of the products most essential for the advancement of agriculture can be manufactured in small local factories using unsophisticated and often traditional production methods. Local, small-scale production has the advantage of being more flexible in turning out products adapted to local soil and other natural conditions. Such establishments can be very useful in overcoming rural unemployment and converting previously wasted human resources to constructive ends. A large proportion of the rural work force is needed only in peak agricultural seasons and remains idle most of the year. With the growth of local industry in the countryside, idle labor power can be put to work in manufacturing and construction and still be on hand when needed at seasonal agricultural peaks.

The important point is that if attention is directed to agriculture and to the health, housing, and education of the vast impoverished masses, the technology and the composition of production required will be in marked contrast to the types and patterns normally associated with the utilization of the most modern technology. I am not denying the importance of such technology; I want only to stress that we need to think in terms quite different from, and more complex than, a simple transplant of advanced Western methods of production.

Self-Reliance

Above all, what is needed is to shift attention from technology and capital to *people*. Ultimately, successful development depends on the transformation of the people themselves. And since this is so, we must be aware of the limits imposed by the prevalence of a dependent psychology among the peoples of the Third World. This dependency is most striking in the rural areas where the majority of the population generally lives. There the domination of the landlord, moneylender, tribal chief, and petty bureaucrat—enforced by local police, goon squads, and if necessary the national army —is deeply rooted and touches almost every aspect of the peasant's and rural laborer's day-to-day experience. The same kind of dependency exists, though in different form, in the cities as well.

On top of all this is the cultural dependence and lack of self-confidence stemming from the whole history of formal and informal imperialism. People have been taught that the best products are made in the Western world, that the only ones who can master technology are superior beings of the metropolitan centers. A combination of class oppression and cultural imperialism reinforces the feeling of inability to handle and cope with modern technology. These factors, in addition to the arrogance of the Western specialists who come to install and operate the modern factories, are important contributors to the isolation of the modern technological sectors in the Third World countries and to the perpetuation of reliance on the West for technology.

Technology does not mean machines alone. There is an art in the use of machines. New problems are always coming up in the operation of factories: parts break down and need to be repaired; materials used in one country differ in composition from materials used in other countries, and machines have to be adapted for these variations; products, and therefore the processes of production, have to be designed to meet local conditions and needs. If the ability to cope with these problems does not develop internally within a country, its dependence on imported industry and foreign specialists will be continuously reproduced and perpetuated.

In order to bring science to agriculture for the solution of food and raw materials problems—and it is important to stress that these problems can be solved in most countries—you need a new breed of farmers, farmers who have confidence in themselves, who are not afraid of bosses or moneylenders and who are willing and able to face up to all kinds of difficulties. Once the farmers are convinced that the location of power has really changed and that they are indeed their own masters, their minds can open up to the culture, science, and experimentation needed to produce new seeds and plants with higher yields, and to the employment of improved methods of farming. A whole new social structure is needed in the villages if labor is to be mobilized for the satisfaction of such crying needs as irrigation and water conservancy, activities which can be successful only when there is a proper social approach and the old atmosphere of fear and lack of self-confidence has been replaced by a new feeling of worth and self-reliance.

In industry, too, a change in people is of utmost importance. A new breed of mechanics has to arise: people who are not afraid of machines, who are able to examine them, study them, and take them apart, who understand what they are working with instead of reconciling themselves to being mere appendages to automatic machinery. All the industrially developed countries went through their own development by precisely such means—creating and nurturing vast numbers of mechanics who were able to develop and adapt new inventions, as well as take care of and repair a wide range of already existing industrial equipment. This situation has changed with modern technology. Nowadays in the advanced countries progress is tied to innovations in physics and chemistry under the leadership of highly trained scientists and engineers. These specialists have become a kind of priesthood, worshipped and respected by the rest of society. And when an industrially backward country imports modern technology, it must also import the priesthood and join in paying it homage. Such a country is then caught in a trap from which the only possible escape is to develop its own technology.

This does not mean avoiding the borrowing of knowledge and learning from modern science and engineering. All of human history is a record of cultural and technological learning by one people from another. No people have a monopoly on the ability to develop science and technology. But the successful borrowers, those who are able to master and advance the knowledge learned from others, are the ones who borrow on their own terms and in their own ways. If an underdeveloped country today wants to become economically and culturally independent, it too must do its own learning and on its own terms. Most especially it needs to have its own master mechanics and its own ability to study and design industrial processes.

In this connection much can be learned from the early history of the United States. One of the greatest boons to U.S. capitalism was the decision by the British toward the end of the eighteenth century to prohibit the export of machines and the emigration of machinists. When an Englishman went before an emigration officer, he had to show his hands: if the hands did not have calluses that are typical of farmers the applicant was denied an exit visa. This prohibition was undoubtedly a powerful spur to the development in the United States of its own industrial revolution. At first, industrial undertakings were imitative of those in England; but as native mechanics emerged, the United States began to discover new and better ways adapted to its own conditions and needs. Japan's industrial development is also significant. The Japanese did it by closing their doors to foreign investment and learning Western technology on their own. This learning process is slow at first, and it entails making many mistakes, but it is the only way to become the master of technology and of one's own destiny.

I recently came across some comments which make a similar point in an interesting fashion. I refer to an interview with Nobel Prize-winning physicist C. N. Yang, an American of Chinese descent, in *New China* (Fall 1975). Professor Yang was asked how rapidly China's science is developing. He replied:

> The fastest way to catch up in modern science and impress visitors from abroad is to establish a super laboratory, buy all the equipment from abroad and then quickly train graduate students and research workers to do the problems which are currently being done elsewhere. China rejects this method because it would be a showcase, unrelated to the general development of the country.
>
> This was brought home to me one morning in 1973, when I visited a laser laboratory at a university in Hong Kong. It was in an air-conditioned room; there was an enormous imported laser tube, very smooth, very nicely made, and very nicely packaged.

They were doing some quite advanced research and I was impressed.

That same afternoon, after I had crossed the border into China, I was ushered into the optics laboratory of Zhong Shang University. I saw room after room of laser equipment, wires sticking out here and there, glass tubing going in all directions. Everything was messy. The contrast was amazing. The tubes weren't nicely smooth; there was no chrome anywhere; and there were all kinds of problems. It was clear to me that in this organic environment there will develop a group of laser scientists who know everything about the whole field, who know the real reason for the existence of the problems that are investigated abroad. I think this philosophy will generate benefits to Chinese science and technological developments.

I too was immensely impressed by the phenomenon described by Dr. Yang in visits to factories in China during a recent trip there. It was exciting to see workers producing the machines that would then be used to make final products in their own factory. According to capitalist standards, these machines were being made inefficiently: highly trained Western engineers would consider this type of production woefully backward. But according to human standards and the needs of the Chinese people at this stage of their development, the inefficient, backward methods were strikingly progressive. In each factory we visited, the workers pointed proudly to machines, some very advanced and precise, that they themselves had made in their own workshops. The practice is to bring together what they call three-in-one teams, including representatives from the shop floor, engineers, and management. These teams, in which workers play a prominent part, begin by taking apart an old machine, figuring out how it works, and then, through trial and error, constructing one of their own. Often, workers had begun by studying machines used in more advanced factories. Or they would travel to a university to consult specialists. Many of the homemade machines we saw were of a truly advanced type, such as precision gear-shapers, which required knowledge of mathematics as well as skill in machine operations. So the factories started their own schools to teach workers the necessary mathematics and mechanical theory.

What we saw in China was an industrial revolution in process, one in which the main reliance is on the initiative and competence of its own people. Even as they borrow from the West, and at times import whole production systems from the more advanced countries, they are creating the conditions for true independence. At the same time they are meeting the highest social standards—seeing to it that the entire population, and not just privileged classes, are fed and provided with medical attention, education, and the means to the satisfaction of other basic needs.

To sum up: what is needed is a wholesale shift in emphasis from faith in capital and technology to faith in people. This, of course, means a society that is impatient, one that is not willing to wait for some future technological miracles. And such societies do not develop without a change in the structure of power, without a transfer of power to those classes which will redirect the basic priorities of society toward the elimination of poverty and misery and which will rely on people as well as on modern science and technology.

REPLY TO CRITICS

10

Is Imperialism
Really Necessary?

How a question is formulated usually defines the limits of its answer. Hence, a most important aspect of scientific inquiry is discovering the right questions to ask. In this context, the very formulation of the question about imperialism by S. M. Miller, Roy Bennett, and Cyril Alapatt takes us off the path of understanding modern imperialism.

Their article is directed to the question, "Is imperialism really necessary?" Imperialism, however, is so intertwined with the history and resulting structure of modern capitalist society—with its economics, politics, and ruling ideas—that this kind of question is in the same category as, for example, "Is it necessary for the United States to keep Texas and New Mexico?" We could, after all, return these territories to the Mexican people and still maintain a high-production and high-standard-of-living economy. We could import the oil,

This is a reply to a critical essay on Harry Magdoff's *The Age of Imperialism* (New York: Monthly Review Press, 1969). The essay (by S. M. Miller, Roy Bennett, and Cyril Alapatt), originally entitled "Is Imperialism Really Necessary?" but finally published as "Does the U.S. Economy Require Imperialism?" appeared with this reply in the September/October 1970 issue of *Social Policy*. It was also published in the October and November 1970 issues of *Monthly Review*.

mineral ores, and cattle from these territories and sell U.S. goods in exchange. Any temporary decline in our gross national product would surely be a small price to pay for social justice. And given our growth rate and supposed ability to regulate our economy, continued economic growth should soon make up any losses resulting from the return of stolen lands.

Or one might ask, "Is Manhattan necessary for the United States?" It would surely be equitable to return land obtained from the Indians in a sharp deal. Such a transfer might at first have some small downward economic effect, but eventually should make for more prosperity. Manufacturing on the island is an insignificant percentage of total U.S. output. The profitable port activity could be shifted to New Jersey or other excellent Atlantic ports. Other economic functions—stock and commodity exchanges, investment and commercial banks, headquarters of large corporations—could be transferred lock, stock, and barrel to the interior. Such a move to wipe out a terrible blot on the conscience of white America could be socially useful. Moreover, a new financial headquarters of the United States (and the capitalist world) could be designed to avoid slum, smog, pollution, and traffic crises; the demand for buildings, housing, and transportation and communication equipment in the new "Manhattan" might spur the economy to new heights.

Such questions might be useful in the classroom to help stimulate students' imagination and to illustrate the contradictions of a capitalist economy. But they will not contribute to an understanding of the role of territorial expansion in the evolution and functioning of the economy, or the unique role of a financial center in the operations of a capitalist economy.

Our Critics* no doubt justify their question on the grounds that some popularizers of the Left formulate the

* To avoid the awkwardness of listing the three authors at each reference, and to somewhat depersonalize the controversy, we will refer to them as the "Critics." We trust they will not take offense. "Critic," to our way of thinking, is an honorable designation.

issue purely in terms of "economic necessity"—as if every political and military action were in response to an immediate economic cause or to a telephone call from a corporation executive. Such a mechanical cause-effect approach is an obvious oversimplification, an inadequate guide to history, and more rhetoric than analysis. But when one merely meets an exaggerated rhetoric head on and makes the rhetoric the focus for debate, one departs from the tasks of scientific inquiry: one may thus be at a ball park, but not where the game is being played. The major task, in my opinion, for the study of imperialism is to discover and understand what Bernard Baruch described as "the essential one-ness of [U.S.] economic, political, and strategic interests."[1] In such a study, we have to seek the key roots—the mainsprings—of this "one-ness" as well as to understand the interactions and interdependence of the economic, political, and military drives.

It takes no deep perception to recognize the limits of the "necessity" formula. Thus, a substantial part of the world, notably the Soviet Union and China, has chosen the path of economic independence and therefore broken the trade and investment ties with the imperialist network. The advanced capitalist countries adjusted to these changes and have in recent decades achieved considerable prosperity and industrial advance. However, important as it is to recognize that such adjustments can take place, it is equally important to understand the route that these adjustments take: via wars, depressions, and huge armaments programs. The economic adaptations emerged in the midst of recurrent struggles for control over spheres of influence—over other advanced countries as well as over Third World areas, it should be noted. And, most important, these adjustments have in no way lessened the intensity of the counterrevolutionary thrust of imperialist states, by wars and other means, directed (1) to preventing a further narrowing down of the territory in which they can freely trade and invest, and (2) to reconquering the space lost to the imperialist world. Nor has this counter-revolutionary activity, which began during the first days of the Bolshevik Revolution, diminished since the United States took the reins as leader and organizer of the capitalist world.

The relevant question is not whether imperialism is necessary for the United States, but to discover the "rationality" of the historic process itself: why the United States and other leading capitalist nations have persistently and recurrently acted in an imperialist fashion for at least three-quarters of a century.

The contrast between speculative hypotheses about the "necessity" of imperialism and the actual course of history is excellently demonstrated by the Critics themselves when they illustrate their interpretation of imperialism by referring to, and endorsing, the theoretical position of Karl Kautsky in his debate with Rosa Luxemburg. Kautsky argued, they point out, that imperialist expansion was sustained by only a small and powerful group of capitalists and that such expansion conflicted with the interests of the capitalist class as a whole. Because of this, Kautsky believed that the majority of the capitalist class would increase its opposition to, and eventually prevent, armed imperialist expansion.

It is strange indeed, in this day and age, to come across a revival of Kautsky's theory—a theory that has been devastatingly refuted by events. Our Critics refer to Kautsky's exposition at the 1907 Stuttgart Conference of the Second International. But only seven years later World War I broke out, to be followed at the earliest practical opportunity by World War II. It doesn't take much insight to recognize the role that Germany's expansionist aims played in both wars: Kautsky's optimism turned out to be mere illusion.

The Critics remind us of the current dissatisfaction of some U.S. businessmen with the Vietnam War. That there are shrewd businessmen who recognize that at times one must cut one's losses should hardly come as a surprise. The surprise is that it has taken them so long to awaken to the reality of a lost war and its social and economic consequences. However, the acid test of Kautsky's and the Critics' position would be: how many of these businessmen would agree (1) to an immediate pullout of U.S. forces from Vietnam, leaving the fate of Vietnam to the Vietnamese people, and (2) to a complete withdrawal of all U.S. military forces and equipment from all of Asia?

The major weakness of Kautsky's theory was precisely its concentration on "necessity." By casting his argument within this sterile framework, he distinguished between capitalists who "need" and those who "don't need" expansionism. He thus ignored what was most important in explaining the course of militarism and imperialism: the industrial and financial structure of the economy, the strategic elements of change, and the special nature of the political system associated with successful monopoly capitalism. (It should go without saying that a full explanation of, say, German imperialism would have to take into account the special socio-economic features and history of Germany.)

On their part, the Critics in effect adopt for their own economic analysis the same limited and crude economic interpretation of imperialism that they are criticizing. Accordingly, they look at only some of the relevant economic elements; those that they examine are treated as isolates, not as part of a social and economic organism; and then they whittle down even these isolates. This shrinking process takes on the following forms: (1) they eliminate from the realm of imperialism U.S. economic activity *in other advanced capitalist nations;* (2) they restrict the field of economic penetration in underdeveloped countries to *exports and direct private investment;* and (3) *concerning foreign mineral resources,* they deal only with the so-called *national interest,* ignoring the drive for control over such resources by monopolistic interest groups.

Imperialism and Relations Between Developed Countries

A large part of the Critics' article is devoted to statistical computations based on the assumption (and argument) that U.S. trade with, and investment in, other advanced capitalist nations have nothing to do with imperialism. Imperialism, they claim, concerns only the relations between advanced and underdeveloped countries.

The assumption misses an essential distinguishing feature

of modern imperialism. The occupation and/or manipulation of a weaker by a stronger nation and the building of empires by powerful military states have occurred frequently in human history, in ancient, medieval, and modern times. Moreover, the birth and adolescence of capitalism were marked by military penetration of noncapitalist areas to bring the latter into the trade and investment sphere of the dominant capitalists.

Because empire-building has been prevalent over long stretches of history, the use of the term *imperialism* to cover all such activities leads to definitions that stress the superficial and avoid the essential. The value of distinguishing different periods of history, to which convenient labels are attached, is to provide a useful analytical framework for discovering and understanding the main operating levers of the particular stage under study. For that reason, it seems to us, the term *imperialism* is best used to designate the international practices and relations of the capitalist world during the distinct stage of mature capitalism that begins in the last quarter of the nineteenth century.

But even if one disagrees with this terminological approach, it still has to be recognized that the international economics and politics of the past seventy to ninety years have certain unique features. Hence some historians follow the practice of calling the new stage *modern* or *new* imperialism, to distinguish it from that of mere empire-building. The rationale for this should become clearer if we spell out some of the major features of this new or modern imperialism.

1. As noted above, capitalism from its earliest days sank its roots in the noncapitalist world. It prospered by adapting (through force and economic pressure) the rest of the world to fit the needs of the more advanced capitalist nations. However, it is in the stage of modern imperialism that its "historic task" is fulfilled: the entire globe is fitted into the world capitalist system (until, in more recent years, parts of this system break away). Prices of commodities produced around the world become dominated by one world price established in the major financial centers. In this period of

modern imperialism, there is a sharp stepup in the international flow of commodities, men, and capital—in response primarily to pressures emanating from the most advanced centers of capitalism, including the pressures of competition among the advanced capitalist countries themselves.

2. The resulting world capitalist system of modern imperialism comprehends an intricate and interdependent set of relations between countries at various stages of industrial development. The most striking aspect of this world system is the freezing of the so-called Third World countries as industrial and financial dependencies of key metropolitan centers— a behavior of capitalist markets. In addition, among the more advanced capitalist nations, there are a variety of relations of dependency of weaker nations on stronger ones.

3. The technical underpinning of the modern international world economy is the growth of what Veblen called the "technology of physics and chemistry": steel, electricity, oil refining, synthetic organic chemicals, internal combustion engines, etc. The technology of modern imperialism became the material base of decisive concentration of economic power in large industrial corporations and large financial institutions. The maturation of this economic concentration of power (called, for convenience, *monopoly capital*) affected the whole economic and political structure of advanced capitalist nations. On the economic side, in contrast with the earlier stage of competitive capitalism, economic change and economic policy are primarily determined by the imperatives of monopolistic-type industries (oligopolies, to be technical). The latter, to protect their assets and maintain their leading positions, are impelled to seek control over supplies of raw materials and over markets—wherever these raw materials and markets may exist. Furthermore, the evolution of an economic structure based on monopolistic firms limits the alternatives open to the political regimes of these countries. Governments, whether liberal or conservative, can operate with a successful economy only if they support, and help make more efficient, the major determinants of the economy: the monopolistic firms and the international finan-

cial arrangements with which these firms operate.

4. Finally, a distinctive feature of the new imperialism is the rise of intensive competitive struggle among advanced capitalist nations. It is this competitive struggle which helps determine the new world economic arrangements and which is a major source of continual turbulence in the world capitalistic system. Before the era of modern imperialism, Great Britain was the undisputed dominant nation in foreign trade, investment, and finance. The rise of industrialized nations, based on advanced technology that permitted economic and military competition with Britain, led to the hectic struggle for conquest of those parts of the globe not yet incorporated into the global capitalist arrangements. It also led to struggles for redivision of colonies and spheres of influence. But, it should be noted most especially, the competitive struggle is not restricted to dominance over the underdeveloped world. It also entails struggle for dominance and/or special influence over other advanced capitalist nations, as was seen in two world wars. Present also as a major element in the power struggle between nations and between monopolistic firms of these nations is the use of investment in one another's territories and/or cartel arrangements for the division of markets.

Thus, if one sees modern imperialism in historical perspective, it should be clear that there are two attributes of the power struggles of this period: (1) the struggle for economic power vis-à-vis other industrial nations, and (2) the struggle for economic power over the underdeveloped nations. Furthermore, to understand the imperialist drives since World War II, and the strategic alternatives confronting the decision-makers of U.S. foreign policy, one must take into account the past and potential rivalries of the industrialized nations. Not the least aspect of the latter is the maneuvering of U.S. government policy, and of U.S. firms, to take over trade and investment outlets of former allies (as well as former enemies) in the underdeveloped world.

Narrowing down imperialism to trade with, and investment in, the Third World thus eliminates a vital sector of international economic and political activity: the imperialist rivalries associated with the investment operations of advanced capitalist nations across one another's borders. In addition, the Critics do not face up to the reality of world economic interdependence and the significance of U.S. international financial and military preeminence. The latter might be better appreciated if we focus on the balance-of-payments situation.

The United States has had a deficit in its balance of payments for all but one or two of the past twenty years, and that deficit shows no signs of disappearing. This is unique in capitalist history. Any other country—and the United States itself prior to its post–World War II dominance—would have had to submit to the discipline of the international marketplace long, long before the twenty years were up. What would this discipline of the marketplace imply? Adoption by the U.S. government of such measures as would produce deflation: a sharp rise in unemployment and downward economic adjustment. Instead, the United States has been able to maintain its kind of prosperity through the 1950s and 1960s without undertaking effective measures to eliminate the international payments deficit. Quite the opposite: its prosperity was sustained by the very kind of activities which have generated the persistent deficit.

Why the deficit? As a rule, U.S. exports of goods and services (on current account) exceed imports. The deficit therefore arises because the U.S. government and investors spend in international markets over and above their "means." The government spends huge sums for its military establishment around the globe, for its wars, and for military and economic assistance to other countries. Corporations spend on investment in foreign business undertakings—in advanced as well as underdeveloped countries. All of these activities, independently of the motives which induce them, contribute to the prosperity of the economy as it is constituted.

The nub of this whole development is that it is made possible by the fact that the other capitalist nations have, willingly and unwillingly, accepted the U.S. dollar as if it were as good as gold.

One need not follow too carefully the financial news to be aware that the other industrialized nations are not too happy about the necessity to accept the U.S. dollar as a substitute for gold; indeed, considerable friction has resulted, and still exists. Yet they do accept it, for several reasons. First, they fear that if they rock the boat too much, all the central bankers will sink in a sea of financial difficulties. Second, they are impressed with U.S. economic strength, though this confidence is being increasingly shaken. Finally, and not the last of the considerations, is U.S. military might and its global presence. In fact, the United States has undertaken the major responsibility for maintaining the world imperialist system. It first supplied the armaments, armies, and Marshall Plan aid to prevent social revolution in Western Europe. It has furnished naval and air bases around the world, sufficient not only to encircle the Soviet Union and China but to act as a threat of military intervention or for actual intervention in the Third World.

Thus the United States provides the main military might for the "security" of the Western world, including Japan. The *quid pro quo* has been the reluctant acceptance of the U.S. dollar as a reserve currency, despite the inability of the United States to provide adequate gold coverage for its dollar debts. And one of the results of this *quid pro quo* is that U.S. business can keep on investing in Western Europe and buying up European firms, in effect paid for by credit extended by other advanced capitalist nations to the United States.

Suppose, however, one does not accept this analysis of the interrelationship between U.S. investment in advanced capitalist nations, on the one hand, and (1) the actual and incipient tensions between imperialist nations, and (2) the maintenance of control and "stability" in the Third World, on the other. Would the Critics then be correct in isolating U.S. investments in advanced countries as a thing apart from economic and political concern with the Third World? In our judgment, they would still be mistaken in such a narrowing down of imperialism. The reason is simple: when firms invest in advanced countries they become directly involved in the ties between those countries and "their" parts of the Third World. The larger U.S. investments in Europe and Japan become, the more extensively are U.S. interests bound up with the spheres of influence and neocolonial arrangements of *the entire capitalist world.*

The simplest and most direct illustration is the oil industry. Some 24 percent of U.S. direct private investment in Europe is in oil: oil refining, production of by-products, and the marketing of these products to Europeans and their foreign customers. But where do the U.S. subsidiaries get the oil to refine? From the Middle East, of course. Note especially that the rapid rise in U.S. oil investments in Europe was accompanied by a decisive change in U.S. ownership of nearby oil deposits: before World War II, U.S. firms controlled some 10 percent of Middle East oil reserves; by 1967, this percentage rose to 59. The success and prosperity of U.S. investment in the European oil industry depends on access to the oil extracted from Third World countries. Conversely, U.S. companies increase their profits on Middle Eastern oil by investing in oil refining and distribution in nearby Europe.

In less dramatic fashion, yet equally relevant, is the growing interest in the Third World entailed by other investments in the advanced nations. Thus, half of all U.S. direct investments in Europe and Japan is in manufacturing other than petroleum refining. Where do these firms get the raw materials to process? A significant portion comes from the Third World.

On top of this is the growing involvement of U.S. firms in the markets of the other advanced nations in the Third World. Manufacturers in the advanced countries have special positions and privileges in some of these markets through treaties and currency arrangements. Some of these preferred market outlets exist because of tariff barriers and distribution channels established in colonial days. U.S. firms thus extend their markets, getting a foothold in the preserves of other advanced countries, by investing in and thus becoming business "citizens" of the mother countries.

We have by no means exhausted the number of ways U.S. investment in advanced nations extends U.S. involvement in the economic affairs of the Third World. Let us look at just one other way. Quite recently, three U.S. banks made investments in England (a developed country, to be sure): Mellon National Bank and Trust Co. acquired a 25 percent stake in the Bank of London and South America Ltd. (BOLSA); New York's First National City Bank obtained a 40 percent share of National & Grindlay's Bank Ltd.; and Chase Manhattan Bank acquired a 15 percent interest in Standard Bank Ltd. Note, however, that while all three of these U.S. bank affiliates are based in London, "their main operations are in broad chunks of the underdeveloped world. National & Grindlay's operates in India, Pakistan, and the Middle East, Standard is in Africa, and BOLSA concentrates on Latin America."[2]

Investment in Underdeveloped Countries

Having disposed of U.S. investment in advanced countries as unrelated to imperialism, the Critics train their guns on the relative smallness of U.S. business interests in underdeveloped countries. In the statistical process of estimating the degree of U.S. economic interests, they reduce the dimensions of this involvement by restricting the discussion to exports and direct private investment. Perhaps they do so because of the availability of export and investment data and the lack of other adequate data. Whatever the reason, this concentration on direct private investment and exports results in overlooking other major involvement. For example:

1. Licenses of patents, processes, and trademarks granted to foreign manufacturers by U.S. manufacturing firms. This represents a growing business interest in the Third World as well as in advanced countries—in part a by-product of the worldwide distribution of U.S. movies, TV, and advertising.

One finds, for example, such ordinary products as inks and paints manufactured in the Philippines under licenses from U.S. manufacturers.

2. An important source of income to U.S. business is profit derived from shipping food and raw materials from the Third World to the United States, and the reciprocal trade. A considerable number of these ships are U.S. ships flying the flags of Liberia and Panama. Investments in such shipping companies are included in the Department of Commerce statistics under the category "International Shipping" and are excluded from statistics on direct private investments in underdeveloped countries. (Incidentally, control over shipping and related insurance required for Third World trade are important elements of the dependency relation between the peripheral countries and the metropolitan centers.)

3. Excluded from direct private investment statistics are such significant and expanding areas of economic involvement as: (a) direct loans by U.S. banks to foreign governments and businesses; (b) many types of foreign bonds floated in the United States; and (c) loans made in foreign countries by Edge Act corporations (subsidiaries of U.S. banks). It should also be noted that a favorite form of financing by Edge Act corporations is the convertible bond, a financial instrument whereby the U.S. banking corporation can convert the bond to shares of ownership in the foreign company if the latter proves profitable.

4. The data on direct private investment do not include or measure the degree of diffusion of U.S. business interests in the economic life of underdeveloped countries. This is especially evident in the case of the operations of foreign branches of U.S. banks and foreign banks owned by U.S. banks. (This is over and above items referred to in the preceding paragraph.) For example, direct private investment in banks abroad shows up in the catchall category of "other investments," which takes in a wide variety of activities, including such investments as those in sugar and banana plantations. Thus, direct private investment in Latin America

under the category "other investments" amounted to $1,057 million in 1968. Since bank investments are only one component of this category, investments in banks as counted by the Department of Commerce would be considerably below $1,057 million. But the assets of the branches of U.S. banks alone in that year amounted to $1,736 million. And this does not include the extent of financial involvement of U.S. banks through (a) Edge Act corporations owned by U.S. banks; (b) finance companies owned by U.S. banks and other financial institutions; (c) assets controlled directly via equity holdings in Latin American banks; or (d) indirect control over Latin American financial assets through branches of European banks, such as noted above in the case of the Mellon Bank stake in BOLSA. The financial assets controlled and influenced represent a diffusion of U.S. interests throughout the interstices of the Third World economies far beyond direct investments—in the day-to-day activities of the native firms as well as of other U.S. investors.

The importance of U.S. business interests in Latin America, for example, is indirectly reflected in the reason given for the partnership arrangement that Mellon National Bank made with BOLSA to enter the Latin American markets:

> By 1961 it was becoming obvious to the bank's management ... that because of its lack of international banking facilities Mellon's share of the domestic market was being threatened. Huge banks from New York, California, and Chicago were taking advantage of their international expertise to obtain larger shares of the domestic business of Mellon's traditional customers.[3]

In this we can see several important aspects of U.S. involvement in the underdeveloped world: (1) it is becoming increasingly important—important enough for banks to be able to win customers from each other based on the services they can give businesses operating abroad; (2) there is an interconnection of domestic and international business activities, one that exists in nonfinancial business too; and (3) competition within an industry spurs further penetration into the underdeveloped economies—also a factor in promoting pressure for investments other than banking in the Third World.

Small and Big Influences

As noted above, the Critics base their interpretation of the current state of U.S. imperialism on what they consider to be the relative smallness of private investment in the underdeveloped world. We have tried to show that the economic involvement is considerably larger than one would infer merely from the statistics on direct foreign investment. However, one needs to dig deeper. While the relative size of a particular economic sector is important, it is by no means the only consideration. It is necessary to understand the influence of the sector on the dynamics of an economy in motion. For example, the stock market in and of itself is a relatively small part of the U.S. economy. Yet what goes on in the stock market far exceeds its insignificant "statistical" contribution to the Gross National Product. The availability of this gambling casino is of the very essence of an advanced capitalist system. In addition, speculative fervor on the upside of the market can act as a goad and prop to boom and inflation, while panic among speculators can spark and intensify a major economic decline.

The vagaries of the balance of payments are a significant illustration of the potential "bigness" of a statistically small category. The chronic deficit in our balance of payments since 1950 has ranged roughly between $1 billion and $4 billion a year. Now this is obviously an insignificant portion of GNP. Statistically, it is hardly worth mentioning: just the statistical error involved in measuring GNP is surely much larger than the balance-of-payments deficit. Yet this "statistically insignificant" deficit, due to its unique function and its effect, contains all the potentials of a major international crisis. Lack of cooperation by the governments and central banks of the other advanced industrial nations—that is, their decision to go off the "dollar standard" and back to the "gold standard"—would undoubtedly lead to a breakdown of the existing international payments system and consequently of international trade, with obvious serious consequences to the world capitalist economy. (Central bankers understand this; it is, in fact, an important reason for their reluctant endurance of U.S. financial hegemony. But such cooperation is a slim reed to depend on in a world of aggressive, competitive, national and business interests.)

Once we recognize the role of the balance-of-payments deficit in maintaining U.S. prosperity and international financial stability, we can better appreciate the special advantages accruing from business involvement in the Third World. As noted earlier, the United States is able to sustain its wars, military posture, foreign investment, and military and economic assistance for two reasons: (1) the large surplus in the balance of its transactions on goods and services (technically, the "current account"), and (2) its relative freedom to accumulate deficits. We have already dwelt briefly on the politics of the latter. Let us now look into the former. Taking the last five years (1964–1968) for which complete annual data are available at the time of writing, we find that the surplus of goods and services in trade with the underdeveloped countries (including the profits on foreign investments) represented 66 percent of the total U.S. surplus on this account. For the last three of these years (years of full-scale war in Vietnam), the U.S. export balance on goods and services with the Third World was no less than 85 percent of the total U.S. surplus.[4]

Examination of the ramifications of the balance-of-payments issue (for example, the interrelations between current and capital transactions and the ensuing contradictions) would take us too far afield. Suffice it to note here that business dealings with the Third World, from the perspective of the balance of payments, are an especially strategic element of the current capitalist economy of the United States. The balance-of-payments data, however, are a summation of many thousands of transactions. If we look into these "small" transactions, we will also find areas of significance that far outweigh statistical "smallness."

The business of individual firms in the Third World arises usually in response to the following motives: (1) to obtain and maintain enlarged markets; (2) to get higher profit rates by taking advantage of lower production costs; and (3) to achieve control over sources of raw materials and food. Given the international maldistribution of income, it is only natural—indeed, inevitable—that trade (and investment for better access to a country's markets) will be much larger in the case of the rich than in that of the poor nations, despite the great disproportion of population in the two. But this does not mean that interest in the markets of the poor nations has slackened or will diminish in the future—any more than one would expect a waning of business interest in the "peripheral" areas within the United States (e.g., Mississippi) in contrast with the metropolitan centers of the country (e.g., New York). Nor would the business community take with better grace the shutting off of lesser foreign markets than they would countenance the secession of poorer regions of the United States.

The economics of the business firm is dominated by the growth imperative: growth of profits, growth of sales, and growth of capital investment. In the early stages of the evolution of a firm or a product, it is usually found that speediest results are obtained by concentrating on the upper-income segments of the native country and on those foreign countries that have a large upper-income population. However, no successful firm can afford to rest there. Under the pressure of competition, it must seek out additional and, if possible, more profitable markets. While these additional markets may be relatively small, their marginal effect can be unusually important because of their role in sustaining growth. This role of the marginal increase in the export market applies also to the marginal investment in a foreign country.

To liberal-minded observers, like our Critics, some of the percentages of business contributed by exports and investments may look small and unimportant. But these small percentages necessarily loom large in the eyes of the owners and managers of a business. The realities of the business world are such that these owners and managers must struggle doggedly not only to hang on to their share of the market but constantly to maneuver to increase it. Their logic is necessarily shaped by these realities. And it is the logic of the owners and managers of business that insists on keeping as much of the world as possible free for capital investment and trade—to provide at least the possibility of still another marginal boost in sales, profits, and investment. By the same token, the closing down of any area to "free enterprise" is a threat to growth potential.

When the "free world" remains free for private enterprise, opportunities do in fact arise for a new spurt in one business field or another—for a new source of growth. Thus the sober-minded *Business Week* in its forecast for the 1970s recognized the differences between trade with the developed and underdeveloped nations, but it also showed that it understands the new opportunities:

> As in the past, exports to industrial nations will rise faster than those to developing countries. In the 1960s, sales to industrial nations climbed from $13 billion to $24 billion, sales to developing countries rose from $7 billion to $11 billion. *An exception will be a boom in U.S. export and import trade with East and South Asia*, excluding Japan.[5] (Italics added)

It would be illuminating if the authors of this projection were to spell out their assumptions concerning the continuation or end of the Vietnamese War and the nature of the U.S. military presence in Asia in the 1970s, as for example, the replacement by the United States of British bases in Southeast Asia.

Raw Materials and the Third World

The Critics gave two reasons for brushing aside the crucial question of the raw materials factor and the ties with the Third World: (1) they themselves have not studied the question of dependency on foreign raw materials in depth, and (2) they think it is necessary to recognize the possibility of substituting one material for another. Their straightforward acknowledgment of limited acquaintance with the facts is commendable; by all means, they should look into these facts. We would suggest, though, that they not restrict their study to the "dependency" angle. Imperialism is not so much a question of dependency on raw materials as of the compulsive behavior of monopolistic-type business organizations.

That the drive for control of foreign resources extends beyond dependency can be seen in the way U.S. corporations sought, fought for, and obtained exploration and development rights for oil, copper, and other minerals *when the United States was blessed with a surplus of these minerals.* A major reason for the oil industry to invest abroad was specifically to protect its foreign markets. (In the 1870s two-thirds of U.S. oil production was exported.) Here is how Professor Raymond Vernon summarizes the early history of the global expansion of the U.S. oil industry:

> The more remote sources of crude oil, such as those of the Middle East and the Far East, were needed by the U.S. companies because of their proximity to established export markets in Asia and the Mediterranean basin. While these markets had been developed by U.S. companies in the latter part of the nineteenth century on the basis of U.S. exports, they were never wholly free from challenge by others. ... For two decades before 1900, the American companies tried to counter this threat by capturing downstream facilities in some of the main markets in which they were challenged. By 1900, however, they seem to have decided that control of marketing facilities was not the appropriate strategy and that control of the crude oil was the key. It was then that the U.S. firms began aggressively to try for acquisition of foreign crude oil sources. More generally, however, the major oil companies had to take some interest in any potential source of oil, wherever there was a risk that the source, when developed, might undersell existing supplies. ... In economic terms, the cost of development could better be attributed to the hedging of risk—the risk of losing control of the price structure in established markets. ... The early history of the major oil companies suggested another principle of a prudential sort. A well-diversified supply of resources, they rapidly discovered, was especially useful in dealing with blockages of supply, whether threatened or actual.[6]

Foreign investment for the development and extraction of resources took place for many reasons. Just profit alone has been a sufficient motive for starting many plantations and mines in the underdeveloped world. But the investment in raw materials by monopolistic-type firms has added a new dimension—a dimension which goes a long way to explaining what the era of modern imperialism is all about.

The concentration of economic power in a limited number of giant firms became possible in many industries precisely because of the control by these firms over raw materials sources. The ability to maintain this concentrated power, to ward off native and foreign competitors, to weaken newcomers, and to conduct affairs in accordance with monopolistic price and production policies depended on the alertness and aggressiveness of the giant firms to obtain and maintain control over major segments of the supplies of raw materials —*on a world scale*. This has been the underlying rationality of foreign investment in the extractive industries during the whole era of modern imperialism: not only in oil but in a spectrum of products, especially minerals.

The issue, therefore, is not dependency of the United States on foreign mineral supplies, but the dependency of monopoly industry *qua* "monopolies" on the control of these supplies. The data on the extent to which minerals used in the United States are obtained abroad are merely one measure of the far-flung interests of U.S. monopolies. Necessarily, large firms that process "scarce" raw materials must be vitally concerned about the *world* production, distribution, and prices of these supplies, not merely the demand for the products in the United States.

On this subject, too, the issue of "smallness" raised by the Critics has little relevance. They point out that only the investment in foreign oil is large; the investment in other minerals is relatively small. The fact that the proportion of foreign investment in other minerals is small compared with oil has no bearing whatsoever on the depth of the concern and involvement of the firms using these other minerals. The proportion of foreign investment in iron ore, bauxite, and copper ore (among others) to investment in oil has little if any meaning to the steel, aluminum, and copper producers who seek to secure their leading positions and their special profit advantages by controlling a major segment of the foreign (as well as domestic) supplies of their products.

The second point on raw materials raised by the Critics concerns the possible substitution of one product for another in order to reduce the "dependency" on foreign supplies. Obviously, they do not mean the substitution of some ore other than iron to make steel or a bauxite substitute to make aluminum. Our alchemists have not learned these tricks yet. What the Critics dwell on is the substitution of, say, aluminum and/or plastics for some uses of steel and of aluminum for copper. To a considerable extent substitution has been going on for years, if not centuries and millennia. Where technical substitution is feasible, competition between raw materials for the same or similar uses has been heated. This competition, however, has been accompanied not by a lessening of "dependency" on foreign sources but by an increase of such "dependency." The reason is quite simple. One cannot substitute at will—even if the price is right or even if the cost of the raw material is unimportant. For example, copper used in electric wire and cable can be replaced only by a material that conducts electricity. Steel, paper, and wood are therefore not usable as substitutes for wire requiring electrical conductivity. However, whereas aluminum is a possible substitute, the result of such substitution is an increase in "dependency" on foreign sources of supply: the proportion of foreign to domestic bauxite is considerably higher than the foreign-to-domestic ratio of copper ore.

Another reason for not relying on substitutability for removing or diminishing the use of foreign sources can be seen in the case of steel. Steel has been on the losing end of many competitive battles, including the competition of plastics made from purely domestic sources. Nevertheless, the weakening competitive position of steel has been accompanied by an *increase* in the use of foreign ore. The reason is the depletion of the great Mesabi iron ore deposit. Furthermore, even though technical breakthroughs have made the conversion of domestic taconite ore economically feasible, the interest of U.S. steel firms in iron ore reserves in Canada, South America, Africa, and Asia has increased.

The upshot is that the problem of substitution of minerals, on the whole, is quite different from that of butter vs. margarine or synthetics vs. silk/cotton. At rock bottom, the replacement of one mineral by another is a technical problem. Economics is often involved, but the economic maneuverability is severely restricted by the technical determinants. One cannot, at the present stage of technology, send an electric current through matter that lacks the properties to transmit it. Nor can one make airplanes that carry passengers and freight without aluminum. Moreover, we don't know how to make an effective jet engine without getting columbium, tungsten, nickel, chromium, and cobalt from the four corners of the earth. Nor do politics and economics stand still, waiting on the sidelines for future imaginative technological breakthroughs.

The Critics, though, make a still more daring hypothesis on the substitution question: "The question of substitutability is affected by possible shifts in the end-products of American industry which, in turn, determine what materials are needed. The main possibility is, of course, a reduction in military production."

But why stop at military production? We could, for example, have our commercial jet airplanes made in France, England, Germany, and Japan. These countries would be happy to get the business, and we would reduce our dependency on foreign raw materials. Better still, we could shift the end-products of our society by restricting the use of automobiles in our crowded cities and reducing truck traffic through vastly increased use of the railroads. We would thereby lower the demand for cars, cut down on our dependence on foreign sources of minerals, and improve the air we breathe.

It is interesting to indulge in speculations on what a

rational society would do to simplify the problem of foreign raw material dependency. Such speculation might even have educational value in exposing the limits and contradictions of a capitalist society whose *primum mobile* is the profit motive. But if we want to understand what capitalist imperialism is all about, we had better pay attention to the mechanics and dynamics of capitalism as it really is, i.e., *capitalism as a world system.*

Fundamental Changes?

The Critics summarize their argument in a section entitled "Fundamental Changes"—changes which, in their opinion, point to the plausibility of a U.S. capitalist economy without imperialism. We do not have the space to tackle all the points made, but we shall comment briefly on a few.

First, they invoke the authority of John Kenneth Galbraith's *New Industrial State* to support their contention that fundamental changes have occurred in capitalism which depart from the "necessity" of imperialism. But what are the changes that Galbraith deals with? The "new" capitalism, he claims, is and must be dominated by a limited number of giant corporations; the success of the "new industrial state" depends on the success of these giants. These industrial giants, in turn, have three imperatives: they must keep on growing; they must control their raw material supplies at consistent prices; and they must control their markets.[7] Precisely. Galbraith, whether he knows it or not, is explaining the mainspring of the imperialism of monopoly capitalism.

Second, the Critics see a fundamental change in the absence of a major economic crisis since the end of World War II. If, however, one of the most important reasons for this "fundamental change" is the huge military machine built up and maintained by the United States,[8] then such a change is hardly an opener of a new dawn of a peaceful modern capitalism. Quite the contrary. It is a harbinger of wars and revolutions. The internal and external conflicts generated by such a "success" do indeed foretell the end of imperialism and the decline of the U.S. empire—but not by a peaceful reform of monopoly capitalism.

Third, the Critics contrast the more rapid growth of "non-imperialist" Germany and Japan with the slower growth of imperialist United States and Great Britain. (Incidentally, they refer to "the tempestuous growth of Japan and Germany in the postwar period, without foreign investments. . . ." They may wish to argue that foreign investments were not *important* for the growth rate, but they are mistaken if they think there have not been considerable foreign investments by Germany and Japan.) What is missing in this sort of correlation is an appreciation of the way the world capitalist system has been working in recent decades.

Under *Pax Americana*, the United States supplies the main military power and the police action to keep as much of the world as possible safe for "free" enterprise. In this arrangement, Germany and Japan, as major and strategic components of world capitalism, are special beneficiaries of the economic and military strategy of the United States. Japan, in particular, has benefited not only from the advantages of a prosperous U.S. market but also from U.S. purchases for the Korean and Vietnam wars. There are, of course, special factors which have contributed to the German and Japanese growth rates, but the very possibility of growth is intimately related to *Pax Americana* and a relatively successful U.S. economy based on militarism.

In sum, the Critics' analytical method is to separate out the various parts of the U.S. and world economy and to sever economics from politics. They arrive at the conclusion that, by tinkering with some of the parts through political pressure, capitalism can be reformed so that it can live and grow without imperialism. Our point of view is that the separate parts must be understood in the context of their inter-relations with the social organism of world monopoly capitalism. Further, it is important to recognize the essential unity of the economics, politics, militarism, and culture of this social organism. We reach the conclusion that *imperialism is the way of life of capitalism. Therefore, the elimination of imperialism requires the overthrow of capitalism.*

Notes

1. Foreword by Bernard Baruch to Samuel Lubell, *The Revolution in World Trade and American Economic Policy* (New York: Harper and Bros., 1955), p. xi.
2. Data and quotation from *The American Banker*, January 28, 1970.
3. Ibid.
4. Calculated from balance-of-payments statistics reported in *Survey of Current Business*, June 1967 and June 1969. The Third World was defined as Western Hemisphere countries, other than Canada, and Asian and African countries, other than Japan and South Africa.
5. *Business Week*, December 6, 1969.
6. "Foreign Enterprises and Developing Nations in the Raw Materials Industries," in *Allied Social Science Associations, Papers and Abstracts to be Presented at the Annual Meeting of the ASSA*, New York, N.Y., December 28-30, 1969.
7. See the author's review of Galbraith's *New Industrial State*, "Rationalizing the Irrational," *The Nation*, September 18, 1967.
8. See Paul A. Baran and Paul M. Sweezy, *Monopoly Capital* (New York: Monthly Review Press, 1966). Also, "Militarism and Imperialism," p. 198, this volume.

11

How to Make a Molehill
Out of a Mountain

Al Szymanski wants to throw new light on the cause and cure of imperialism. Introducing what he believes to be a rigorous analysis and empirical tests, he reaches the conclusion that most radical critiques of imperialism are ultimately based on false dogmas. The structure of his argument, in barest outline, runs along the following lines:

1. Lenin, Luxemburg, and those who follow in their path claim that capitalism cannot exist without imperialism.

2. The facts on U.S. private investment and U.S. raw material needs demonstrate that capitalism can exist without imperialism.

3. Since capitalism can exist without imperialism, it is possible to eliminate imperialism and maintain capitalism. Not only that, but other contradictions of capitalism can meanwhile also be resolved.

The trouble with these arguements, as I see it, is that the first proposition misstates the position of Lenin and other

This is a revised version of an article that appeared in the Spring 1977 issue of the *Insurgent Sociologist* entitled "Imperialism and the State: External and Internal Effects." It was prepared as a response to an essay in the same issue by Al Szymanski on "Capital Accumulation on a World Scale and the Necessity of Imperialism." The article also appeared in the March 1977 issue of *Monthly Review*.

radical analysts of imperialism; the data discussed in the second proposition are irrelevant as tests; and proposition three has no logical connection with the other two. On the whole, Szymanski substitutes a broad faith in the feasibility of substantially reforming capitalism for what he considers to be conventional radical dogma. Let us examine his arguments in order.

Lenin vs. Luxemburg

Throughout his essay, Szymanski insists on equating Lenin's and Luxemburg's views on the indispensability of imperialism to the capitalist system. This theme is at the heart of his argument and is repeated again and again, as for example: "Both [Lenin and Luxemburg] argued that the process of accumulation *could not proceed* without imperialism. . . ." "For Lenin and Luxemburg, it is not merely a question whether or not overseas investments are *more* profitable than domestic investments but whether or not *any* profitable investment can be found, i.e., whether or not capital accumulation can proceed. . . ." "Lenin and Luxemburg claimed that capitalism would be impossible in the absence of imperialism."

Szymanski is substantially correct with respect to Rosa Luxemburg. She did advance the theory that capitalist economies could not grow in an isolated, self-contained system. The alleged reason was that the markets provided by workers and capitalists are insufficient to support investment in expanded capacity (accumulation); in other words, surplus value cannot be fully realized within the framework of capitalist markets. And since capitalist economies must grow in order to exist, "third markets" have to be opened up in noncapitalist sectors inside and outside the capitalist country. The role of imperialism, then, is to invade noncapitalist areas in other countries and bring them into the capitalist fold, thus prolonging the life of capitalist societies. But in the long run, she argued, the whole world comes under the sway of capitalism; and in the absence of any more new markets to conquer, capitalism can no longer exist. This ultimate limit may never be reached, for the road thereto is paved with wars and economic and political catastrophes which prepare the ground for workers' revolutions and the transition to socialism.

Correct as Szymanski may be in his characterization of Luxemburg's views, he is equally incorrect in putting Lenin in the same camp. As a matter of fact, Luxemburg herself identified Lenin as a theorist with whom she totally differed on the very issue of whether capitalism could live and grow on the basis of internal markets alone. (In Luxemburg's *Accumulation of Capital* Lenin is referred to as V. Ilyin, the pseudonym Lenin used as author of the publications on which Luxemburg bases her criticisms.) Lenin, it should be recalled, was an active participant in debates with the populists (*narodniki*), a major trend in Russian social thought during the latter part of the nineteenth century. Influential populist thinkers had advanced the following line of reasoning: the growth of capitalist industry results in a shrinking of internal markets; as a result, surplus value could not be realized unless capitalists had access to foreign markets; in view of the constraints on expansion of foreign trade for a latecomer, a full capitalist economy could not develop in Russia.

Lenin aimed his heavy artillery against this strain of populist thought in two major works: *A Characterization of Economic Romanticism* (1897) and *The Development of Capitalism in Russia* (1908). We need not be concerned here with all aspects of Lenin's critique of the populists. What is relevant to the present subject is Lenin's approach to the role of foreign markets, which is exactly opposite to that of Rosa Luxemburg:

> But what about the foreign market? Do we deny that capitalism needs a foreign market? Of course not. But the question of a foreign market has *absolutely nothing to do with the question of realization*, and the attempt to link them into one whole merely expresses the romantic wish to "retard" capitalism, and the romantic inability to think logically.[1]

> This brings us to the question of why a capitalist country needs a foreign market. Certainly not because the product cannot be realized at all under the capitalist system. That is nonsense. A foreign market is needed because it is *inherent* in capitalist production to strike for *unlimited* expansion. . . .[2]

Lenin develops this theme more fully in his later work. There he points out that "capitalism makes its appearance only as a result of widely developed commodity *circulation*, which transcends the limits of the state." Thus, historically, international trade provides the natural environment for the operations of capitalist enterprise, and given the persistent pressure of capital to expand, foreign trade also grows and eventually "links all countries of the world into a single economic whole." In addition, the uneven development of the separate branches of industry within a country also contributes to the drive for foreign trade. Many of these branches are interdependent: they sell their products to each other. But since each of the industries expands without full knowledge of its markets, and since some grow faster than others, those that advance more rapidly than the rest of the economy are especially in need of foreign markets. Therefore, Lenin concludes that behind "the need for a foreign market are . . . causes of a historical character. In order to understand them one must examine each separate industry, its development within the country, its transformation into a capitalist industry—in short, one must take the *facts* about the development of capitalism in the country. . . ."[3]

Of course, Lenin is here disputing with the Russian populists, and not with Luxemburg whose book had not yet appeared. But he is addressing the very same question that Luxemburg deals with at a later date, and it is precisely the question on which Luxemburg takes issue with Lenin. In view of Szymanski's equating Lenin's and Luxemburg's theories, it is instructive to underline not only the stark contrast between the two sets of ideas, but also the marked difference in their methods of analysis.

Luxemburg's method is to start from Marx's reproduction

schemes in the second volume of *Capital*, one of the tools Marx developed for examining and explaining in a general way how the capitalist system as a whole is able to function and grow. She thinks she finds an error in Marx's treatment, and she corrects for this supposed error. Then, using very limited assumptions and magnifying the applicability of the reproduction schemes beyond what, in our opinion, is reasonable, Luxemburg arrives at an almost mathematical formula which is supposed to prove on the one hand the impossibility of capitalism's existing without noncapitalist markets, and, on the other hand, the inevitability of an absolute limit to the life of capitalism. This is model-building *par excellence:* a tightly knit, rigid mechanism in which all the component parts fit neatly into place.[4]

Lenin's approach is clearly the direct opposite of this sort of mechanistic thinking. While he of all people is fully conscious of the contradictions of capitalism and the necessity of a workers' revolution to finish off capitalism, he regards all talk about *automatic* limits to capitalism as romantic and unrealistic. Thus, his analysis of the "necessity" of foreign trade has nothing at all to do with mathematical or absolute limits to capitalism, but is instead based on history, an understanding of the dynamics of capitalist development, and the concrete *facts* about the way capitalist enterprise operates.

Thus far we have dwelt on Lenin's writings before he began his study of imperialism. Did he perhaps reverse his thinking about the limits of capitalism when, seven to eight years after the publication of *The Development of Capitalism in Russia,* he entered on an intensive study of imperialism?[5] And did he at that time come anywhere close to either Luxemburg's theory or to Szymanski's attempted synthesis of Lenin's views? The answer to both of these questions is purely and simply: no.

The plain fact is that Lenin's and Luxemburg's theories of imperialism are miles apart. Her theory is (1) completely rooted in the "realization" problem discussed above; (2) concerned exclusively with relations between capitalist and noncapitalist areas; and (3) an intended explanatory device for the entire history of capitalist expansion. Lenin's theory, in contrast, differs substantially on each and every one of these counts.

To begin with, Lenin is primarily concerned with explaining the major historical changes that show up toward the end of the nineteenth century when, among other things, competing empire-builders emerge among industrialized nations; England's dominant position in trade, military power, and colonial empire is challenged; and there is a marked and sudden speedup in colonial acquisitions and wars associated with empire.[6] Lenin concluded that the underlying explanation for this concatenation of events was to be found in a major structural change in capitalism. The long-run tendency for the concentration and centralization of capital had reached a point where the leading capitalist economies were dominated by a relatively small number of large firms. With the emergence of this monopoly stage of capitalism, during which finance capital (the merger of bank and industrial interests) is in the ascendancy, capitalism becomes capitalist imperialism.

Whereas Luxemburg centers her theory on the supposed inability of capitalists at all stages of their history to make profits in a closed system, Lenin locates the nature of imperialism in the modes of behavior of monopoly capitalism to protect and increase their profits. The context of Lenin's analysis is the uneven development of the assorted capitalist nations, the tendency to stagnation in the monopoly stage, and the special features of monopolistic competition as contrasted with "free competition." Under these propelling forces, certain crucially important characteristics of the imperialist stage come to the fore: capital export becomes increasingly important; the world's economic markets are divided up among international monopoly groups; the territorial division of the world by capitalist powers is completed; not only colonies but semicolonies and weaker capitalist nations become enmeshed in a net of financial and economic dependence on the centers of world finance capital; and antagonisms among imperialist powers for the redivision of the world intensify. In contrast with Luxemburg and many other writers on imperialism, Lenin's theory is not restricted to the relations between metropolitan centers and the periphery. Among the essential features of the imperialist stage, according to Lenin, are the economic struggle (and alliances) among sectors of finance capital for division of markets and investment opportunities in the advanced as well as the underdeveloped nations, and the military and diplomatic struggle among the imperialist powers for control and influence over weaker nations, industrialized as well as non-industrialized.[7]

It is specially noteworthy that despite the many changes that have occurred during the sixty years since Lenin's *Imperialism* appeared—a second world war, the spread of socialism, decolonization, and the forward surge of American empire—the theory he sketched still serves as the most useful framework for understanding the course of capitalist imperialism, provided of course that it is applied in a nondogmatic fashion. The reason for this, I believe, is the way Lenin identified the new monopoly stage of capitalism and then put his finger on its most important distinguishing traits. While this achievement is a tribute to Lenin's great theoretical capacity in interpreting his times, we must never forget that he was primarily concerned to understand objective reality as a basis for preparing for a socialist revolution. The last thing in the world he was interested in was idle speculation about conceivable future variations in the relations between capitalism and imperialism.

Where then does Szymanski get his far-fetched notions about Lenin's theory? To a large extent, unfortunately, by the simple process of misinterpreting what Lenin wrote. Let me give but two illustrations out of many.

1. Szymanski:

> These two [Lenin and Luxemburg] maintain that capitalism during its monopoly phase is absolutely unable, because of the low living standards of the masses and the inability of the state to spend enough on public welfare, to find sufficient domestic

markets for all it produces, and that consequently outlets for otherwise unrealizable profits must be found in ways that result in the domination of Third World countries if the capital accumulation process is to continue.

What is wrong in this sentence? (1) The monopoly phase does not enter into Luxemburg's analysis. (2) Lenin says nothing about the inability of capitalism "to find sufficient domestic markets for all it produces," nor is there any reason to infer this from his analysis. (3) Luxemburg's argument about insufficient domestic markets is not concerned with the low living standards of the masses. (4) Neither of the two deals with "the inability of the state to spend enough on the public welfare." (5) There is nothing in Lenin to justify the statement that "outlets for otherwise unrealizable profits must be found . . . if the capital accumulation process is to continue." He nowhere deals with the problem of "unrealizable profits," only with the opportunities for finding new investment opportunities and for getting more profits in a capitalist world system.

2. Szymanski:

In the models of Hobson, Lenin, and Luxemburg the motive force for the export of goods was the inability to realize surplus value in the metropolitan countries and hence the necessity to attempt to realize it overseas where there was available purchasing power, i.e., trade results in the net transfer of value to the periphery.

And what do we find mistaken here? (1) The first part of the sentence (up to the "i.e.") is wrong as far as it applies to Lenin. (2) It is only partially correct with respect to Hobson and Luxemburg, since the reference to "available purchasing power" oversimplifies and thus misses the essence of their argument. (3) The concluding part of the sentence about "the transfer of value to the periphery" has no logical connection with what precedes it; in other words, the "i.e." introduces a non sequitur. Furthermore, it has nothing to do with the ideas of Lenin, Hobson, or Luxemburg, all of whom maintain that the capitalists in the metropolitan centers get richer at the expense of the periphery.

If Szymanski has a grain of a valid argument, it relates to Lenin's discussion of export of capital. In order to uncover this grain, however, Szymanski has to (1) substitute for Lenin's definition of imperialism his own, which he restricts exclusively to relations between the metropole and the periphery; (2) insist that only one facet of Lenin's complex theory (capital export) is the essential one; (3) select only one of Lenin's explanations for the growth of export capital; and (4) interpret export of capital, which includes loans, as meaning only direct investment. This sort of compression and selection leads, in my opinion, to a distortion of Lenin's theory and a misunderstanding of his vital contribution to the understanding of our times.[8]

What Szymanski and like-minded commentators latch on to is a short passage in chapter 4 ("The Export of Capital") of Lenin's *Imperialism*, which concludes: "The necessity for exporting capital arises from the fact that in a few countries capitalism has become 'over-ripe' and (owing to the backward state of agriculture and the impoverished state of the masses) capital cannot find 'profitable' investment."[9] Much depends on how much weight is placed on this sole passage and how it is interpreted. In view of Lenin's writing style, and considering this excerpt in the context of his *entire* essay, one could properly argue that Lenin did not intend at this point to lay down a law of monopoly capitalism, rather that he was directing his fire at the shortsightedness of petty-bourgeois radical critics. Thus, in the same paragraph from which the above-cited sentence is taken, Lenin states with respect to the conditions of his times:

> It goes without saying that if capitalism could develop agriculture, which today lags far behind industry everywhere, if it could raise the standard of living and the masses, who are everywhere still poverty-stricken and underfed, in spite of the amazing advance in technical knowledge, there could be no talk of a super-abundance of capital. This "argument" the petty-bourgeois critics of capitalism advance on every occasion. But if capitalism did these things it would not be capitalism; for uneven development and wretched conditions of the masses are fundamental and inevitable conditions and premises of this mode of production.[10]

Do these words sound so strange in today's world? In the midst of mass unemployment, extensive poverty, urban crisis, etc., do the capitalists invest to eliminate these evils? Of course not. The obvious reason is that they see too little profit and too much risk in such ventures. But at the same time, of course, our giant firms have expanded, and continue to expand, their overseas enterprises.[11]

By harping on one phrase in a major work of analysis—about capital not being able to find "profitable" investment (note Lenin's use of quotation marks here)—Szymanski, in effect, makes a molehill out of a mountain. One might well argue that Lenin was imprecise, unclear, and contradictory in some of his formulations about the export of capital (and other matters as well.)[12] But what is really significant (and merits attention by aspiring theoreticians) is how right Lenin was sixty years ago in selecting (from among many variables) the growing importance of capital exports (relative to exports of goods) as a key feature of the stage of monopoly capitalism. Thus, a recent United Nations study reports that in 1971 the sales of foreign affiliates of the world's multinational corporations (in other words, the production activity resulting from the direct foreign investments of the imperialist powers) exceeded the total export of goods by all capitalist nations combined.[13]

By now it should be clear that I, and I hope the reader too, see no justification whatsoever for Szymanski's claim that Lenin entertained ideas about capital accumulation's collapsing in the absence of imperialism, even though at one point he refers to the difficulties of capital in mature economies in finding profitable investments. Stranger still is the way Szymanski projects this notion to the next step in his private logic to the effect that because Lenin did advance such a theorem he must also have believed that capitalism would cease to exist if imperialism evaporated. This inference cannot be refuted by quoting from Lenin, since Lenin never indulged in such nonsensical speculations. Considering the whole of Lenin's writings, I find it impossible to conceive of Lenin believing that any society ever has collapsed by itself and ceased to exist or ever will. Allow me to quote at length what I wrote on this subject some years ago:

> A corollary of the argument that imperialism was a way out of depression is the idea that capitalism will collapse as the area for imperialist expansion shrinks. This thesis is based on an unrealistic and rigid view of how capitalism works. Cutting off markets and sources of raw materials creates serious problems for capitalist enterprise but does not necessarily portend collapse.
>
> It should hardly be necessary to point this out after the many years of experience during which sizable sections of the globe have removed themselves from the imperialist orbit. Yet oversimplified, mechanistic formulations seem to have a life of their own. It is important to understand the degrees of flexibility that exist in capitalist society and which make the system more durable than its opponents have often supposed. Biological organisms may show the same quality: the closure of one heart artery may be compensated by the enlargement of another artery to take over its function. To be sure, these organic adjustments are not eternal and they often lead to other and greater complications. But a significant lesson to be learned from the history of capitalism is that great troubles do not lead to automatic collapse.
>
> The post-World War II experience provides a good example of this flexibility. The enlargement of the U.S. military machine became a powerful support to the U.S. economy. In turn, the success achieved by the United States as the organizer of the world imperialist system on the verge of breaking down gave other advanced capitalisms an important boost, creating markets and enlarging international trade. This flexibility, however, is not limitless. Cracks in the most recent imperialist arrangements are clearly evident in the strains on the international money markets as well as in the mounting difficulties of the U.S. economy itself. Further shrinkage of imperialist territory will create more troubles: it might lead to a sharpening of the business cycle, prolonged depression, mass unemployment. Nevertheless, as we know from historical experience, these do not necessarily bring the downfall of the system. In the final analysis, the fate of capitalism will be settled only by vigorous classes, and parties based on these classes, which have the will and ability to replace the existing system.[14]

While this denies the collapse theme, it is still quite different from Szymanski's optimism about the ease with which capitalism can supposedly adjust to drastic changes in the world imperialist network. But before getting on to that subject, we had better deal with Szymanski's effort at statistical proof.

The Evidence

Szymanski presents data on U.S. investment in, and foreign trade with, Third World countries. Then by showing that the amounts involved are relatively small compared with domestic capital investment, he believes that he has proven that "neither investment nor trade . . . acts to facilitate the continuation of the capital accumulation process by acting as mechanisms for extensive capital accumulation," and therefore "the Third World is not used as an outlet for surplus capital as Lenin and Luxemburg argue."

Since Luxemburg never held that the Third World was used as an outlet for surplus capital, any evidence to the contrary is irrelevant to her position.[15] As far as Lenin is concerned, we showed above that he had a much more realistic explanation of the sources of export expansion, such as the history of capitalism as a world system and the role of anarchy of production. This explanation had nothing to do with the relative size of exports or the export surplus. Hence, Szymanski's statistics, and his inferences from them, are irrelevant here too.

We have also tried to demonstrate that Lenin's reference to superabundance of capital was not crucial to his much more complex theory of imperialism and its relation to the functioning of monopoly capitalism. But even if Szymanski's interpretations were correct, his data would be insufficient to support his argument. He seems to think that capital *accumulation* and capital *investment* are the same thing. This is not correct since investment consists of two components: replacement of used-up plant and equipment, and capital goods for expansion of capacity. It is only the latter that represents capital accumulation.

The trouble here, however, is not with this or that statistic, but with the whole line of reasoning. Szymanski and too many others look for a simple, neatly packaged formula to explain an intricate set of contradictory relations, the concrete forms of which change in different historical circumstances. And if they fail to find such a simple formula, then the sky is the limit: it is even possible to relegate imperialism to the status of a mere policy option.

But if one really wishes to understand the imperatives of imperialism, one needs to examine (among other things) the growth, influence, and methods of operation of multinational corporations throughout the entire capitalist world; the struggle for power and hegemony by and among leading nations, singly or in allied groups; how Third World countries are used economically and politically as instruments in the struggle for power; and how power itself is related to international exchange rates, international banking, international money markets, and the balance of payments. This is the context in which Lenin's theory of capitalist imperialism needs to be tested, and not the few sentences about superabundance of capital.

In all fairness, it should be noted that in addition to exports of capital and commodities Szymanski discusses, and subjects to empirical tests, the question of the Third World as a source of raw materials. For this purpose he presents data for two years on imports of strategic raw materials from the Third World as percentages of estimated U.S. consumption. He then finds that in a majority of cases there has been a decline between 1965 and 1971 in dependency on Third World sources. In some instances the changes are hardly meaningful. For example, the decline in this measure of dependency for manganese is from 95 to 91 percent, and for iron from 13 to 12 percent. Interestingly enough, oil is counted as one of the items showing a marked decline, from 16 to 8 percent, while we know that today the ratio of imports from the Third World to consumption amounts to over 30 percent and is expected to keep on climbing. But there is a more serious difficulty with these numbers. Most of the materials for which declines in dependency are supposedly registered are part of the U.S. government stockpile program. Hence, if Szymanski wants to draw meaningful conclusions from these data, he should first determine to what extent the percentage changes were influenced by differences, if any, in government stockpiling practices in the two years—a factor having little if any relation to the subject he purports to throw light on.

Let us assume, however, that the data do indeed reflect a downward trend in dependency on the Third World's resources. Does anyone imagine that the National Security Council, having inspected such a statistical table, will decide that there is no need to trouble itself further with what goes on in Africa? Surely no one with the slightest knowledge about the affairs of government and business. I doubt that Szymanski thinks so either. What he says is that if push came to shove we—that is, the capitalist economy—could get along without the raw materials from the Third World. True, but how? "We" could tell the multinational corporations to go to hell, along with their struggle for monopoly control, growth, and profits. "We" could cut down on the production and use of autos. "We" could ration the distribution of goods using scarce materials. "We" could invent and produce more expensive substitute materials. "We," especially the working class and the poor, could pull in our belts and reduce our standard of living. If one moves from the real to the speculative, one can dream of many things, without worrying too much about how the dream could be realized or what its consequences might be.

The Abolition of Imperialism

Szymanski acknowledges fully and forcefully that imperialism grows out of capitalism. What really concerns him is the association of that relationship with the dread word "necessity." Having demolished Lenin's and Luxemburg's "necessity," he turns to Magdoff and other necessitarians. Although he concedes that these *epigoni* supply a lot of useful information, they too fail to demonstrate "necessity." It thus follows, as spring follows winter, that if there is no absolute *proof* of necessity, the opposite is true: there ain't no necessity. That being the case, it is possible, indeed feasible, to wipe out imperialism—and not only keep capitalism, but make it more prosperous and flourishing.

Szymanski even has a game plan for, in his words, the "liquidation of imperialism." The contradictions of imperialism—growing national liberation movements, the consequent burdens on the population of the metropoles involved in suppressing revolutions, the eventual support of those capitalists who lose out from imperialism—will pave the way. Somehow or other, imperialism will be replaced. Presumably popular reform movements will supersede the capitalist control of the state, and the capitalist organism will bow to the will of the people. To be sure, large sections of the capitalist class would suffer during the liquidation process, even though they too can expect to benefit in the long run. It will be possible, again in his own words, "to appease these groups" by expanding the state's role to make up for the slack in military spending and other lost imperialist business.

It is extraordinarily interesting that the first task Szymanski assigns to the proposed enlarged state activity is to increase productivity and subsidize wages "so as to preserve and increase the U.S. competitive advantage in both domestic and international markets." Little does he realize how quickly this brings him back into the old ball game. If he deems it crucial for U.S. capitalism to increase exports and hold down competitive imports, he had better understand that foreign trade is no gentlemen's game in which the better product and lower prices are automatically successful. All of capitalist history and today's real world of business show that foreign trade advantage is tied up with much more than having a better mousetrap. Needed in addition are more powerful banking, shipping, and insurance facilities; protection of trademarks and patents; effective local advertising and sales promotion; and control or influence over wholesale and retail channels.

For U.S. capitalism to give up imperialism, if we wish to

indulge in such a fancy, means to give up these advantages to competitors in other leading capitalist nations and to take the consequences. For it should not be imagined that the fantastical, voluntary dissolution of imperialism means merely pulling out of the Third World. It must also include closing down the operations of U.S. banks and manufacturing concerns in the advanced capitalist countries, since these activities are closely tied up with the imperialist networks of the other metropoles.

It should also be understood that pulling out of the rest of the capitalist world and giving up the worldwide military machine would mean folding up U.S. influence over international exchange rates, banking, and money markets—all clearly crucial props to U.S. prosperity as well as critical elements in sustaining, let alone supporting growth of, U.S. exports. These comments are not intended to provide a scenario of the consequences of the "liquidation of imperialism." Their purpose is simply to emphasize that in the real world—as in capitalist history from the beginning—foreign trade, international economic relations, and power (military, economic, financial) are all closely interrelated.

Perhaps none of this would faze Szymanski, since he has still another solution. Economic planning and massive government spending will not only overcome imperialist and export losses; they will also bring about higher growth rates and a reduction in unemployment. Presumably these panaceas will also cure other ills in addition to stagnation and unemployment: inflation, the consequences of the debt explosion, shaky financial institutions, the financial morass of cities—all of which matured while one of his remedies (federal, state, and local government spending for nonmilitary goods and services) was already being vigorously applied. How interesting that someone with such a high regard for rigor and proof when it comes to the question of the "necessity" of imperialism, can derive so much comfort, in the midst of all the economic problems of world capitalism, from a few vague generalizations!

Notes

1. *A Characterization of Economic Romanticism*, in V. I. Lenin, *Collected Works*, vol. 2 (Moscow: Foreign Languages Publishing House, 1963), p. 162.
2. Ibid., p. 164.
3. This paragraph is a summary of chapter I, section 8, of *The Development of Capitalism in Russia*, 2nd ed. (revised and expanded), 1908, in V. I. Lenin, *Collected Works*, vol. 3, pp. 61-67.
4. Please note that we are here referring only to Luxemburg's imperialism/breakdown thesis, and that we have absolutely no intention of classifying this brilliant theorist and revolutionary as a mechanistic thinker. In addition to her other extremely valuable writings, the two books on imperialism are most definitely still worthy of study. For even though her solution may be unsatisfactory, the theoretical problem she poses is an important one, and in addition, the historical material is outstanding. We are, of course, referring to Rosa Luxemburg, *Accumulation of Capital* (New York: Monthly Review Press, 1964) and *The Accumulation of Capital—An Anti-Critique*, published together with N. Bukharin, *Imperialism and the Accumulation of Capital* (New York: Monthly Review Press, 1972).
5. Those who think that all Lenin did was to pull together a few strands of thought then floating about, or those who imagine that useful theory on social matters comes from intuition or pure deduction from other theories, would do well to consult the extensive notebooks Lenin wrote in preparation for his brief essay on imperialism. His notes on his research in this field constitute the over-800-page volume 39 of his *Collected Works*.
6. For a brief overview of the historical background of the new imperialism, see "European Expansionism Since 1763," this volume.
7. As examples of the striving for control over developed areas, Lenin cites German appetite for Belgium and French appetite for Lorraine.
8. See "Imperialism: A Historical Survey," this volume.
9. V. I. Lenin, *Imperialism the Highest Stage of Capitalism* (New York: International Publishers, 1939), pp. 62-63.
10. Ibid.
11. It seems to me reasonable to believe that Lenin had no intention of contradicting Marx's opinion on the reasons for foreign investment:

> If capital is sent abroad, this is not done because it absolutely could not be applied at home, but because it can be employed at a higher rate of profit in a foreign country. But such capital is absolute excess capital for the employed labouring population and for the home country in general. It exists as such alongside the relative over-population [i.e., unemployment], and this is an illustration of how both of them exist side by side, and mutually influence one another. (*Capital*, vol. 3 [Moscow: Progress Publishers, 1959], p. 256)

12. In my own work I have tried to evaluate the "superabundance of capital" theorem, and concluded that the most useful hypothesis for explaining the growing importance of foreign investment is to be found in the imperatives of monopolistic firms, and that short-cut formulas such as the pressure of surplus capital or the declining rate of profit are either irrelevant or inadequate. This is in line with the position of the late Oskar Lange who wrote many years ago: "The pursuit of surplus monopoly profits suffices to explain the imperialist nature of present-day capitalism. Consequently, special theories of imperialism which resort to artificial constructions, such as Rosa Luxemburg's theory and Fritz Sternberg's, are quite unnecessary." ("The Role of the State in Monopoly Capitalism," in Lange, *Papers in Economy and Sociology, 1930-1960* [Oxford: Pergamon Press, 1970].)

    Some may take this argument as a basic criticism of Lenin. I think, on the contrary, that, based on subsequent developments, it substantiates Lenin's encapsulation: "If it were necessary to give the briefest possible definition of imperialism we should have to say that imperialism is the monopoly stage of capitalism." See "Imperialism Without Colonies," this volume.

13. Department of Economic and Social Affairs, *Multinational Corporations in World Development* (New York: United Nations, 1973), pp. 13-14.

14. "Imperialism Without Colonies," this volume.

15. Nor do Szymanski's data on trade have a bearing on Luxemburg's theory, since she focused on exchange with noncapitalist production areas. Those interested in a review and evaluation of Luxemburg's theory should consult Paul M. Sweezy, *Theory of Capitalist Development* (New York: Monthly Review Press, 1956), pp. 202-7, and Joan Robinson's Introduction to Luxemburg's *Accumulation of Capital*.